Employee Relations in Europe

Human Resource Management in Action Series

Series Editor: Brian Towers

Other HRM books from Blackwell Business

Employee Relations in Europe

JEFF BRIDGFORD AND JOHN STIRLING

First published 1994

Blackwell Publishers
108 Cowley Road
Oxford OX4 1JF
UK

238 Main Street
Cambridge, Massachusetts 02142
USA

British Library Cataloguing in Publication Data

A CIP catalogue record for this book is available from the British Library.

Library of Congress Cataloging-in-Publication Data

Bridgford, Jeff.
    Employee relations in Europe Jeff Bridgford and John Stirling.
      p.   cm. – (Human resource management in action series)
    Includes bibliographical references and index.
    ISBN 0–631–18683–2 (pbk. : alk. paper)
    1. Industrial relations – Europe. I. Stirling, John, 1949– .
II. Title. III. Series: Human resource management in action.
HD8376.5.B73 1993
331'.094–dc20   93–16874
                                   CIP

Typeset in Plantin on 11/13 pt
by Graphicraft Typesetters Ltd., Hong Kong
Printed in Great Britain by Page Bros, Norwich

This book is printed on acid-free paper

Contents

List of Tables and Figures

Figures

Foreword

When the UK became a member of the European Community it was perhaps not widely foreseen that, within 20 years, membership would be beginning to have far-reaching and irreversible effects on the UK and its partners and, because of this, acute differences over the extent and pace of integration would become a live political issue – even to threatening the stability of individual governments and shaking the self-confidence of those riding the European integration horse. More immediately, there is, at the time of writing, a real possibility that the Maastricht Treaty will fall and that even if it does not it will need to shed a great deal of federalist weight if it is to clear the ratification hurdle.

As always, there are other perspectives. The Community has already weathered bouts of acute political and economic turbulence as well as the dangers inherent in immobility on a becalmed ocean. Furthermore, the old Treaty of Rome and the new Single European Act remain as the twin blades propelling the still seaworthy EC vessel. There is also the single market from 1993 – arising out of the Single European Act – which is potentially the biggest and richest single market in the world.

Few blessings are unmixed. Is, for example, the vast single market clearly a positive step on the road of progress? Some stress the benefits to consumers from the large scale, low cost provision of goods and services which such a market can bring. Others see dangers in continent-leaping corporate capital, the marginalizing of consumers, the brow-beating of employees and the arm-twisting of governments. There is something in both of these ways of looking at the single market. The continental European tradition is to recognize both by giving large corporations freedom to operate but within the constraints of the law as well as the further safeguard of institutionalized collective bargaining to protect the interests of consumers and employees. This approach explicitly and formally legitimizes the role of trade unions, an approach which has not been followed in the UK since 1979.

Yet the changes in the UK since 1979 only partly explain the differences in the approach to the employment relationship (and its contexts) between the UK and its EC neighbours; there are also explanations of much longer standing, deriving from both philosophy and historical development and it would be wrong to believe that Mrs Thatcher's lengthy ascendancy has transformed much, if anything at all. Furthermore, despite the series of legislative interventions of the 1980s, and earlier, in the UK the form and degree of State involvement on matters of individual and collective employment rights cannot yet be described as having been transformed and the system, in substance, still remains very different from that prevailing in the other parts of the EC forest.

This book is about these different systems. But it is also about how far British customs, practices, and institutions within the employment relationship are presently changing, and are likely to continue to change, under the influences of EC membership. We have already seen this in relation to, for example, equal value legislation, health and safety and transfer of undertakings. Also in the Directive pipeline is legislation on pregnant workers and perhaps limitations on the working week. Aside from these legal changes employers and trade unions are beginning to tool up for the internal market and could yet make progress on the development of European works councils through the voluntary route and without the encouragement of the Commission and the Social Dialogue which at the time of writing is under review in Brussels.

More broadly, readers will find here a detailed mapping of the EC's employment dimension and its actual and potential impact on the UK. As such it is an up-to-date and comprehensive work of reference for all those active, or interested in the European single market as well as those contemplating their entry into that still relatively uncharted territory.

Brian Towers
Series Editor

Acknowledgements

Jeff Bridgford would like to thank David Foden and Rachel Woolf for reading draft chapters, Eva Berger for efficient secretarial assistance and colleagues at the Documentation Centre of the European Trade Union Institute for their diligent support.

John Stirling would like to thank his colleagues and students at the University of Northumbria, the staff at the European Documentation Centre at the University and his family for putting up with the book.

We would both like to thank our editor, Paul Stringer, for his invaluable contribution.

List of Common Abbreviations

BDA	Bundesvereinigung der Deutschen Arbeitgeberverbände
CBI	Confederation of British Industry
CCOO	Comisiones Obreras
CEEP	Centre Européen de l'Entreprise Publique
CFDC	Confédération Française des Travailleurs Chrétiens
CFDT	Confédération Française Démocratique du Travail
CGIL	Confederazione Generale Italiana del Lavoro
CGT	Confédération Générale du Travail
CISL	Confederazione Italiana Sindicati Lavoratori
CNV	Christelijk Nationaal Vakverbond
Cobas	Comitati di base
CSC	Confédération des Syndicats Chrétiens
DAG	Deutsche Angestelltengewerkschaft
DC	Christian Democratic Party (Italy)
DGB	Deutscher Gewerkschaftsbund
EC	European Community
ECSC	European Coal and Steel Community
Ecu	European Currency Unit
EETPU	Electrical, Electronic and Plumbing Trades Union
EFTA	European Free Trade Association
EMS	European Monetary System
EP	European Parliament
ESC	Economic and Social Committee
ESF	European Social Fund
ETUC	European Trade Union Confederation
FGTB	Fédération Générale des Travailleurs de Belgique
FNV	Federatie Nederlandse Vakbeweging
FO (or CGT-FO)	Confédération Générale du Travail – Force Ouvrière

GATT	General Agreement on Tariffs and Trade
GDP	Gross Domestic Product
GNP	Gross National Product
GSEE	Geniki Synomospondia Ergaton Ellados
ICFTU	International Confederation of Free Trade Unions
ILO	International Labour Organization
IMF	International Monetary Fund
IOE	International Organization of Employers
IRI	Istituto per la Ricostruzione Industriale
ITS	International Trade Secretariat
LO	Landsorganisationen
MEP	Member of the European Parliament
NATO	North Atlantic Treaty Organization
OECD	Organization for Economic Co-operation and Development
OEEC	Organization for European Economic Co-operation
ÖGB	Österreichischer Gewerkschaftsbund
OJ	Official Journal of the European Communities
ÖTV	Öffentliche Dienste, Transport und Verkehr
SAK	Suomen Ammattiliittojen Keskusjärjestö
SEA	Single European Act
SMEs	Small and Medium-size Enterprises
TCO	Tjänstemännens Centralorganisation
TGWU	Transport and General Workers' Union
TUC	Trades Union Congress
UGT-E	Union General de Trabajadores (Spain)
UGT-P	União Geral de Trabalhadores (Portugal)
UIL	Unione Italiana del Lavoro
UNICE	Union of Industries of the European Community
WFTU	World Federation of Trade Unions

Introduction

The subject of this book is European employee relations, a subject that is characterized by a continual process of development and change. A part of that process is the increasing influence of European employee relations policies on EC Member States. Human resource management policies are now developed within a global context through transnational companies. Labour too is developing international trade union bodies that have an increasingly important role in policy making. Isolation is no longer an option and that makes it necessary to increase our understanding of the European dimension to employee relations. These international developments are taking place at a time when employee relations in the United Kingdom, for instance, are experiencing radical challenges. Many industrial relations shibboleths have been challenged by human resource management policies and the long period of office of the Conservative government. The key features of change have been well rehearsed. The trade unions have suffered a dramatic membership decline since 1979 and a major reduction in their political influence. Their role at the workplace has been subject to wider debate regarding the relative importance of continuity and change (Bassett, 1986; MacInnes, 1987). Traditional management practices have been challenged by the confrontational styles developed in highly unionized industries such as printing and mining. More significant has been the growing adoption of human resource management practices and the example set in this respect by Japanese companies investing in the United Kingdom. In the public sector, privatization in all its forms has had a major impact on management practice in the employee relations field. The role of the State in employee relations has also shifted significantly. The neo-corporatism of the 1970s has been replaced by an open hostility to trade unionism and an encouragement of private sector management methods in public sector organizations. There has been a decade of employment legislation designed to reduce trade union power and limit State intervention in the labour market.

In Western Europe, we have witnessed an overall decline of national corporatism and the growing influence of the European Community. The Community itself continues to expand in size and it has an increasing influence on national governments. The Single European Act was signed in 1986 and created the Single European Market. This gave a new stimulus to the development of a Social Dimension as did the EC Community Charter of the Fundamental Social Rights of Workers, which is commonly known as the Social Charter and was signed in 1989 by all the Member States, with the exception of the United Kingdom. Further decisions affecting employee rights were made at the inter-governmental conference in Maastricht in 1991 at which the Treaty of European Union was agreed. The United Kingdom refused to sign the Social Chapter and opted out of its specific social provisions. However, as other Member States will go ahead with decision making in the sphere of social policy, and Britain is still covered by the Treaty of Rome and the Single European Act in such areas as equal opportunities and health and safety, it must be doubtful whether Britain can isolate itself from the outcomes.

It is clear that British industrial relations is increasingly becoming part of a European framework and yet British understanding of continental systems has been limited by parochialism and the different development of the UK system. The British Government's refusal to participate in European employee relations developments in Maastricht in 1991 is the most recent example of an isolationism that has a longer history. For example, in his discussion of European trade unions, Kendall (1975, p. xiii) observes that 'too often it has been assumed that the mode of operation of labour movements in Britain and the United States conforms to some objective norm from which labour movements in other countries diverge for unexplained, but by implication irrational, reasons'. In this book we set out to establish the differences and the commonalities in European employee relations. We do not start from a perspective of Britain either as 'market leader' or in desperate need to catch up. Rather, we are concerned to develop an overall picture of European employee relations practice.

Comparative Analysis

As we have argued elsewhere (Bridgford and Stirling, 1991, p. 263), comparative analysis is not simply an end in itself. An understanding of employee relations in other countries can inform policy making in the United Kingdom, but there is a need to draw a balance between what is culturally specific and what is generally applicable. On the one hand, the pioneering study by Kerr and his colleagues (1962) emphasized the 'convergence' of industrializing economies and focused on a systems model of employee relations in which the common features were stressed. In broad terms, the emergence of trade unions in one form or another appears inevitable and with them come employers' organizations and collective bargaining. The State necessarily intervenes in the employee relations process to a greater or lesser degree and the actors establish a system. On a global scale, the industrialized western economies become a model for developing countries and an institutionalized employee relations system becomes a part of the package. On the other hand there are those authors who stress the importance of cultural diversity (Poole, 1986). In this approach, attention is focused on social, cultural and political differences which are seen as likely to remain and even grow rather than be smothered by industrialization.

It is fruitless to join battle with one side or other of a false dichotomy. There are factors working in both directions and at different speeds and levels. In reality, both managers and workers face common problems in industrialized market economies and a comparative analysis explores the different responses to them. In this respect, comparison can be informative but should not be prescriptive. Bean (1985) has gone as far as to suggest that

> The most important and overriding purpose of comparative studies is not for any practical policy implications which may be derived. Rather, by exploring the determinants of similarities and differences found between national systems, they can help promote the development of industrial relations as an academic discipline. (p. 7)

This is a necessary caveat for those who would wish to 'import' employee relations systems as if they were manufactured products. For example, it is clear that the 1971 Industrial Relations Act drew heavily on the American experience. The legislation proved disastrous in the United Kingdom and was effectively abandoned by the Conservative government, even before it was repealed by the following Labour government. However, this is not to say that there were no lessons for the United Kingdom to draw from the United States or that similar legislation could not have been introduced in other circumstances. American laws made an important contribution to the development of British legislation on equal opportunities, and Japanese companies with plants in the United Kingdom have become 'market leaders' in the development of human resource management.

There are a number of common features in the Western European economies covered in this book which underline the necessity of developing a comparative analysis. In general terms we are discussing liberal capitalist democracies with independent trade union movements and free collective bargaining arrangements. More specifically, these countries have experienced a number of similar changes. Firstly, there is the industrial restructuring that has affected most European economies since the oil crises of the 1970s. This has led to changes in employment patterns which have a considerable effect on the development of human resource policies (we discuss this in detail in chapter 1). Secondly, there has been the post-war development of global companies which now dominate the world economy. These organizations have developed their own employee relations policies and have often attempted to export them through the power of the dollar or the yen. Thirdly, there is the growing influence of the European Community. The EC is now a significant actor in the field of employee relations policy development either directly through its own legislation or indirectly through its encouragement of the process of social dialogue between European trade unions and employers' organizations. Each of these factors means that comparative analysis is essential to understanding, evaluation and policy making. In what follows we hope to indicate the variety of employee relations in Western Europe and also the common reactions to common problems.

Approach of the Book

Our focus of attention is on those matters of direct concern to employee relations students and practitioners. We have opted for English translations for the sake of consistency. However, this has its problems given that some words carry with them meanings beyond the literal translation. For example, Schregle (1987) argues that

... it may have been a mistake (now past remedy) to translate the German word *Betriebsrat* by the English expression 'works council'. This term has a definite meaning in the English-speaking world where it usually refers to a joint body composed of management and labour representatives with advisory or consultative functions that are kept separate from the collective bargaining functions of a trade union. By contrast, the works council of the Federal Republic is not a joint body but consists of elected workers' representatives only. It is an instrument for labour–management cooperation and has both advisory and collective bargaining functions. (p. 320)

Terms such as manager or shop steward can also be confusing. As Lane (1989) notes in relation to managers

... the word 'manager' is of Anglo-American origin and has entered French and German usage only in recent decades. In France and Germany the term still coexists, and competes with, indigenous titles which have different social and organizational implications. (p. 87)

On the trade union side, as we shall see in chapter 3, 'workplace representative' as a term cannot cover the different roles of the French '*délégués du personnel*', the Danish '*tillidsrepraesentant*' or the British 'shop steward'. In general we have retained the common English usage except where this would be misleading and have explored the differences between managers, union representatives and employee participation systems in the appropriate sections.

We have tried to stress European issues that have a direct influence on employee relations in the United Kingdom. Inevitably, this means that we give considerable weight to the decisions of the EC. However, the increasing internationalization of business, the growing geographical mobility of managers and the increasing importance of transnational trade unionism means that European employee relations systems and working conditions are likely to have an increasing impact on the United Kingdom. A British manager would be unable to make decisions in a European subsidiary without a basic understanding of issues such as dismissal or equal opportunities policies. Similarly, British trade unionists would make little headway unless they understood the organization of the European movement or the collective bargaining arrangements in other countries.

Finally, we have tried to address the pace at which change is taking place in Europe. For example it is evident that the development of human resource management strategies are rapidly gaining popularity. We have responded to some of the features of this approach but would record that the changes are occurring within the well-established employee relations frameworks that are the central focus of this book. Change cannot and should not be ignored but it must be placed clearly in context. It is this context that is our focus here. We have been as up to date as deadlines and the slow workings of the EC allow but our primary purpose is to provide the context which explains change.

Outline of the Book

In line with what we have said above about commonalities we have organized our book around themes rather than on a country by country basis. We have devoted a brief section to the EC as an institution but we have been more concerned to integrate the most significant EC decisions into the relevant chapters. In the first three chapters we develop an analysis of the employee relations context by focusing on labour market developments and the changing role of managers, unions and the State.

The changing pattern of employment in Europe is critical to an understanding of the development of human resource management policies. There have been major structural readjustments in different sectors of the European economy which have had significant implications for both State policy making and the trade unions. We explore the global changes in employment patterns and the specific trends in employment patterns for men and women, young and old, and those outside traditional full time employment. There is a variety of often competing evidence in these areas and it is clear that while there are very broad European trends the pattern and pace of change is by no means universal. Related to the changing patterns of employment has been the development of human resource models based on core and peripheral workforces and 'flexible specialization'. As we discuss in chapter 1, such developments have considerable implications for employee relations in general and trade unions in particular.

In chapter 2 we look at the influence of public authorities on employee relations. We begin by exploring the traditional 'voluntarist' approach of the State developed in the United Kingdom in contrast to much of the rest of Europe where more legalist traditions prevail. The role of the State is important in countries such as Spain, Greece and Portugal which moved from dictatorships to western democracies and where socialist governments played a leading role in establishing workers' rights. In other European countries neo-corporatism was a common feature of Social Democratic or Labour government policies and this gave a key political role to the trade unions. This approach has now weakened considerably, most obviously in the United Kingdom and also, albeit to a lesser extent, in the Scandinavian countries with their long traditions of social democracy. We discuss the role of the State as law-maker in the employee relations field and the ways in which the EC is now assuming a role as a supranational political actor. We also focus on the State's role as a mediator in industrial conflict and as an employer.

Chapter 3 is concerned with the two other major actors in industrial relations: management and the unions. We look briefly at historical developments and at the characteristics of employers' organizations and trade unions. Trade unions in particular have developed different trajectories in the different European States in terms of levels of membership, methods of organizing and political orientation. We also consider the increasing importance of transnational trade union and employers' bodies. The European Trade Union Confederation (ETUC) and the European employers' federation (UNICE) are now, clearly, political actors at the European level and partners in the 'social dialogue' which provides a forum for the potential development of new European collective bargaining arrangements.

The relationship between managers and employees through participation and bargaining structures is the subject of chapter 4. We begin by looking at the different levels at which collective bargaining takes place and then explore the question of whether Europe-wide company bargaining is on the agenda. In the field of employee participation schemes, there are marked differences between the *laissez-faire* approach which prevails in the United Kingdom and the statutory provision which is common in most other Western European countries. Finally, we consider the question of the failure of the bargaining and participation process. Strike incidence varies considerably between Western European States, and a range of explanations of the variations in industrial conflict is examined.

In chapters 5 and 6 we turn to the variations in terms and conditions of employment across Western Europe. In an area where change is constant and accurate comparisons are often difficult to draw we have confined ourselves to the main features of key bargaining areas. We have developed a common format for a number of areas. Firstly, we describe the general features of a particular area (such as retirement or working time) over a number of European countries. We then discuss the role of the EC in shaping policy in those areas and conclude by looking at the implications of developments at the European level for the United Kingdom. We cannot seek to be comprehensive (that is the job of reference documents) but we hope to indicate the variety of practices across Europe and the ways in which they are established.

Our conclusion draws together some of the common themes established in the preceding chapters and explores the future of European employee relations. We particularly wish to discuss the question of the 'Europeanization' of employee relations, and we return to our initial concerns with divergence and convergence. Our overall intention is to give a European perspective which will inform both analysis and policy making. It is becoming increasingly difficult for students and practitioners of employee relations to understand current developments in the United Kingdom without placing them in a European context. Our aim is to provide that context in this book.

1
Employment and the Labour Market

Labour markets both reflect and shape human resource policies. Enterprises seek to control their own internal markets and nation states attempt to manage employment and training. They do this within a framework of individual choice at one end of a spectrum and macro-economic change at the other. The interaction of these factors on a European scale alongside the national differences in employment patterns increases the difficulty of developing arguments and analysis that are universally applicable. This is further complicated by cultural assumptions, interpretation difficulties and the availability or otherwise of accurate data.

Employee relations policies are developed in relation to labour markets just as much as in relation to the status of the trade union movement or the role of legislation. For example, the development of equal opportunities policies in relation to the increases in women's employment or the development of 'two-tier' employment conditions in response to the development of a 'core' and 'peripheral' workforce. Thus, in order to develop an adequate understanding of European employee relations, an overview of labour market conditions must be established.

There is no doubt that post-war Europe has seen major changes in the nature of employment, and that this is continuing and, indeed, escalating. It is also becoming commonplace to suggest that labour market changes are a permanent feature of a fundamentally restructured economy. As the Commission of the European Communities (1989a) suggests:

> Firstly the economic conditions which gave full employment prior to 1973 – at least in the northern areas of the Community – will not

recur, at least in the form that they took then. The days when whole economies or regions could be dependent on heavy industry with vast workforces in individual factories are gone. Either the products or the technology of the industry have changed, so that the pattern and content of the work remaining is totally different, or the work is now done elsewhere in the world where the countries are in an earlier stage of development, where labour costs are substantially lower and where plants are often more modern than in the Community. (p. 8)

New patterns of employment are most commonly related to three factors: shifts between economic sectors and occupations; the changes in women's employment patterns and the alternations in demographic structure in relation to age. However, the distribution and pace of change is not evenly spread across the EC. Neither is there unanimity in discussions on the degree of change that is taking place in the development of a core and peripheral workforce. What has become supposedly commonplace in the United Kingdom may still be novel in countries such as Greece and Portugal or in the former command economies of Eastern Europe.

In the rest of this chapter we will be exploring these similarities and differences, as well as assessing the extent of change, by looking first at the broad developments in employment and unemployment patterns. We then move on to more detailed analysis of change by gender, age and through migration. The next section looks at the types of jobs people do and how they are employed. This brings us into the contemporary debates about flexibility and core and periphery workers which we shall review within a European context. Finally, we will look at the role of State policies in regulating employment.

Workforce Size

It is an often neglected point that in most industrialized capitalist countries the majority of the population is not in paid employment. For example, in only one of the EC Member States, Denmark, does the number at work or seeking work exceed half of the population (table 1.1). At the opposite extreme to Denmark are Ireland and Spain where little more than a third of the respective populations are economically active. The pace of change is also different between the Member States. While there has been an overall growth

Table 1.1 Labour force participation (total civilian working population as a percentage of the total population)

	1970	*1980*	*1989*	*Change 1970 to 1989*
Belgium	39.7	42.2	40.8	+1.1
Denmark	48.3	52.0	56.5	+8.2
Germany	44.2	44.2	47.1	+2.9
Greece	39.0	37.7	39.6	+0.6
Spain	38.6	36.0	38.2	−0.4
France	42.2	43.4	42.3	+0.1
Ireland	37.9	36.7	36.4	−1.5
Italy	38.8	39.8	41.2	+2.4
Luxembourg	40.0	41.8	43.4	+3.4
Netherlands	36.8	38.1	44.6	+7.8
Portugal	–	46.2	44.7	–
UK	45.5	47.6	49.4	+3.9
EC 12	–	42.5	44.0	–

Sources: Adapted from tables in Eurostat (1989) *Employment and Unemployment*; Eurostat (1991) *Basic Statistics of the Community*

in the percentage employed across the Community, Ireland and Spain have both experienced slight drops which contrasts with the substantial growth in Denmark and the Netherlands.

The EC as a whole falls behind the United States and Japan which had economically active populations of 50.1 and 49.8 per cent respectively in 1987. Moreover, the high unemployment levels of the Community has meant that a larger proportion of the economically active population is without jobs. As the Commission of the European Communities (1989a) records:

> The proportion of the population of working age which is in employment is still below the level achieved at the end of the 1970s. Furthermore, with the growth of part time employment, the overall volume of employment has grown much less, if at all. (p. 13)

As well as the social and individual costs of unemployment there are significant economic costs. These include the financial payments necessary to support a large non-working population and the foregone contributions of potential employees to economic growth.

Table 1.2   Unemployed persons as a percentage of the civilian labour force (1964–1993)

	1964–73	1974–83	1985	1987	1989	1991	1993*
Belgium	2.0	7.3	11.8	11.3	8.6	8.3	9.4
Denmark	0.9	6.1	7.2	5.6	7.7	8.6	9.1
France	2.2	5.7	10.1	10.4	9.4	9.7	10.4
Germany	0.7	3.7	7.1	6.3	5.6	4.3	4.9
Greece	4.2	3.2	7.8	7.4	7.5	8.6	10.0
Ireland	5.7	9.7	18.2	18.0	15.7	16.1	18.4
Italy	5.2	6.9	9.6	10.3	10.6	10.3	10.5
Luxembourg	0.0	1.4	3.0	2.5	1.8	2.0	1.9
Netherlands	1.3	7.1	10.5	10.0	8.5	7.0	7.8
Portugal	2.5	6.6	8.8	6.9	5.0	3.8	4.4
Spain	2.8	9.4	21.6	20.4	17.0	15.9	16.3
UK	2.0	6.1	11.4	10.4	7.1	9.4	11.0
EC 12	2.4	6.0	10.8	10.3	8.9	8.9	9.7
USA	4.6	7.5	7.2	6.2	5.3	6.7	6.8
Japan	1.2	2.1	2.6	2.8	2.3	2.1	2.1

* Forecast

Source: *European Economy*, Supplement A, No. 5/6, May/June 1992

Unemployment levels generally in Western Europe grew rapidly from the mid-1970s until the peak at the end of the 1980s. This is illustrated in the European Community in table 1.2. Rapidly rising unemployment has been associated with major economic reconstruction in the advanced capitalist States and many factors have been suggested to explain this. It is not our purpose to explore them in detail here, but those most commonly cited relate to changes in the global economy, such as oil price rises and the growth of low-cost manufacturing centres in newly industrializing countries. This was exacerbated in the advanced capitalist countries by the decline in profitability and an associated slump in investment (Armstrong et al., 1984). This has been linked with changing wage costs and productivity levels (Boyer, 1988). In addition, it is suggested that the substitution of capital for labour through technological change in industry has increased unemployment. Moreover, the late 1970s saw a substantial increase in the number of women and young people entering the labour market and an inadequate rate of new job creation. Between 1985 and 1990 employment in the EC increased by 1.5 per cent a year but only one-third of these jobs were filled by workers previously unemployed (Commission of the European Communities, 1991, p. 9).

Since 1987 there has been a persistent, if uneven, decline in European unemployment levels in most countries as economic growth and job generation have generally recovered. However, as we shall see, a significant component of this growth is related to part time employment and State training schemes. Furthermore, the trend had been reversed in many countries by 1991 and forecasts were for further expansion in unemployment (table 1.2). In these circumstances, there is no doubt that, even with changing demographic patterns and the predicted decline in entry to the labour market, unemployment will remain a major issue.

Even if the present (i.e., 1989) economic performance continued into the medium term it would still only bring unemployment down by 0.5 per cent a year, which would mean the unemployment rate in 1995 still being above the 1980 level. (Commission of the European Communities, 1989a, p. 21)

Sectoral Employment Patterns

Unemployment growth has been paralleled by shifting patterns of employment. The main features of the changes in sectoral employment patterns are longstanding and well known. Table 1.3 illustrates the points and makes a comparison between the European Community States and the United States and Japan. It is clear that there has been a substantial fall in agricultural employment which would have been even higher but for countries such as Greece and Portugal (table 1.4). No other nations match the figures for these two but Ireland, Spain and, to a lesser extent, Italy retain significant agricultural sectors. Much of this employment is regionally centred and encompasses countries other than those already mentioned – for example, southern Germany and north-west France. The significance of this for employee relations resides in the continuing importance within the sector of self-employment, the consequent low levels of unionization and the lack of other features associated with independent collective bargaining.

Table 1.3   Sectoral composition of the workforce in the EC, the USA and Japan (per cent)

	1970	1975	1980	1985	1987	1991
Agriculture						
EC	13.7	11.2	9.4	8.5	7.8	6.2
USA	4.4	4.0	3.5	3.1	3.0	–
Japan	17.4	12.7	10.4	8.8	8.3	–
Industry						
EC	40.8	38.8	36.9	32.8	32.1	31.3
USA	33.0	29.9	29.9	27.5	26.6	–
Japan	35.7	35.9	35.3	34.9	33.8	–
Services						
EC	45.6	50.0	53.6	58.7	60.1	62.3
USA	62.6	66.2	66.6	69.5	70.5	–
Japan	46.9	51.5	54.2	56.4	57.9	–

Sources: Eurostat (1989) *Employment and Unemployment*; Commission of the European Communities, 1992

Table 1.4   Economic sectors as a percentage of total employment

	Agriculture			Industry			Services		
	1970	1990	Change	1970	1990	Change	1970	1990	Change
Belgium	4.7	3.3	–1.4	41.6	30.7	–10.9	53.7	66.0	+12.3
Denmark	11.3	5.5	–5.8	37.1	27.3	–9.8	51.7	66.7	+15.0
France	13.2	6.4	–6.8	38.1	30.3	–7.8	48.7	62.9	+14.2
Germany	8.5	3.7	–4.8	48.4	40.1	–8.3	43.1	56.2	+13.1
Greece	38.8	23.9	–14.9	23.8	25.8	+2.0	37.4	50.2	+12.8
Ireland	26.9	15.2	–11.7	29.6	28.6	–1.0	43.5	55.7	+12.2
Italy	19.6	9.0	–10.6	38.4	32.4	–6.0	42.0	58.6	+16.6
Luxembourg	9.3	3.8	–5.5	44.1	29.3	–14.8	46.6	66.9	+20.3
Netherlands	6.1	4.6	–1.5	38.1	26.1	–12.0	55.7	68.5	+12.8
Portugal	–	18.1	–	–	34.0	–	–	47.6	–
Spain	28.5	11.9	–16.6	36.0	33.5	–2.5	35.5	54.6	+19.1
UK	3.2	2.2	–1.0	44.1	32.1	–12.0	52.7	65.1	+12.4

Sources: Eurostat (1989) *Employment and Unemployment*; Commission of the European Communities, 1992

The change in agricultural employment levels has been evident since the 1960s whereas the marked decline in industrial employment has been a more recent phenomenon. As table 1.3 illustrates, the industrial workforce fell by 9.5 per cent between 1970 and 1991, with the decline evening out since the mid-1980s. However, this also conceals as much as it reveals. The decline in employment has been in those industries which have had a particular force in shaping industrial relations policies. Mining, shipbuilding, the dockyards, steel making and heavy engineering have all suffered from disproportionately high levels of unemployment across Western Europe.

It is interesting to note that industrial employment did not fall as dramatically in the United States and, particularly, Japan as it did in the EC. However, both started from a lower base and the difference has now narrowed. Within the EC, there is a narrower range of employment levels in industry compared with agriculture (table 1.4). The Federal Republic of Germany retains the highest level of industrial employment while Denmark, Greece and the Netherlands have only around one-quarter of their workforces in that sector. These shifts from agricultural and industrial employment are in contrast to the growth in the service sector.

The service sector now accounts for over sixty per cent of employment in the Community, compared with little more than forty per cent twenty years ago. While part of this shift is a 'statistical illusion' – the result of industry increasingly contracting out business services such as cleaning and computing to firms who are classified in the service sector – the changes are far more extensive than this and reflect a major restructuring of the way we live our lives, as well as the way we work. (Commission of the European Communities, 1989, p. 9)

Again, it is clear that there are important international differences in the growth of employment in the service sector. The United States remains clearly in advance of the EC figure as a whole. However, Portugal, Greece and, to a lesser extent, Spain deflate the Community's overall percentage, and countries like Belgium, the Netherlands, the United Kingdom and Denmark are approaching the United States. Within individual nation states, employment in different services is growing or contracting at differential rates. Lindley (1987), for example, suggests that

Transport and storage is expected to decline at 0.5 per cent per annum in Germany and rise at the same rate in the Netherlands (remaining stable in France and the UK). Financial institutions are expanding in the German and the UK scenarios and contracting in the French and Dutch assessments. The other producer services appear to be declining in the Netherlands and expanding at almost 2 per cent per annum in the UK, with more modest growth in France and Germany. (p. 56)

Within the service sector, public employment has also played a significant role in post-war employment growth. Even leaving aside State owned industries, the public sector expanded considerably across the EC until the mid-1980s. This was in line with global trends which showed an increase in public service employment in countries of the Organization for Economic Co-operation and Development (OECD) from 14.2 per cent of the total labour force in 1970 to nearly 18.0 per cent in 1979 (International Labour Organization 1984, p. 49). In the Federal Republic of Germany, for example, public employment increased by nearly 60 per cent between 1960 and 1980. The major contributors to this growth were not central government agencies but, rather, areas such as health, education and social welfare. In France and the United Kingdom these sectors accounted for around a half of public sector employment and of 3.4 million public employees in Italy in 1979, 0.9 million were in education and 0.6 million in the health services.

During the 1980s the rate of growth in public sector employment slowed and the United Kingdom has not been the only nation seeking to divest itself of civil servants. Looking at public sector employment in the industrialized market economies as a whole the Economic Commission for Europe (1988) records that

> ... the general weakening of the growth of public sector employment can be seen from the fact that prior to the recession employment increased more rapidly than total service sector employment in all countries except the United States; during the recovery from the recession this was the case in only three of the seven countries for which data were available. (p. 49)

As with the other shifts in employment, these changes have important implications for employee relations policies. Public sector service employment has often been well unionized, with a highly formalized industrial relations framework. However, the private sector can provide a marked contrast, with much less traditional employee relations policies and, in many cases, lower trade union membership levels. Boyer (1988, pp. 203–6) has suggested that the growth in the service sector across Europe alters the balance of bargaining power in favour of management.

Developments in sectoral employment patterns are linked with other changes in relation to gender, occupational structure and atypical employment contracts.

Male and Female Employment

In the broadest terms, male employment has been declining in Western Europe and female labour force participation has been rising. Areas of declining employment in traditional industrial sectors have been associated with men's work whereas job creation has been overwhelmingly in sectors where women are more likely to participate. As Bakker (1988, p. 19) notes, similar trends have occurred in most other industrialized economies: 'a decline in male rates has occurred in most Organization for Economic Co-operation and Development countries while . . . the female participation rate has been on the increase everywhere and has, in some countries, more than doubled'. These generalizations are now the conventional wisdom but they conceal considerable variation across Europe and disguise the seemingly paradoxical growth in women's unemployment.

Table 1.5 looks at the growth of women's employment as a percentage of the employed workforce. In each of the EC Member States there has been an increase in the proportion of women employed. However, there are differences in participation levels, ranging from 31.9 per cent in Spain to 45.9 per cent in Denmark. Also, women's increased involvement in the workforce is not characterized by secure employment. Female unemployment rates across the EC are typically higher than for males (table 1.6). It has also been suggested that official statistics under-represent female unemployment because women are less likely to register since there is often no material benefit in terms of social security payments.

The changes in male and female employment levels are related to developments in both economic and occupational structures as well as the development of atypical forms of work. The most significant economic shift has been from industrial to service sector

Table 1.5   Percentage of women in the employed workforce

	1985	1990	Increase
Belgium	35.1	37.5	2.4
Denmark	44.9	45.9	1.0
France	41.6	42.4	0.8
Germany	39.0	40.4	1.4
Greece	34.0	35.2	1.2
Ireland	30.9	33.1	2.2
Italy	32.2	34.2	2.0
Luxembourg	33.8	34.4	0.6
Netherlands	34.1	37.9	3.8
Portugal	40.0	42.1	2.1
Spain	29.3	31.9	2.6
UK	41.7	43.2	1.5
EC 12	37.2	38.9	1.7

Source: Calculated from figures in Commission of the European Communities, 1992

employment. It is this sector which is most closely associated with the growth of women's employment (table 1.7).

> Most women in employment work in the service sector – 73 per cent of the total in the Community as a whole – where their numbers are now almost as high as men. By contrast, only 20 per cent of women work in industry, less than half the proportion of men employed in this sector. (Commission of the European Communities, 1989a, p. 85)

The growth of service sector employment for women has been linked with the expansion of the public sector. As we have seen, post-war development saw considerable job creation in central and local government as well as in related welfare, health and education services throughout Western Europe. In countries where the service sector has not grown so rapidly at the expense of industrial employment, women's participation rates have grown less steadily. In the Federal Republic of Germany, for example, industry has retained a higher proportion of jobs, often of a skilled nature, and women's employment has increased by one of the smallest percentages in the European Community (table 1.5). In Italy, service employment

Table 1.6   Unemployment rates (annual averages)

	1983	*1984*	*1985*	*1986*	*1987*	*1988*	*1989*	*1990*	*1991*
Males									
Belgium	8.6	8.4	7.5	7.4	7.5	6.7	5.4	4.8	5.0
Denmark	8.2	7.4	5.6	4.0	4.5	5.2	5.8	7.3	7.9
France	6.3	7.9	8.4	8.5	8.3	7.7	7.1	6.8	7.3
Germany	6.2	6.1	6.1	5.2	5.1	4.9	4.4	4.0	3.7
Greece	5.8	6.0	5.6	5.1	5.1	4.9	4.9	4.3	–
Ireland	14.6	16.3	17.5	17.5	17.4	17.0	16.1	13.9	15.4
Italy	5.8	6.3	6.3	7.1	6.9	7.2	7.4	6.5	6.9
Luxembourg	2.6	2.4	2.1	1.8	1.8	1.6	1.4	1.2	1.2
Netherlands	11.1	11.0	9.2	8.4	7.5	7.2	6.8	5.6	5.3
Portugal	5.3	6.5	6.7	6.4	5.1	3.9	3.4	3.2	2.8
Spain	16.5	19.4	20.3	19.2	16.8	15.0	12.7	11.9	12.2
UK	11.9	11.9	11.7	11.8	10.8	8.7	7.1	7.4	10.0
EC 12	8.7	9.4	9.4	9.2	8.6	7.8	7.0	6.6	7.3
Females									
Belgium	19.0	19.3	18.4	18.5	17.6	15.2	13.3	11.9	11.4
Denmark	10.5	10.2	9.1	7.4	7.0	7.4	7.8	8.8	9.5
France	10.8	12.3	12.6	12.8	13.3	12.8	12.7	11.8	12.2
Germany	8.0	8.6	8.7	8.1	7.9	7.8	7.3	6.0	5.2
Greece	11.7	12.1	11.7	11.6	11.4	12.5	12.7	11.7	–
Ireland	16.5	18.0	19.7	19.9	19.3	18.9	18.8	15.5	17.5
Italy	14.6	15.5	15.5	16.6	16.0	16.9	17.3	15.5	15.9
Luxembourg	5.3	4.4	4.3	4.0	3.9	3.1	2.7	2.5	2.3
Netherlands	14.7	14.9	12.8	13.4	14.0	13.1	13.2	10.6	9.7
Portugal	11.9	11.9	11.7	10.9	9.2	7.9	7.2	6.4	5.7
Spain	20.8	23.3	25.2	25.2	27.7	27.5	25.2	24.0	23.6
UK	9.9	10.6	11.0	11.0	9.9	8.1	6.1	6.5	7.9
EC 12	11.8	12.7	12.9	13.0	12.9	12.5	11.8	10.8	11.0

Source: *Unemployment*, Eurostat 4/1990 and 7/1992

is also at the lower end of the range and the public sector plays a minor role in job provision for women (del Boca, 1988, p. 128) but this is counterbalanced by the importance of women's employment in the 'informal' sector of the Italian economy dominated by small firms.

Alongside changes in sectoral employment patterns are developments in occupational structures. It is clear that occupational

Table 1.7 Female employment by economic sector (percentage of total women's employment)

	Agriculture			Industry			Services		
	1985	1990	Change	1985	1990	Change	1985	1990	Change
Belgium	3.1	2.3	−0.8	16.7	15.9	−0.8	80.3	81.8	+1.5
Denmark	3.4	2.8	−0.6	15.8	15.9	+0.1	80.6	80.8	+0.2
France	7.1	5.2	−1.9	19.2	17.7	−1.5	73.3	76.7	+3.4
Germany	6.3	4.1	−2.2	25.6	25.2	−0.4	68.1	70.7	+2.6
Greece	37.8	30.2	−7.6	16.5	17.3	+0.8	45.6	52.4	+6.8
Ireland	7.0	4.8	−2.2	19.1	18.9	−0.2	73.3	76.1	+2.8
Italy	11.5	9.4	−2.1	24.5	23.2	−1.3	64.0	67.4	+3.4
Luxembourg	4.0	3.7	−0.3	10.0	9.3	−0.7	86.0	88.9	+2.9
Netherlands	3.1	3.3	+0.2	11.8	11.0	−0.8	84.2	84.9	+0.7
Portugal	25.9	21.3	−4.6	24.5	25.7	+1.2	49.5	52.8	+3.3
Spain	13.8	10.1	−3.7	16.8	17.7	+0.9	69.2	72.2	+3.0
UK	1.2	1.1	−0.1	19.2	17.2	−2.0	78.1	81.1	+3.0
EC 12	7.7	5.7	−2.0	20.2	19.2	−1.0	71.7	74.8	+3.1

Source: Calculated from data in Commission of the European Communities, 1992. (Figures have been rounded)

segregation by gender remains deeply rooted within European and other industrialized nations. It also appears that this segregation is not being reduced as more women participate in the labour market. As Bakker (1988, p. 29) says, 'in general, the countries with the highest levels of participation also have greater measured occupational segregation'. In particular, women are located in service occupations at lower skill, pay and status levels. In France, Germany and the United Kingdom, for example, around three-quarters of the female labour force work as clerical, professional, sales or service personnel. No more than 1.5 per cent in 1985 worked in managerial grades (Bakker, 1988, p. 29). This contrasts with the figures of 4.8 and 5.9 for Canada and the United States respectively although these levels still represent a tiny proportion of female employment.

The developments in the gender distribution of employment have important consequences for human resource management particularly when they are related to changes in demographic structure. Potential labour shortages in the next century are likely to see employers balancing the need for numerical flexibility with the desire to recruit and retain women workers. Equal opportunities policies have already been given a stimulus by EC legislation, and national governments and trade unions will also have to turn their attention to that area if they wish to increase female membership. Thus, the focus of collective bargaining may move to incorporate issues such as equal access to promotion and training opportunities as well as maternity pay and equal value claims.

We return to gender differences in European employment when we examine atypical employment later in this chapter but we now turn our attention to the age distribution of employment.

Young and Old Workers

From the mid-1970s onwards job opportunities for workers entering the labour market or approaching retirement have become increasingly scarce. Companies introducing large-scale redundancies or public sector employers facing financial stringency have often adopted non-recruitment policies or early retirement schemes as coping mechanisms. School leavers and older workers have been likely to face long periods of unemployment with, in the latter case, perhaps little chance of ever returning to a job. This has been exacerbated by the regional nature of employment, work opportunities being associated only with one or a small cluster of employers operating in declining industries, such as in mining, steel and shipyard communities. Current demographic changes and projections into the medium-term future suggest that this position may soon be reversed and that it is labour shortages rather than over-supply that may be a problem for the EC.

After peaking in 2005, by 2010 the population of Europe will be only 2 per cent more than now [1989] . . . The Community share of the world's population is expected to fall from 6.4 per cent to 4.7 per cent by 2010. By 2025 there will probably be about 2 per cent fewer people in Europe than at present. (Commission of the European Communities, 1989a, p. 93)

These changes will be differentially distributed between European countries – table 1.8 shows projected changes in the over-65 population. It is interesting to note that the predicted peak year is 2030 when, for example, there will be a difference of over 7

Table 1.8   Percentage of the population aged 65 and over for selected European countries

	1980	1990	2000	2010	2020	2030	2040	2050
Finland	11.98	13.14	14.43	16.76	21.73	23.78	23.14	22.70
France	13.96	13.79	15.28	16.26	19.45	21.76	22.72	22.33
Germany	15.51	15.51	17.12	20.35	21.74	25.82	27.60	24.48
Italy	13.45	13.77	15.31	17.28	19.37	21.92	24.15	22.61
Netherlands	11.51	12.69	13.46	15.13	18.89	22.96	24.77	22.61
Sweden	16.29	17.74	16.58	17.47	20.81	21.70	22.47	21.40
UK	14.87	15.13	14.48	14.61	16.27	19.24	20.43	18.74
OECD States	12.20	12.95	13.94	15.36	17.96	20.62	22.09	21.36

Source: Adapted from Euzeby, 1989, p. 13

percentage points between the Federal Republic of Germany and the United Kingdom. Ten years later, it is predicted that the percentage of older workers in the labour force will have declined overall and the difference between the top and bottom countries will have been reduced to under 6 per cent. We also need to look at activity rates among older members of the population and bear in mind that statutory retirement ages are becoming less significant with the growth of early retirement arrangements. In many European countries, the real retirement age is now consistently below the statutory level.

Young people are also experiencing different employment patterns. As is clear from table 1.9, unemployment among people under 25 is significantly higher than the overall rates across the EC. The Community average unemployment rate of 8.3 per cent in 1990 was almost half of the 16.0 per cent figure for the under 25s. There is considerable speculation about the future development of young people's employment, particularly in the light of predicted demographic changes.

Over the next 35 years the numbers of young people aged between 15 and 19 is projected to decline from over 7 per cent of total population to around 5 per cent . . . Overall the decline in numbers across the (European) Community might be as much as 15 per cent over this period. (Commission of the European Communities 1990a, p. 113)

Table 1.9 Comparative unemployment rates (per cent)

	1983	1984	1985	1986	1987	1988	1989	1990
Males and females, all ages								
Belgium	12.5	12.5	11.6	11.6	11.4	10.0	8.5	8.1
Denmark	9.3	8.7	7.2	5.6	5.7	6.5	7.7	7.9
France	8.2	9.8	10.2	10.3	10.4	9.9	9.4	9.0
Germany	6.9	7.1	7.1	6.3	6.2	6.1	5.5	5.1
Greece	7.8	8.1	7.8	7.4	7.4	7.7	7.5	7.5
Ireland	15.2	16.8	16.2	18.2	18.0	17.4	16.0	15.6
Italy	8.8	9.3	9.6	10.5	10.2	10.8	10.7	9.8
Luxembourg	3.5	3.1	2.9	2.6	2.6	2.1	1.8	1.6
Netherlands	12.4	12.3	10.5	10.2	10.0	9.3	8.7	8.1
Portugal	8.0	8.7	8.8	8.2	6.8	5.6	4.8	4.6
Spain	17.8	20.6	21.8	21.1	20.4	19.3	17.1	16.1
UK	11.1	11.3	11.4	11.4	10.4	8.5	7.0	6.4
EC 12	9.9	10.7	10.8	10.7	10.3	9.7	8.9	8.3
Males and females under 25								
Belgium	27.2	27.7	24.9	23.3	22.6	19.6	17.0	16.0
Denmark	17.3	13.8	10.6	7.7	8.1	8.7	10.8	11.0
France	21.5	26.0	25.7	24.8	23.7	22.2	20.0	18.6
Germany	11.8	11.4	10.3	7.6	6.9	6.5	5.3	4.5
Greece	22.8	23.9	23.9	24.1	24.8	25.8	24.8	24.8
Ireland	22.3	24.2	26.1	26.8	26.3	25.1	21.9	21.6
Italy	30.1	31.7	31.8	33.2	31.7	32.4	31.4	28.9
Luxembourg	8.1	6.8	6.7	6.1	6.0	5.0	4.0	3.5
Netherlands	22.3	21.3	17.7	16.8	17.1	14.7	13.4	11.6
Portugal	18.5	19.7	19.9	19.2	15.9	13.0	11.1	10.0
Spain	42.7	46.9	48.1	46.0	43.0	40.0	34.0	31.5
UK	20.2	19.2	18.3	18.1	15.5	12.5	9.8	9.4
EC 12	22.8	23.8	23.1	22.3	21.0	19.6	17.8	16.0

Source: *Unemployment*, Eurostat, 3/1991

Long-term unemployment has also been a problem for both young and old workers. In the former case this has meant that they have been denied job opportunities altogether and, in the latter case, that there has been a premature end to their working lives. There has been a substantial growth in long-term unemployment in all the EC Member States. In 1990, almost half of the unemployed in the Community had been out of work for at least one year and a further third for at least two years (Commission of the European Communities, 1992). In all of the Member States, apart from Denmark and the Federal Republic of Germany, at least one-quarter of the long-term unemployed were under 25 and in Italy it was just over 60 per cent (Sexton, 1988, p. 38). The gender distribution shows that, in general, long-term unemployment has been rising for women and declining for men. There are also differences between economic sectors, with building, distribution and metal manufacturing tending to have higher levels. 'The greater emphasis which the industrial sector assumes for the long-term unemployed is noticeably present in the case of Belgium, Greece, the Netherlands and the United Kingdom' (ibid., p. 46).

Migration

Europe has been characterized by shifting populations and changing national boundaries throughout much of its history and the developments in Eastern Europe in the 1990s are a contemporary manifestation of that tradition. Within the EC, freedom of movement was one of the founding principles and the development of the Single European Market has strengthened that commitment. The movement of labour within Europe and migration from the outside is not a new phenomenon. Some nations have experienced considerable population movements between regions and others have relied on migrant workers from beyond Europe to undertake jobs in important sectors of their economies.

The modern period of mass migration within, and into, Europe occurred during the economic expansion of the post-war period. Immigration from non-European States was largely associated with ex-colonial countries, although the Federal Republic of Germany also developed close links with Turkey and received refugees from the Eastern European States. Within Western Europe, migration was generally a south–north movement. The southern regions of Italy, Spain, Portugal and Greece were the major losers. For example, in the thirty years from 1945 to 1975

Fifteen million immigrants and their families settled in northern Europe, drawn mainly from the Mediterranean countries (Greece, Spain, Turkey, Portugal, Italy and Yugoslavia). The Greeks, Turks and Yugoslavs went to Germany. Algerians, Portugese, Spaniards, Italians and West Africans went to France. Britain drew its migrant population from its former colonies (India, Pakistan and the Caribbean). Holland's immigrant population is also drawn from its former colonies of Indonesia and Surinam. (Gerhardt et al., 1985, p. 14)

Countries such as France, the Federal Republic of Germany and the United Kingdom established recruitment offices overseas to encourage emigration and by the 1970s 'in France, Belgium and Switzerland, one-quarter of the industrial workforce was immigrant' (Webber, 1991, p. 12). The United Kingdom offered its immigrants citizenship in contrast with other European States, which adopted 'guest worker' systems offering little security and few legal rights. As we shall discuss in chapter 6, this has had important consequences for the development of legislation on race relations and employment.

Changing economic circumstances and stricter immigration controls for non-European residents have combined to restrict such mass movements of labour from the mid-1970s onwards. Firstly, transnational companies have shifted their investment strategies and work has moved to sources of labour rather than the other way around. Secondly, economic development in the new EC States and elsewhere in the world has encouraged some nationals to return to their own countries. For instance, the number of foreign residents in France decreased by 130,000 between 1982 and 1990 and this is largely attributable to such developments (Garson, 1992, p. 21). Thirdly, there has been a Europe-wide movement to introduce or strengthen laws on immigration. From the mid-1970s countries such as France, the Netherlands and Belgium imposed strict controls and began to deport guest workers whose permits were no longer valid. The United Kingdom also tightened its policies although its immigrants had the right to settle. These restrictions on immigration have been stimulated in the 1980s and 1990s by the break-up of the old command economies in Eastern Europe and growing expectations of large population movements (Read and Simpson, 1991). Thus, as the movement of labour within EC States is eased, the barriers to entry from the outside are raised.

In 1989 there were 12.5 million foreign residents in EC States of whom 5.5 million were EC nationals. The bulk of these lived in the Federal Republic of Germany, France and the United Kingdom although the Netherlands and Belgium also have significant populations. The non-EC nationals will not have the same rights to free movement as other workers.

In reality, the 'free movement' of EC citizens will continue to be restricted by cultural, social and language barriers. One exception to this may be the creation of cross-national labour markets within multinational companies for professional and senior managerial staff. Teague (1989, p. 18) suggests that this may become the most significant form of mobility within the Community and we return to this in our discussion of management in chapter 3.

Migration has brought with it a number of issues related to employee relations policies. Non-professional migrant workers have often found employment opportunities restricted to low status, low skilled and low paid jobs. They have also tended to experience higher than average unemployment levels. This has led to the development of equal opportunities legislation in relation to permanently settled immigrants, although at EC level such laws have confined themselves to gender rather than national differences. Employers and trade unions have also sought to develop equal opportunities policies. However, it is clear that practice has not always matched policy.

Atypical Employment

So far, we have considered the changes in patterns of employment and unemployment. We now turn to the sort of jobs that people do when they are employed. In particular, we will look at the significance of employment in various types of company and explore the contribution of small and medium-size enterprises (SMEs) and self-employment to job creation. We will begin this section by looking at what has come to be called 'atypical' work and then move on to consider employment in the clandestine or 'black' economy.

Considerable attention has been focused on so-called non-traditional forms of work and, as we shall discuss later, they have become an important component of arguments suggesting a fundamental shift in the economic structure of capitalist industrial economies.

The new forms of work first appeared in practice slightly more than ten years ago. The innovation which they introduced did not consist in the actual content. Fixed-term employment, part time working, home-based work, and temporary employment already existed in some countries . . . What is new about them now is mainly: (a) their 'irresistible', unprecedented spread in all member states, with or without an employment contract: self employment, or employment in the black economy; (b) their recognition by certain legal systems, not always without some hesitation, using regulations which are not consistent with the principles governing labour law, so that it has some difficulty in accommodating them; (c) the fact that as they are encouraged – and promoted – by both governments and employers, the trade union organisations (currently in a weakened position) have no option but to accept them. (European Foundation for the Improvement of Living and Working Conditions, 1988, p. 19)

However, before we proceed down this 'irresistible' road, a number of important reservations need to be established. Firstly, employment in the EC countries remains dominated by full time work on a permanent basis undertaken by employees working for employers other than themselves. Secondly, atypical forms of work are, as suggested, not new and have, indeed, been typical in some areas of the economy – home-working in some sectors of the clothing industry or part time work in cleaning or catering, for example. Thirdly, while there are indications of change across Europe the pattern is uneven. With these caveats in mind, we will turn to developments in part time employment as the most commonly quoted change in employment patterns.

Part time Employment

It is clear that there has been an increase in part time employment in most countries. Figures from the early 1990s suggest an average of 15 per cent of workers are employed on a part time basis across the EC. However, the distribution of part time employment is uneven. In particular there is a clear gender division – almost 30 per cent of women were in part time employment in the Community in 1990 compared to just 4 per cent of men (Commission of the European Communities, 1992, p. 15). On a national basis, the United Kingdom and the Netherlands accounted for 42 per cent of female part time employment in the EC whereas there were still very low levels in countries such as Greece, Italy and Spain (ibid.). Commenting on the overall pattern in the EC countries, the Commission of the European Communities (1989a) concludes:

> Part time work is very much concentrated among women in the
> middle and older age groups . . . With the exception of the young in
> Denmark and the Netherlands, levels of part time work among men
> are still very low and show no signs of increasing. (p. 74)

However, we must be careful in drawing conclusions from the raw
data. For example, while the changes for men are small and generally less than those for women, Organization for Economic Co-
operation and Development figures do show an increase in male
part time employment rates. In the case of Denmark the increase
for men is higher than that for women, and in Norway a decline in
women's part time employment is partly offset by a growth in
men's. It is also clear that changes have occurred at different rates
across the European States. In some cases, statistical changes may
have influenced figures but, even taking them into account, Dale
and Glover (1989) argue that broad comparisons between nations
are valid. They conclude

> . . . that while the UK and Denmark have high levels of both labour
> force participation and part time working among women, the Nether-
> lands has low rates of labour market participation but high rates of
> part time working among women. On the other hand, France, which
> has a high rate of labour force participation, has a relatively low rate
> of part time working. This leads to the conclusion that, for women,
> high levels of labour force participation are not necessarily related to
> part time working. (p. 306)

Much of the increase in part time employment is related to the
growth of the service sector where it is the traditional pattern in a
number of occupations, such as catering and cleaning.

There is some debate about the 'voluntary' nature of much of
women's part time employment. Traditional arguments have suggested that it fits with the responsibilities they are given or assume
for the care of children or the elderly. However, the 'voluntary'
nature of such part time employment is questionable. There is evidence to suggest that it is 'involuntary' part time work as a substitute
for full time employment that is rising (Bakker, 1988, p. 21; International Labour Organization 1984, p. 50). On the other hand, an
EC survey concludes that 'of full time employees 21 per cent would
prefer a part time job, and of part time employees 30 per cent of
employees would rather have a full time job' (*European Economy*,
March 1991, p. 19).

Temporary Work

Temporary work may fall into a number of different categories. It may be full time or part time. It may be seasonal and also subject to fluctuations in demand for goods or services. Other temporary contracts may be for a pre-determined fixed term in order to complete a particular job or to cover for an absent employee. Temporary workers may also be registered with employment agencies and remain with them while taking a series of short-term appointments. A further category exists which strictly falls outside the scope of temporary employment but which is a growing phenomenon. This covers permanent employees working in foreign locations for their employer.

Given the wide range of temporary employment it is not a straightforward exercise to track changes or to quantify the extent. One survey of EC Member States in 1989 concluded that:

> Only some nine per cent of employees in the Community are currently on temporary contracts . . . For a third of workers with a temporary contract, the contract period runs for up to half a year. In the member states in which the proportion of temporary contracts is disproportionately high, seasonal work is likely to have been a major factor. (*European Economy*, March 1991, p. 31)

In the United Kingdom, evidence of a dramatic expansion of temporary employment has been challenged although there are some indications of slow growth, particularly in the public sector (*Labour Research*, August 1988, pp. 11–12). It also seems that temporary employment through agencies in those EC States where they are legally permitted has increased (*European Industrial Relations Review*, March 1989, pp. 11–16). In spite of the legal restrictions in Greece and Spain, they have, alongside Portugal, the most significant incidence of temporary employment in the EC. In this respect it can hardly be the case that temporary employment is related to the 'flexible firm' model that we discuss later. Rather it would seem to link with the more traditional seasonal activities of agriculture and tourism. Denmark and the Netherlands are the only other EC countries with a temporary workforce of marginally more than 10 per cent.

As with part time work there is some question about the voluntary nature of temporary work. In this case there seems to be a higher level of workers whose temporary status is involuntary. The European Commission's evidence suggests that, within the Member States, '50 per cent of women and 70 per cent of men doing temporary jobs are doing so because they could not find a permanent job' (1989a, p. 75). However, British evidence suggests that this might be changing. The 1989 Labour Force Survey records a fall to 25 per cent in the number of workers who took temporary jobs as substitutes for permanent ones (*IRS Employment Trends*, April 1990, p. 7). This change in attitude may be linked with changes in human resource management policies as organizations begin to adapt to changes in labour markets and shape working arrangements to fit individual life-styles. In any case, temporary employment needs to be viewed as both part of management strategy and individual choice as well as subject to State regulation such as the draft EC Directives on atypical employment.

The Clandestine Economy

The legal restrictions surrounding temporary work in some countries and its often clandestine nature brings us to an analysis of forms of work that exist outside the official European economy.

The nature of work outside the formal economy inevitably makes accurate information difficult to collect and levels of activity hard to quantify. It is also the case that a public image of unemployed workers taking on illicit low skilled work does not tally with the evidence of professional employees taking on second jobs. The size of the unofficial economy in Western Europe is impossible to estimate accurately. Inter-country comparisons are also problematic because of the different legal frameworks and social attitudes. Commenting on the EC alone, the Commission of the European Communities (1989a) has estimated that:

> In many regions of the Community, the 'black economy' is a regular fact of life involving a large proportion of the population. Surveys suggest that 30 per cent of people do some 'black work' on a regular basis, and a further 20 per cent occasionally. However, the amount of 'black work' performed by each individual is generally very small since it involves only occasional hours of work. This makes the total value of 'black work' low compared with the value of declared work. In most northern parts of the Community it is probably around 5

per cent or less, somewhat more in France and Belgium, and possibly reaches 10–20 per cent in the southern countries. (p. 130)

It is important to put the clandestine economy in its proper perspective and avoid exaggerated claims. However, it is equally important to notice its longstanding significance in some European States and in some sectors of the economy. For example, in Italy, the importance of unofficial work has been long known. Estimates of employment are very wide and range from about two million in 1974 to between four and seven million in 1979 (International Labour Organization, 1984, p. 51) and about 4.7 million in 1984 (Negrelli and Santi, 1990, p. 161). This latter figure would amount to nearly one-quarter of the labour force. Alongside Italy, Spain, Portugal, Ireland and Greece have higher levels of irregular employment. It is clear that much of this work is well established and traditionally linked to particular sectors such as agriculture, building, the retail trade, tourism and small-scale home-based activities such as the manufacture of clothing.

However, there is some evidence to suggest that irregular employment is growing and extending beyond these traditional boundaries. In this respect it is second jobs for workers already in employment that is the most significant category. It is also not surprising to find that it is the service sector of the clandestine economy that appears to be expanding at the expense of traditional areas and 'regular' employment in the sector is being replaced by a wider variety of arrangements. Temporary work appears to be concentrated in either professional activities or very low skilled jobs.

The significance of this changing pattern of irregular employment outside the official economy for employee relations lies in its relationship to the emergence of flexible working patterns. Unofficial employment is attractive to employers for two reasons. Firstly, it allows them the numerical flexibility to cope with fluctuating demands or one-off pieces of work. Secondly, it reduces labour costs by eliminating contributions to State benefit schemes and cutting out non-wage benefits to the unofficial worker. As well as the anticipated State hostility that this generates it may also create problems for competitor employers. The unofficial work is effectively undermining established wage rates for particular jobs to the detriment of trade union bargaining power. It will also mean competition on price and potential reductions in market share for those employers who do not benefit from the unofficial 'wage rates'.

Small and Medium-size Enterprises

The clandestine economy, while often officially condemned, is also sometimes regarded as a flexible and dynamic sector. It is characterized by small businesses and self-employment which are often viewed in the same way. As Rainnie (1989) records in relation to the United Kingdom, 'small is supposed to be not only beautiful, but also dynamic, efficient, competitive and, perhaps most important, a source of new jobs' (p. 1). The distribution of self-employment and small and medium-size enterprises (SMEs) across Europe shows wide variation and has been particularly low in the United Kingdom which may help to explain the British panegyrics. However, EC policy has been supportive of SME development and some Member States have developed schemes to encourage new businesses (the United Kingdom, Ireland and France) or to provide them with easier and cheaper access to loans (the Federal Republic of Germany, the Netherlands and Belgium).

Their contribution to employment generation must be treated with considerable caution partly because of the statistical difficulties inherent in collecting data and making appropriate international comparisons in this field (Lindley, 1987, pp. 60–1), and partly because of the need to get the small firm figures in perspective. For instance, it is unrealistic to expect small firms to create enough jobs to counterbalance the loss of employment created by just one factory closure of a large transnational company. As Storey and Johnson (1987) point out:

> Over a period as long as twelve years, only a very small minority (less than ten per cent) of small firms grow out of the smallest size category, and less than one per cent of firms grow sufficiently to become large enterprises (with more than 100 employees). (p. 16)

However, with these reservations in mind, 'the evidence also suggests that the share of employment accounted for by SMEs is increasing' (Commission of the European Communities, 1989a, p. 81). There is wide variation in the EC when comparing SME penetration of manufacturing industry. The Greek and Italian manufacturing sectors have over half their employees working in companies of less than a hundred people. Most of the other Member States have stable employment levels of around one-third or just over. The United Kingdom is unique in its recent expansion of the small firm sector in manufacturing but it still remains at one of the lowest rates, accounting only for around 20 per cent of employment.

Growth in Europe in small firm employment has been part of the expansion of the service sector, in which over half the jobs are now provided by SMEs. Further significant growth in small business employment is therefore dependent on the continuing expansion of that sector. Given the dominance of services in the SME sector it is not surprising to find a link between small firm employment and women's part time work. As Storey and Johnson (1987) argue:

> Small firms tend to employ a greater proportion of female workers and particularly part time females. A Dutch survey . . . suggests that 37 per cent of small firm employees (i.e. with 1–9 employees) are female compared with 26 per cent of large firm (100+) employees. In the Federal Republic of Germany, it is found that a disproportionate number of female small firm employees were working part time. Firms with less than 20 workers employed 30 per cent of all female workers, but 40 per cent of all female part time workers. (p. 20)

What are the implications of small firm employment for human resource management? The ideal typical model is one of close personal relations, high levels of communication and, as a consequence, good employment conditions. Small businesses are often contrasted with the impersonal bureaucracy of large corporations where work is characterized by personal isolation and alienation. The picture of industrial harmony in small firms has been increasingly criticized for neglecting the terms and conditions of employment that exist. As Rainnie (1989) suggests in relation to the United Kingdom, 'we have then a mounting body of evidence that small is brutal, not beautiful' (p. 7). On a wider scale the Commission of the European Communities (1989a) has suggested that:

> Employment in small firms tends to be more unstable than in large firms. Small firms experience much higher levels of turnover than large firms which have a hard core of 'permanent' workers who tend to be better paid than their counterparts in small firms. In France, for example, wages in large firms are up to sixty per cent higher than in small firms. (p. 82)

It is also clear that smaller firms are more able to stand outside the formal processes of employee relations and avoid collective agreements and high levels of unionization. Such flexibility may fit into an increasingly deregulated European economy but it raises substantial questions for the Social Dimension of the European Community.

Self-employment

Self-employment, like the SME sector, is often regarded as a significant job generator which is growing in importance across Europe. This view may be arrived at by projecting recent British trends. However, the United Kingdom has started from a lower base of self-employment when compared to the rest of the EC. The numbers of self-employed in the EC increased by 12 million between 1979 and 1989. 'However, since the increase was only marginally more than the rise in employment, the relative importance of self-employment increased only slightly over this period' (Commission of the European Communities, 1991, p. 10). It is also the case that self-employment is unevenly distributed both across Western Europe and between economic sectors. For example, while agriculture is diminishing as a source of employment, it retains the highest proportion (over 50 per cent of all jobs) of self-employment (Commission of the European Communities, 1989a, p. 83). This means that European States which retain significant agricultural sectors such as Greece, Ireland and Portugal have higher than average levels of self-employment.

In the more industrialized northern European States, the expansion of self-employment is associated with the growth of the service sector. It should be noted that, here too, the growth is by no means even. In Denmark, Luxembourg and Ireland there has been a recent fall in the number of self-employed and in France and the Federal Republic of Germany, growth has been minimal (ibid., p. 84).

Self-employment outside agriculture may be regarded as a response to the high levels of unemployment in much of Europe. Its growth may therefore be regarded as a transitory phenomenon if this is the case. However, it would appear that the continuing growth of the service sector, with which new self-employment is associated, is more likely to ensure a slow and stable level of growth.

Alongside the gradual expansion in conventional self-employment and small businesses there has also been a development in the co-operative sector. Workers co-operatives have often been regarded as a precarious form of enterprise whose radical pretensions made them unlikely to survive for long in a capitalist economic environment. However, this would not necessarily be the view in France or Italy where there are long-established co-operative movements and supportive legal frameworks. In Spain, the Mondragon co-operatives of the Basque region have provided an example of the development of a commercially successful sector. While there are clear indicators of growth throughout the European co-operative sector (Mellor et al., 1988, ch. 2), Italy remains the dominant country with perhaps half a million co-operators, (McDonald, 1989, p. 27). However, in absolute terms, co-operatives provide a very small amount of employment opportunities in Western Europe.

From a different perspective, co-operatives provide the basis for a radically different approach to human resource management. Control of the enterprise rests with those who work within it and decision making is formally based on democratic principles. However, the implementation of such an approach in the highly competitive market sectors in which co-operatives tend to be concentrated is fraught with difficulties. There is a considerable likelihood that co-operatives will 'degenerate' into a form that is indistinguishable from conventional small businesses (Mellor et al., 1988).

Core and Periphery Work

So far, we have described the changing labour markets in Western Europe and made reference to the implications that they might have for employee relations. We have not attempted to deal with the underlying causes of those changes or to look at the wide ranging debate about developments in the labour market. In this section we will bring together the salient features of the changes and examine the significance of dual labour market analysis and the notion of flexibility for the development of human resource management in Western Europe.

It is clear from the brief descriptive evidence we have presented that labour market developments are by no means uniform in the European Community. In particular, there is a broad distinction between north and south, with the newer Member States of Greece, Spain and Portugal having features of an industrializing agricultural economy. However, even this division is not always appropriate because Ireland and France, for example, retain significant agricultural sectors.

Nevertheless, a cultural particularism could leave us not seeing the wood for the trees. In spite of the often wide differences between nations, broad trends can be discerned which are likely to have a significant impact on employee relations in the EC. The most important change is the shift of employment into the service sector of the economy. We have noted (see p. 22) that some of this is related to a statistical quirk deriving from the development of sub-contracting and the movement of the same workers from an 'industry' to a 'services' classification. However, there can be no doubt that there is a real movement to service employment which is not a transitory phenomenon.

Clearly related to this change has been the expansion in womens' employment, part time and temporary work, small and medium-size enterprises and self-employment. The growth of these so-called non traditional work patterns has been analysed in terms of the development of a core and periphery workforce. As these terms can appear to be value laden, the notion of 'flexibility' is often used as an interchangeable concept – we may not want to be peripheral but we should be happy to be flexible. However, there are differences between these approaches, and values are not so easily expunged. It is clear that some Western European States have embraced and encouraged changes in the labour market much more willingly than others and that the United Kingdom's Conservative administration has taken the lead in deregulation. On the other hand, it is suggested that workers themselves do not welcome the changes. As Bachy (1986) makes very clear in a report to the European Parliament:

> All the studies which have been carried out, including some by the employers' associations, on the development of certain 'flexible' forms of work (temporary work, fixed term contracts . . .) show that, in the majority of cases, these are neither chosen nor valued by the employees, who accept them only because they have no other choice in the absence of stable and permanent jobs. Generally speaking the idea that workers, in particular women, find in such 'atypical' jobs a new source of individual and collective freedom is just a myth . . . This demand for flexibility in the workforce is also . . . a means of destroying the solidarity between workers by adopting an individualized approach to contracts, jobs and conduct, as a way of weakening the trade union movement. (pp. 10–11)

Individual decisions in this area will depend on a range of factors including the level of household income, child care arrangements, personal work preferences and the availability of different types of jobs.

Global Flexibility

There is often ambiguity and a lack of conceptual clarity in discussions of changing labour markets and it is as well to identify these at the outset. There are several options open and we intend to develop our discussion at three different levels. Firstly, there is the relationship between the core Western European economies and the peripheral nations in the global economy. Secondly, there is the development of core and peripheral regions within the EC. Finally, there is the development of the 'flexible firm' at the European level. In human resource terms, the most significant development is in the flexible firm but we shall briefly touch on the other two points in order to set the context.

Using the catch-all, core and periphery concepts to describe whole economies is, of course, fraught with difficulties. Economies are dynamic phenomena in which change can be very rapid and distortions can be caused by a single commodity, such as oil. In addition, each of them has its own unique labour market. However, it is possible to predict some general trends in the global economy, partly because the changes occurring in Europe the United States and Japan have consequences elsewhere in the world, and partly because of the domination of international markets by transnational companies. The relative freedom with which such organizations can move capital has allowed the shifting of production on a global scale. Thus, as the service sector and non-manufacturing employment has grown in northern Europe in particular, the production of manufactured goods has developed in the newly industrializing countries.

Non-European investment for transnational manufacturing capital was attractive for a number of reasons. Firstly, within the industrialized European States, wage costs had grown almost continuously within the framework of Keynesian economic expansion. Increasing real incomes were an important factor in underwriting growth and were initially matched by rising productivity. Thus, Boyer (1988) argues, a 'virtuous circle' becomes possible: 'rapid growth is fostered by a stable relationship between wages and profits and consumption and investment' (p. 6). 'However, from the late 1960s wage rises began to outstrip productivity and depress profits' (p. 21). Hence overseas investment in cheaper labour markets become increasingly attractive to transnational companies.

As well as cheaper wage costs, the less industrialized countries had other advantages. A 'compliant' workforce was supplied in a number of ways. Repressive governments often restricted the right of workers to organize and provided little in the way of welfare or health and safety rights. The recruitment of women to light engineering and textiles also provided a workforce that was often culturally conditioned to a subordinate and subservient role. Underlying all of this was a sentiment clearly expressed by the Sri Lankan civil servant quoted by Gerhardt et al. (1985):

> In a Third World country, I would like to see a person work for even a small wage rather than starve because of pride by saying that wages are not good enough by Western standards. I have gone to rural areas and I have seen how people suffer without employment, and they're willing to work for any price. In that situation, the question of cheap labour never enters the mind of a Sri Lankan worker. It enters only the mind of a Western observer. (p. 40)

With that background it is hardly surprising to find governments willing to provide a whole range of fiscal and financial benefits to attract transnational investment. However, does this mean that Third World nations have become peripheral economies servicing the industrialized west through the utilization of cheap labour? This is clearly too simplistic a notion. There remain considerable differences in the rate of development of non-industrialized countries and there is no necessary inevitability in progress down a particular road. Much of the growth that has occurred has been in a small number of countries and they still account for a small proportion of world trade in manufacture. As Armstrong et al. (1984) observe:

> The three biggest Asian exporters – Taiwan, South Korea and Hong Kong – together account for about half of all Less Developed Countries (LDC) exports of manufactures to the advanced countries. Brazil and Mexico provide another 15 per cent, and Singapore, Yugoslavia, Malaysia and the Philippines account for a further 15 per cent . . . The share of manufactures in LDC exports to the advanced countries more than doubled over the seventies, rising from 22.1 per cent to

45.0 per cent. By 1980 8.5 per cent of manufactures imports into the advanced countries came from the third world as compared with 4.5 per cent in 1970. (p. 357)

The last figure quoted above had increased to 10 per cent by the end of the 1980s as a new wave of industrializing economies began to develop export markets (Commission of the European Communities, 1989a, p. 44) As well as this unequal distribution between countries there is also an unequal distribution within them. Disparities in the availability of jobs and the continuing wide divergences in incomes would suggest that these countries too are developing their own core and peripheral labour markets.

While we must remain cautious in grafting an analysis of western labour markets onto the global economy we must equally be aware that the developments will inevitably have implications for European human resource management. For instance, the shipbuilding industry was long dominated by western economies but their share of the world market has declined dramatically in recent years. The most immediate consequence has been loss of jobs and the need to manage redundancy programmes. However, in the United Kingdom and France for example, there have also been implications for union organization and policy, collective bargaining, and pay and conditions (Stirling and Bridgford, 1985).

The developments in world capitalism have a parallel European dimension. Economic development becomes concentrated within a relatively confined geographical area and other regions become peripheral. This is an already existing trend within the European Community and a 'golden triangle' containing the prosperous population centres in Europe has commonly been identified. The situation for the peripheral areas is further complicated by the development of market economies in the former socialist bloc. The difficulties of some regional economies have been recognized for some time and considerable resources have been invested through regional aid programmes. However, the regional imbalances remain and may be accentuated by the impact of the Single European Market. On the other hand, low wage costs in some regions may act as a pull on investment particularly if the EC's Social Dimension makes less progress than the deregulation of markets. This fear of 'social dumping'. is the motivating factor behind the growth in interest in the Social Dimension in the EC following the introduction of the Single European Act.

A Flexible Workforce?

Industrialized European economies have sought to respond to changes in the global economies and developments in their own through changes in their labour markets. The process is not a new one and, as Rosenberg (1989, p. 364) notes, dual labour markets were identified by academic studies of urban labour markets in the United States in the 1960s. He goes on to identify key features of the analysis.

> Dual labour market theorists initially conceptualized the labour market as being divided into primary and secondary sectors. The former is characterised by high wages, relatively good working conditions, employment stability and opportunities for advancement; the latter by low wages, poor working conditions, high labour turnover and little chance of advancement. (p. 365)

Since the 1960s, there has been considerable development in the analysis of internal labour markets and more sophisticated divisions have emerged. Hakim (1990), following Loveridge, has developed a fourfold typology (p. 159). In summary, she identifies a primary internal sector of jobs which would be 'permanent and full time, typically middle management and above, combining flexible but firm-specific skills with a high span of discretion and long term stable earnings'. Another sector would be a secondary internal market covering, for example, lower status and part time work. Then there are primary and secondary external markets, the former comprising professional or high skilled workers working on a self-employed or contract basis, the latter covering low skilled workers on temporary or seasonal contracts.

These developments in the labour market have considerable implications for employee relations policies and the role of trade unions. This is particularly the case when they are linked with notions of flexible specialization and the flexible firm. This is not the place to enter into the considerable debate on flexibility but its importance cannot be neglected given the related analysis regarding the development of a 'post-Fordist' economy. In essence, the analysis suggests the breakdown of mass consumer markets and the replacement of mass production factories. A bewildering variety of market niches will be satisfied by firms exploiting a diversified labour market and high technology. This is linked to the notion of a flexible firm which is able to adapt rapidly to changes in the product market. Pollert (1988) suggests that this

> ... is dependent on the firm's workers offering two different kinds of 'flexibility': the first group offer 'functional' flexibility in the labour process, by crossing occupational boundaries and multiskilling, and also flexibility by time, in terms adjusting more closely to production demands. The second group provide 'numerical flexibility': they may be insecurely or irregularly employed, or they may not have a direct relationship with the firm at all, being, for example, sub-contracted or self employed. (p. 283)

As Phillimore (1989) has suggested there have been a number of responses to the advocates of a post-Fordist economy and we will follow his division into 'optimists', 'pessimists' and 'sceptics'. The former see the development of flexible specialization as central to economic growth in the European economies. They note the importance of Japanese production methods as well as the growing significance of skill, quality and variety. Pessimists tend to focus on the disproportionate benefits to capital and suggest, for example, that 'Japanese methods of work organization can be seen primarily as a means of work intensification based upon the elimination of wasted time in production' (Tomaney, 1990, p. 37). Furthermore, the pessimists focus on the importance of the peripheral labour market and note the lack of unionization and the poor terms and conditions of employment. Commenting on the 'sceptics' Phillimore (1989) notes that they

> ... doubt the significance of flexible specialization (FS) at all. Some argue that, quantitatively, mass production is still very much more important than FS, which is at present confined to relatively few regions and industries. Also, mass production is much more 'flexible' than critics give it credit for ... Others argue that the spread of Fordism itself has been exaggerated, and that FS is in fact more common in those sectors which were resistant to Fordism, such as batch engineering. Still others argue that the whole debate misses the point. FS enthusiasts are manufacturing enthusiasts – but manufacturing is declining in significance and thus FS is not the wave of the future. (p. 82)

However, commentators on the flexible firm are not necessarily arguing for its current prevalence but rather for its development at the 'leading edge' of the economy. The pace of change for many

Fordist companies is inevitably constrained by existing investments and flexible firms are seen as developing in new market sectors among smaller enterprises (Rosenberg, 1989, p. 394; Pollert, 1988, p. 285). Such an approach to the flexible firm raises questions as to whether it is itself an atypical model. Furthermore, it returns us to an earlier point about value judgements. The flexible firm can be adopted or discarded depending on its usefulness as an analytical tool but it can also be advocated as a model for future development. It is this point that many critics find disturbing. As Pollert points out: 'It is important to evaluate the "flexible firm" model at the level of "best practice"; for whatever one's criticisms as an empirical model, it has certainly had an effect as a policy model, and should be taken seriously as, potentially, a "self fulfilling prophecy".'

For this to happen would require changes in the approach of management to consciously adopt the model rather than make *ad hoc* responses to the employment needs of their businesses. This would require cost benefit decisions about recruitment policies, particularly in relation to work carried out on non-standard forms of contract. Laurie Hunter (1988) has suggested that there are a number of factors concerning costs and productivity that could have both advantages and disadvantages to firms (p. 224). Among the former are likely to be reduced wage costs, lower national insurance costs, reduced costs of other employment benefits, lower employment protection costs and lower levels of unionization. Among the disadvantages are higher supervision costs, higher absenteeism and turnover, lower commitment and morale. Ultimately, the balance between these factors will depend on the circumstances of each firm but they are far more likely to influence management decision making in a pragmatic way than any moral exhortations to develop a flexible firm.

As we said at the outset of this section, the debates on labour market changes in Western Europe are as likely to obscure as to elucidate. What is clear are the general trends in employment patterns that we have already identified. The pace and direction of change is too uneven and, often, too recent to make unqualified predictions about the future shape of the labour market. As one Dutch study concluded:

> Would it be impossible to re-industrialize again? Before we say no, it should be remembered that in 1899 there existed some very small

sub-sectors like electrochemical manufacturing or chemical industry, which became very large . . . Such tiny yet unidentified sectors, may exist now as well. (Van der Vegt, 1988, p. 567)

What is clear, is that changing labour markets have clear implications for human resource management policies. In many cases, 'flexibility' is part of.a human resource package which focuses on individual and human relations as opposed to collective bargaining. Linking this with the reorganization of work poses significant challenges to traditional employee relations mechanisms and employee representation systems.

The Role of The State

So far we have looked at the developments in European labour markets in isolation from the influence of State policies. However, Western European governments and the EC itself, at a supranational level, have a key role to play in shaping patterns of employment and labour markets. Such a role has never been non-controversial as the movement from interventionist to non-interventionist stances has indicated. Furthermore, State involvement in employment policy has significant implications for employee relations. Just one example of this would be policies in relation to nationalization and privatization which have major implications for employment and the resultant human resource management policy. It is also important that we put government measures into context. The vast majority of people enter and leave the labour market in Western Europe without State assistance in job finding. In the EC the public sector's 'market share of total placements at most reaches 20 or 30 per cent and is usually barely into double figures' (Commission of the European Communities, 1989a, p. 164).

Nevertheless, there is a range of ways in which Member States and the EC as a whole can become involved in employment policies affecting labour markets. At a general level, macro-economic decisions in areas such as taxation and interest rates will obviously have their employment implications. Social security schemes, or the lack of them, will also have an effect. Similarly, changes in the area of labour law will work through to influence employer decisions regarding recruitment, retention and dismissal. However, we wish to focus here on government policies that relate more directly to employment and which operate in a number of areas.

Firstly, there is the role of the nation State itself as an employer. This is clearly an important feature of European labour markets because of the growth of public sector employment and the State's role in setting patterns for employee relations policies. Secondly, there is the role of the State in providing financial incentives and disincentives in relation to jobs. There are a number of common features across Europe in this respect although the detail of particular schemes will inevitably vary. State subsidies of various forms for ailing industrial sectors have been commonplace in the past although EC competition policy now imposes considerable restrictions on Member States. Direct payments to individual entrepreneurs have also featured in State schemes, particularly related to the development of new businesses. Money has also been invested in State redundancy schemes and this has sometimes been enhanced in declining industries and depressed regions by support from EC Social Funds. Finally, States have intervened directly through the development of job generation programmes. There have been a bewildering variety of these and they have often been aimed at specific sectors of the unemployed; young people in particular have been the subject of a range of schemes as have the long-term unemployed.

The development of employment policies have given Western European governments an important determining influence on labour market strategies. We need now to look in more detail at the policies and their significance for the changing patterns of employment we have identified in this chapter.

Employment Policies

The most significant role of Western European States in relation to employment has been in the provision of financial benefits for those without work. Direct job creation through State-sponsored programmes of work have been introduced to cope with specific periods of economic crisis, such as the inter-war years, but, in general, government intervention has been directed at the social consequences of unemployment. The provision of social security remains the major function of labour market policies in Europe. As Reutersward (1990) records:

> The largest part of labour market policy, measured in terms of spending, consists of income transfers to the unemployed, such as

unemployment benefits and early retirement pensions. These transfers alone account for more than two per cent of GDP in several countries (Belgium, Denmark, France, Ireland, Netherlands and Spain) and over one per cent in many others. (p. 31)

The payment of benefits was the initial response to the high levels of unemployment in Member States following the economic recession of the mid-1970s. However, this was more a matter of inertia than policy and, as high unemployment levels persisted, Western European countries began to explore measures designed to encourage job creation. Numerous schemes were developed and large numbers of the unemployed participated in them. It is significant that the policies have gone beyond providing temporary employment schemes directly for the unemployed. Labour market policies have also been developed to encompass those in employment and those normally classified as economically inactive. Measures aimed at those at work have been designed to reduce or bring to an early end their role in the labour market in order to generate jobs for others. In relation to the economically inactive, measures have been designed to reduce the likelihood of their labour market participation. However, this must be counterbalanced by the changing demographic trends within the EC which could lead to measures with the opposite effect, such as the ongoing development of equal opportunities policies designed to encourage the increased participation of women in the workforce.

Youth unemployment was a major feature of the recession and although this is changing there is still a clear commitment from the EC States to continuing training programmes. As Teague (1989) notes, the European Commission is seeking to co-ordinate policies within the Community in this area and it has adopted a resolution 'stipulating that a Community-wide social guarantee should be established for young people as regards to training' (p. 29). This has been backed by a decision to commit at least three-quarters of the EC social funds to tackling youth unemployment (Brewster and Teague, 1989, p. 84).

It is training that has provided the main focus of youth employment schemes in Europe. The major thrust of the programmes is to increase the skills level of the young people and to provide them with some sort of work experience. The development of such schemes across the EC are summarized by the Commission of the European Communities (1989a):

Special schemes to provide qualifications for young people are particularly widespread in the United Kingdom, Italy, Greece, Ireland,
Spain and Luxembourg. These schemes range from theory in training establishments to practical work experience with firms, but normally an attempt is made to combine both aspects. The schemes can
only be understood in the context of the vocational training system
in the Member State in question . . . There are considerable differences in these programmes, both in terms of time and as regards
content. They can be either full or part time (Greece, Spain) and
can include an apprenticeship which provides a recognized leaving
certificate. (p. 11)

In addition to training schemes, young people have been the major
beneficiaries of job creation schemes: these exist in all the EC
States and are normally related to work that is of benefit to the
local community. In many Member States the schemes will also
have an element of vocational training (France and Belgium) and
may operate on a part time basis in order to attract young people.
More controversially, there has been debate about the level of
payment for workers on such schemes, particularly where they are
employed in subsidized conventional, rather than community,
employment. It is argued both that the young people are providing
unfair competition with non-scheme workers and that they themselves are being exploited through low wage levels. This has not
halted the spread of such schemes and they are more likely to
decline through changing demographic trends than as a political
response to public criticism.

Training and job creation schemes are by far the most dominant
means of tackling youth unemployment and it is clear that large
numbers of young people have participated in such schemes across
the EC. Other schemes have had only a minor impact but perhaps
the most significant of these have been policies, in France and Belgium for example, which have allowed employed workers to take
early or phased retirement and their jobs to be taken by unemployed
young people.

The Long-term Unemployed

The concern for unemployment among young people has been
paralleled by a similar one for the condition of the long-term unemployed (generally, those who have been out of work for over a

year). As with the young, the major problems are those of skills matching and the lack of a work routine, and, hence, programmes for dealing with the problem are similar. The focus is on training or retraining schemes to change or upgrade skills, and job creation projects. In Denmark, there has been a particular focus on preventing long-term unemployment and schemes have been developed to a greater extent than in most of Western Europe. The essential element of one such programme was that all unemployed people must receive a job offer before their period of unemployment benefit expires. The job should be for at least nine months in a private sector company or, failing that, the public sector must provide a job for at least seven months. The workers would receive the standard wage or have their benefit cut if they refused. The employer is given an allowance of 70 per cent of the unemployment benefit paid to the unemployed person in the previous year.

Another approach to long-term unemployment has been to encourage self-employment. As we have seen, self-employment is differentially spread across Europe and remains particularly significant in agriculture in spite of that sector's overall decline. New self-employment is being generated in the service sector and often with the encouragement of government aid. This has been a more recent innovation than traditional schemes to help the unemployed and has been particularly significant in the United Kingdom and France. In the former, the numbers participating in the Enterprise Allowance Scheme rose from 20,000 in 1983 to 96,000 in 1987 and by 1990 was providing 200,000 places annually. Other EC States, such as France, Spain, Italy and Germany have developed similar programmes. There is a wide variety of schemes available and they are normally based on individual payments rather than training programmes, although counselling and training would be encouraged.

> At its simplest, this aid takes the form of a sum of money calculated according to the maximum unemployment benefit due. In addition to a fixed payment (France, Ireland, Spain, Portugal, United Kingdom), the following benefits are provided: continued payment of unemployment benefit for a fixed period (Federal Republic of Germany, Spain, Portugal), loans at low rates of interest, investment grants, tax relief, etc. (Commission of the European Communities, 1989c, p. 15)

Self-employment schemes have not been totally successful and countries like Denmark and the Netherlands have been reluctant to establish them. In Ireland the number of people participating in such schemes fell by around 50 per cent between 1985 and 1987. Nevertheless, they remain a significant innovation in unemployment programmes and one that is unlikely to disappear even if European unemployment levels fall significantly.

This may not be the case with other forms of initiatives. Programmes to aid the unemployed have been so disparate within Western Europe that there is a need to rationalize the provision and avoid the scatter gun effect of *ad hoc* responses. It is likely that in the future schemes aimed at disadvantaged groups such as the long-term unemployed or the disabled will be refined and retained. There is also a commitment in the EC to retain training programmes for young people. In this respect and others, the Community itself is taking an increasing role. In particular, the European Social Fund is being used to support employment initiatives for young people and the long term unemployed. Local employment initiatives have also been an important focus of Community involvement but, 'these programmes and actions are carried out in co-operation with the Member States. Their role is not to replace Member States' own actions but to provide backing or encouragement for the implementation of policies designed to promote employment' (Commission of the European Communities, 1989c, p. 169).

What are most likely to decline in importance, particularly if overall levels of unemployment fall, are the job creation programmes. These have often been the most controversial of government programmes on the grounds that they subsidize jobs that would have existed anyway and that they have often provided low levels of earnings for the participants. This has led to the argument that such schemes have become part of the peripheral economy and the secondary labour market. They are seen as creating a cheap and flexible supply of labour to employers and as low paid, low status, and insecure jobs for workers.

It is clear that Western European States will continue to play a significant role in labour market intervention through programmes to alleviate unemployment. This will continue to influence industrial relations in a number of ways. At the level of the Community, trade union and employer representatives will be involved in the creation, development and implementation of programmes. However, trade unions may have a declining role in the operation of the programmes and, as we have seen in the United Kingdom, training schemes have not provided fertile recruiting ground. Less directly, the schemes influence employee relations by providing another source of labour for employers. This can affect union bargaining power and increase management's flexibility in employment policies.

Conclusion

Employee relations policies are created in response to changes in the labour force and developments in labour markets. The last 20 years have seen major shifts in employment and significant changes in human resource strategies, so much so that there are those who argue that an irreversible change has occurred. It is clear from this chapter that Western European labour markets have been the subject of important developments. Firstly, there are the demographic changes affecting the old and the young. Europe's age profile reflects the expanding population of the elderly and retired and the decline in the numbers of young people joining the labour force. Secondly, there has been a clear shift in economic sectors. Over 60 per cent of the EC's workforce is now employed in the service sector. This parallels developments elsewhere in the advanced industrialized nations and, again, it has been argued that this is an irreversible process. Thirdly, there has been a growth in forms of employment outside of traditional full time, permanent jobs. Atypical contracts based on part time work, temporary or self-employment or government training schemes have undoubtedly expanded. There has also been growth in small and medium-size enterprises and the clandestine economy. A significant feature of atypical and, particularly, part time employment is its dominance by women. Finally, technological change has been linked with workforce flexibility to provide new methods of production to match product market changes. The outcome of this process of change has been the identification of core and peripheral labour markets.

The extent and significance of all these changes is much debated and it is certainly necessary to place them in context. For example, the highest percentages of part time work are in the Netherlands, Denmark and the United Kingdom where they amount to about one-quarter of the working population but this still leaves most employed people in full time jobs. The pattern of employment is changing but there remains considerable stability and significantly different rates of change across Western Europe. As proponents of the 'flexible firm' accept, their arguments apply to a relatively few organizations at the leading edge of developments. Nevertheless, while the pace of change may be uneven there can be no doubt that changes in the labour market are directly linked to the development of employee relations policies.

2

The Public Authorities and Employee Relations

At the national level, States, or more specifically governments and their agencies, are major actors within employee relations systems and have a number of significant roles to play. Firstly, they condition the style of employee relations that exists within a country, either regulating many issues by means of the legal system (a legalist approach), or choosing to leave these issues mainly to employers and employee representatives to decide upon by means of voluntary collective agreements (a voluntarist approach). Secondly, States may intervene directly in the practice of employee relations in a more structural way, by drawing socio-economic interest groups (employers' and employees' representatives) into a joint decision-making framework in order to tackle problems associated with the management of social and economic policy making and most notably the regulation and distribution of wages. Thirdly, States provide services for conciliation, mediation and arbitration in order to help settle industrial disputes. Finally, States are major employers and are directly involved in employee relations in the public sector. In this way they can expect to extend their influence beyond the public sector so as to participate in setting the agenda within the private sector also. For purposes of academic enquiry it is useful to separate these different roles, but in practice there is a tendency for some of them to become confused, particularly in the public sector where the roles of employer, mediator and regulator of incomes are difficult to disentangle.

Increasingly, with the gradual drift towards economic convergence in Europe and the establishment of a political superstructure at the European level, the EC is developing its own framework for employee relations both at the transnational and national levels. While it plays no significant role as a mediator, only a tiny role as an employer and a limited one as a forum for social and economic policy making, it is beginning to play a significant role as a legal regulator. In this chapter we propose to examine these four roles of the State from a comparative perspective and to examine the ways in which the EC is beginning to have an impact on employee relations issues.

Employee Relations Traditions – Legalism and Voluntarism

The degree of legal intervention in employee relation systems differs significantly from one country to another. In order to resolve employee relations issues, some States have a tradition which encourages legal intervention (legalism), while others generally have more recourse to collective bargaining (voluntarism). Voluntarism tends to be identified with employee relations systems in the United Kingdom and Ireland, while legalism prevails in continental Europe. Within each tradition, systems differ somewhat. Some legal systems are formal, as in the Federal Republic of Germany, for example, where there is a greater tendency to believe in the rule of law and the approach of social problems from a legal perspective; at the other end of the spectrum, in Italy, 'informality carries the day' (Blanpain, 1991, p. 65).

As will be seen throughout the book, there are numerous examples of employee relations norms, such as working time and holidays. The bases for these have been set by legal means in most countries of continental Europe but by collective bargaining in the United Kingdom and Ireland. However, this does not mean that the United Kingdom and Ireland are free from legal constraints or that collective bargaining is an insignificant feature of employee relations in the rest of Europe.

Legal intervention has traditionally been the norm for the regulation of certain aspects of employee relations in all Western European countries, including the United Kingdom, notably to cover issues such as health and safety and, more recently, sex discrimination. Moreover, all legalist countries have a significant place for collective bargaining, and Denmark, in particular, resolves many of its employee relations issues via collective bargaining procedures. In France, legalist means were recently introduced to achieve voluntarist ends, and one of the so-called Auroux laws (a series of laws affecting employee relations introduced in the early 1980s by Jean Auroux, the then French Minister of Employment) aimed specifically to encourage the practice of collective bargaining. French employers and trade unions now have an obligation to negotiate at national industry level once a year on wages and once every five years on job classification, and, at the level of the firm, annual negotiations are to be held on real wages and working time. (Bridgford and Morris, 1987, p. 53) The United Kingdom, on the other hand, has resorted increasingly to the introduction of new legal procedures to regulate employee relations issues. According to McIlroy (1991) 'the disintegration of voluntarism, which has seen the UK under Mrs Thatcher move from one of the most loosely to one of the most tightly legally regulated systems of employee relations in advanced democracies, has its roots in changes within the economy, changes within the trade unions and the failure of alternative methods of solving the problems of British capitalism' (p. 5). The succession of laws introduced by the Conservative government has led to a significant transformation in the pattern of employee relations in the United Kingdom. However, the Conservative governments' legislative approach has focused primarily on the power of the trade unions, while the terms and conditions of employment remain largely determined by collective bargaining in a generally unregulated marketplace.

Even within an employee relations area such as health and safety, which has traditionally been regulated by legal intervention in all Western European countries, considerable divergence still remains. In the view of the British Health and Safety Commission (1990) there are the following differences in philosophy and practice between the United Kingdom and other Member States of the EC.

- Some Continental law tends to be highly prescriptive, resembling the pre-1974 pattern of British law and in marked contrast to the new-style British law – acceptance of this is made possible in other Member States by the Continental normative pattern of law where literal interpretation is not expected.
- In some north European States, there is a tendency to ban processes or substances, or to apply strict quantitative limits, where the United Kingdom would think a more flexible approach both desirable and necessary, particularly where we would regard strict calculation as impossible.

• Some countries use licensing systems for regulating areas where, in the United Kingdom, we would consider this approach excessively bureaucratic and expensive.
• In some countries (particularly Germany) standards for industrial plant tend to be more detailed and descriptive of particular (nationally manufactured) articles than are UK standards – sometimes this is accompanied by informal arrangements for derogations.
• In certain countries – particularly France which has a State controlled occupational health service – there is more law and provision for occupational health matters than in the UK.
• Some Continental codes provide for absolute liability of the employer or plant manufacturer/supplier in case of accident, as opposed to the British system of tort backed by State social security.
• Systems and standards of enforcement differ between Member States. (p. 15)

This divergence in employee relations traditions has been explained in different ways. Poole (1986) has drawn attention to the existence of written constitutions which 'may provide the crucial underpinning for extensive legal regulations, not least because these wider legal provisions are endorsed by all the main parties to employee relations' (pp. 26–7). However, Ireland has a written constitution but, because of its historical links to Britain, a voluntarist tradition. The existence of a written constitution is itself a reflection of an already existing legalist tradition. Another explanation has been put forward by Bean (1985, pp. 103–4). Employee relations in the United Kingdom were established as a result of a process which relied little upon regulation by legal procedures. As British trade unions acquired and maintained significant bargaining powers at an early stage of economic development, they never saw the need to mount a sustained campaign in favour of legal intervention as a means of promoting collective bargaining. Moreover, they were suspicious of any later attempts made to interfere with this process. He quotes Kahn-Freund who noted that the 'formative period' of the relationship between law and industrial relations in Britain (i.e. 1850–1906) was unique because of a combination of three circumstances which were not to be found elsewhere. Firstly, the labour movement was relatively strong, and trade unions achieved bargaining status without legal assistance at a relatively early stage; secondly, this was obtained without the aid of a working-class political party (the Labour Party was born only in 1906); thirdly, the basic trade union laws were established before universal male franchise. As Bean points out, 'one important consequence was that the legal form of collective trade union rights consisted largely of negative statutory protection, or 'immunities' from the sanctions that would otherwise attach in law, rather than positive legal rights to associate, to bargain and to strike as in many comparable countries' (ibid.).

It is this difference of approach which helps to explain why the United Kingdom and most of the other Western European States often have such divergent views concerning the resolution of many employee relations issues within the European Community.

The State and Employee Relations

Neo-corporatism

The strategy of the State is often defined in terms of its control of employee relations (*laissez-faire* or interventionist) and the degree of freedom of trade unions (autonomous or heteronomous). The two most prevalent types in post-war Western Europe are pluralism on the one hand, whereby the State plays a relatively interventionist role in employee relations, but whereby trade unions retain a considerable level of autonomy, and neo-corporatism on the other, whereby the State plays an interventionist role and also attempts to incorporate trade unions into its own decision-making process (Poole, 1986, p. 105).

It is neo-corporatism which has received the most attention from specialists in employee relations. According to Panitch (1980), it is a strategy which 'integrates organised socio-economic producer groups through a system of representation and cooperative mutual interaction at the leadership level and mobilisation and social control at the mass level' (p. 173). This process has three dimensions: trade union confederations and employers' federations represent their members, they bargain with government and, finally, they participate in implementing policy. However, not all political systems are neo-corporatist and Taylor (1989) has suggested a three-fold typology – integration, inclusion and marginalization (p. 97). Integration is where trade union confederations are accorded the status of governing institutions, in exchange for which they are expected to reconcile sectional demands with a national mutually agreed policy consensus. Sweden and other Scandinavian States most closely approximate to this model. Inclusion is where trade union confederations obtain representational status, are frequently consulted by government but are excluded from effective decision making. They may strive for integration and may obtain it intermittently, however, this integration is never institutionalized. This has traditionally been the case in the Federal Republic of Germany and the United Kingdom, particularly when left-of-centre parties have been in government, as during 'social contract' period of British employee relations in the 1970s. Marginalization is where trade union confederations obtain representational status but are confined to the periphery of the political process, either as a result of government policy (as is increasingly the case in the United Kingdom), the unions' own organizational weaknesses (as in France), or the dispersal of government power (as in Switzerland). Countries can be ranked according to their degree of 'societal' corporatism based on the degree of organizational centralization and non-fragmentation of the trade union movement. According to this definition, the most neo-corporatist States are Austria, Norway, Denmark, Finland and Sweden, while the least neo-corporatist are Italy, Great Britain, France, and Ireland (Schmitter, 1981, p. 294).

Threats and challenges to neo-corporatism are manifold. Neo-corporatism only succeeds as long as trade unions, employers' representatives and government departments continue to participate in the appropriate structures. However, actors will abandon them when there is no apparent benefit in participating. This means that neo-corporatist structures are often highly unstable. Trade union leaders in countries with voluntarist traditions may experience enormous difficulties within their organizations when they agree to some form of wage restraint, particularly if governments are unable or unwilling to exercise any control over other macro-economic variables, such as consumer prices, profits, and investments. Neo-corporatist structures have collapsed when trade union leaders are unable to 'deliver' their members, or when governments have sought to deregulate employee relations. Increasingly in the 1980s and 1990s right-of-centre governments and employers' federations have tended 'to recalculate their positions with the result that the main threats to neo-corporatist pacts currently are management and, under certain political circumstances, government' (Keller, 1991, pp. 83–4). Employers' federations advocate more flexible conditions within the labour market which means fewer legal constraints, the individualization of wages, and looser working-time arrangements. Some

Labour and Social Democratic political parties have been voted out of office and replaced by right-of-centre governments, which have been unwilling to establish structures enabling employers and trade unions to participate in the policy-making process. This has been the case in the United Kingdom and, to a lesser degree, the Federal Republic of Germany. Even the Swedish model of close government links with trade unions has been challenged by the changing approach of the employers' federations and the 1991 elections which removed the Social Democratic party from office.

One major advantage for the State of integrating trade unions into a neo-corporatist structure is to regulate incomes. An incomes policy can be defined as 'any measure taken by the public authorities which affects the distribution of incomes at the time of incomes formation or after they have been received . . . In the narrow sense an incomes policy is any measure by the public authorities affecting incomes formation which aims to be comprehensive, consistent and, in general fair' (Commission of the European Communities, 1980, pp. 2–3). Incomes polices aim, above all, to control wage inflation, either by freezing wages, normally for a short period, as was the case in France in 1976 and in Denmark in 1979, or by limiting increases to a specific ceiling figure, as in the United Kingdom during the mid-1970s, or to appropriate increases in the retail price index as in France in 1977. In exchange for an agreement to limit wage increases other elements may be negotiated. Firstly there may be an attempt to redistribute incomes, at least among employees, requiring flat-rate or digressive wage increases or by raising the guaranteed minimum wage for the low paid. Secondly, attempts may be made to control price increases, a regular element in overall packages. Thirdly, attempts may be made to improve the employment situation, by means of specific subsidies for depressed sectors, or by reorganization or restructuring of loans or expenditure on improving the working environment. Finally, in some cases, there may be attempts to change social legislation. The Danish trade union confederation campaigned for a bill to be passed on the employees' investment fund, and in the Federal Republic of Germany the 1976 law on co-management has been seen as a reciprocal concession for the wage and salary restraint accepted by the unions (ibid., p. 27).

By the end of the 1970s and the beginning of the 1980s there were moves in certain countries away from the use of incomes polices. In the United Kingdom the Conservative government elected in 1979 was committed to the rejection of a formal incomes policy. Its monetarist policies aimed to reduce inflation and the level of wage increases, albeit at the cost of soaring unemployment. In this way, it was argued that a formal incomes policy became unnecessary as an element of macro-economic policy making, since control over prices and incomes would in theory be regulated by market forces. The role of government was simply to control the money supply. Conservative governments have nevertheless exercised strict control over wages in the public sector by means of 'cash limits' and calls for 'reasonable' wage demands directed at trade unions in the private sector. Moreover, in the early 1980s the Conservative government announced specific increases in pay for central government services: 4 per cent in 1981–2, 3.5 per cent in 1982–3, 3 per cent in 1983–4, and 3 per cent in 1984–5. During 1992 a further limit of 1.5 per cent was set for the forthcoming pay round. In other countries, however, formal incomes polices have continued to be used on occasions. In the Netherlands for example, the real minimum wage was reduced in 1982, and in 1984 there were cuts in nominal public sector wages; in 1982, the Belgian government introduced a package of measures suspending or eliminating wage indexation as well as increasing taxes, reducing public expenditure, and also freezing some prices; the Danish government suspended wage indexation in 1982; Ireland froze special pay increases in the public sector in 1987; France introduced a temporary freeze on prices and wages in 1982 and 1983; and Italy began the process of dismantling wage indexation in 1983 although it did not finally occur until the abandonment of the *scala mobile* in 1992. In addition incomes policies were introduced in Greece in October 1985, in Portugal in 1987 and in Finland in 1992 (*European Industrial Relations Review*, December 1985, p. 24; November 1986, p. 28; March 1992, pp. 20–2).

Conciliation, mediation and arbitration

Although governments tend to avoid intervening directly in the collective bargaining process in the private sector, the incidence of industrial conflict has nevertheless encouraged public authorities to set up permanent systems of intervention in industrial disputes, providing conciliation, mediation and arbitration services, such as the Advisory, Conciliation and Arbitration Service (ACAS) in the United Kingdom and the Labour Court in Ireland.

Settlement procedures of a conciliatory nature generally form a part of the process of collective bargaining in all Western European countries. Disputes are usually resolved by those same bodies which are responsible for ensuring that agreements are negotiated. These procedures generally allow for the intervention of public authorities, but normally only after the arrangements established by the collective parties themselves have failed to settle the dispute.

Here again, there is a problem of terminology. In countries with a legalist tradition, arbitration is generally considered to be a procedure leading to a third party decision which is legally binding upon the parties to the dispute. This is not the case in the United Kingdom and Ireland, for example, where arbitration is carried out through non-judicial procedures and is therefore not legally binding. The borderline between conciliation and mediation is more difficult to draw. In general terms, however, conciliation is considered to be a procedure whereby a third party merely brings the parties together so that they can find their own solution, while a mediator plays a more active role and may formulate proposals for settlement of the conflict.

A survey by the *European Industrial Relations Review* (1989b) has indicated differences in the approach to the resolution of conflict, according to whether the dispute is one of rights or of interests. 'A dispute of right relates to an existing collective agreement and will arise out of a failure to agree on the interpretation of its provisions or where one of the parties has acted in breach of the agreement. A dispute of interest, by contrast, relates essentially to matters not covered by an existing agreement and is most likely to arise during the course of negotiations for a new agreement' (p. 3).

In most Western European countries collective agreements are normally legally binding and so any dispute will be sent to the appropriate legal authorities – Labour Courts in the Federal Republic of Germany, Denmark, Sweden and Finland, arbitration boards in Denmark and arbitration tribunals in Luxembourg. The judicial authorities may be approached also in Austria, the Netherlands and Italy, although only as a last resort. In Ireland and the United Kingdom, on the other hand, as collective agreements are not normally legally binding, a dispute of rights will be settled by the parties concerned. Disputes of interest are often resolved through formal procedural arrangements which have been written into collective agreements and which have been administered by the same bodies that are responsible for negotiating agreements in the following countries – Belgium, Germany, Ireland, Sweden and the United Kingdom. In these instances the line between collective bargaining and the settlement of disputes is unclear, the latter being an extension of the former. In other countries conciliation procedures are less formal in the private sector. In Italy the emphasis lies with direct action rather than institutionalized procedures, and in France such procedures are rarely used and rarely successful with the result that informal procedures are used increasingly. State intervention is normally optional and, therefore, in the case of conciliation and mediation, the agreement of at least one of the parties to the dispute will be needed, while in the case of arbitration the agreement of both parties is normally necessary. In the event of a deadlock in negotiations, State intervention is mandatory in Luxembourg, Finland and Greece, while in Spain, in order to bring lengthy strikes to an end, the government has the power to submit an industrial dispute to compulsory arbitration (*European Industrial Relations Review*, 1989b, pp. 3–4).

If a typology were to be drawn up according to the degree of State intervention in terms of prevention and settlement of disputes, most countries (Belgium, Luxembourg, Italy, France and even the Federal Republic of Germany and the United Kingdom) would be placed in an intermediate group between Denmark and the Netherlands on the one hand and, on the other, countries where informality has been the norm (Commission of the European Communities, 1984, pp. 150–1).

Disputes procedures in the public sector have been slower to develop. This can be explained in part by the fact that the State in most countries has been unenthusiastic about giving up power to a third party over its relationship with its own employees. As arbitration would constitute a direct challenge to the sovereignty of the State, it is, unsurprisingly, not favoured by governments. Some form of institutionalized conciliation or mediation service exists in Denmark, the Federal Republic of Germany (for public employees under contract), the Netherlands, Sweden and the United Kingdom. Clearly, one of the key issues is the choice of conciliation service, since the neutrality of government departments cannot always be maintained. This was one of the main reasons why in the United Kingdom an independent agency, ACAS, was established in 1975. In the Netherlands, an independent body, the Advisory and Arbitration Committee, was set up in 1984. These two conciliation bodies have been established by law. In the Federal Republic of

Germany, on the other hand, an agreement covering public employees under contract was concluded between public sector unions (the ÖTV and DAG) and government (at the national, regional and local level) which made it possible to refer disputes to a mediation board composed of an independent chairman and an equal number of representatives of each party. This agreement was used in 1976, 1982 and 1983 and, according to Ozaki (1987, pp. 407–9), proved acceptable to all parties.

The State as Employer

The role of the State as an employer is important for two major reasons: first, it employs large numbers of people in the public sector; second, it serves as an example to the private sector of what 'a good employer' should be.

The public sector is increasingly difficult to locate in comparative terms because of the varying relationships that exist between the State and the Civil Service on the one hand and society and the economy on the other. Rose (1985) has chosen to define public employment in its broadest sense as 'persons working for organizations that are headed by elected officials, such as Cabinet Ministers or local councillors, or by appointees of an elected government, such as heads of nationalized enterprises, and/or principally supported by government funds, for example, doctors in countries with a national health service' (p. 3). He concluded that between 1961 and 1981 total public sector employment rose considerably and was the most obvious source of growth in employment (28.5 per cent in the United Kingdom, 39 per cent in France, 55 per cent in Germany, 82.8 per cent in Italy and a remarkable 182 per cent in Sweden). As can be seen from table 2.1, the pattern of public employment at the beginning of the 1980s varied considerably in his sample of Western European States. Social programmes (primarily education and health) were the major areas of public employment, and in Sweden they made up a little over one-fifth of the total workforce, but less than one-tenth in Italy and in the Federal Republic of Germany. However, economic programmes (nationalized companies for the most part) accounted for a relatively similar percentage of the total workforce, just under one-tenth in all countries. Concerns of State (military, police, courts, prisons, tax collectors, etc.) varied around the 5 per cent mark, with Italy on the low side and the United Kingdom on the high side.

Table 2.1   Public employment (1981) as percentage of workforce

	Social	Economic	Concerns of State
Germany (FR)	9.7	8.2	6.4
France*	12.3	7.3	5.2
Italy	9.3	7.5	3.6
Sweden	20.7	9.9	5.4
UK	14.2	9.9	7.3

* Figures are 1980 for France

Source: adapted from Rose, 1985, p. 16, 17, 19

During the 1980s there was a trend towards the privatization of the public sector in some countries, particularly in the United Kingdom, but, as can be seen from table 2.2, the overall percentage change in government employment (which in OECD statistics corresponds best to Rose's term 'concerns of state') is positive in all Western European countries for the 1979–89 period, with one exception, the United Kingdom where government employment fell on average by 0.3 per cent per year.

Changes have been most dramatic in the economic and social areas of public employment. In this, the United Kingdom has led the way. The British government has sold off shares in a variety of public corporations (British Aerospace, Cable & Wireless, Britoil, Enterprise Oils, Amersham International, Jaguar, British Telecom, British Gas, British Airways, Trustee Savings Bank, Rolls-Royce, the electricity and water supply industries). It has encouraged direct sales and management buy-outs (National Freight, Scott Lithgow, Sealink, Inmos, Yarrow Shipbuilders, Vosper Thornycroft, Swan Hunter Shipbuilders, Vickers Shipbuilders, Leyland Bus and Truck). Finally, it has encouraged the contracting out of public services. In employment terms over 850,000 jobs were shed from public corporations in the period from 1981 to 1987. In other countries privatization fever has been less virulent, but some analogous symptoms are apparent. The French government announced a five-year plan in 1986 to privatize a number of companies, most of which were nationalized during 1981 and 1982. Thirteen firms had been sold by June 1987, including St. Gobain, Paribas, Crédit Commercial de France, Compagnie Générale d'Electricité, Havas, Société Générale and TF1. In the Federal Republic of Germany, the government sold a 14 per cent stake in the energy and chemicals conglomerate VEBA in 1984, a 40 per cent stake in VIAG, the aluminium and chemicals group, and a 45 per cent stake in IVG, which has interests in the transport and property industry, in 1986. It sold off its remaining VEBA shares in 1987. In Italy the State holding Istituto per la Ricostruzione Industriale (IRI) sold off 23 smaller industrial enterprises between 1983 and September 1986. It has also sold shares in a number of larger enterprises, including STET and SIRTI (telecommunications), SIP (telephones) and Alitalia (airlines) (Hemming and Mansoor, 1988, pp. 7–9).

The State in many countries has often acted as a model of good employment by encouraging trade union membership, guaranteeing pay comparability and providing favourable working conditions. Modern unionism has flourished largely in this 'hothouse area' of government protection. As table 2.3 shows, trade union density has tended to be higher in the public sector then in the private sector in a variety of Western European countries. In France, the Netherlands and Switzerland the difference is spectacular, and in Great Britain trade union density in the public sector has been almost twice as high. Only in Denmark is there relative parity between the two sectors. In terms of wages, there has been some sort of comparability between public and private sector pay. In Sweden, for example, there was a similar wage increase in the two sectors between 1979 and 1982. In Italy the private sector led between 1969 and 1976, when the situation was reversed. In the Federal Republic of Germany comparability was widely and consistently respected. In the United Kingdom comparability was implemented and supported, but the results were uneven and tensions frequent. France was the major exception, and evidence suggested that the wages levels of public employees were considerably lower than those found in the private sector (Treu, 1987, p. 8, 85). As for working conditions, job security and pensions have been standard in the Civil Service (which in Continental countries refers to a broad sector of the labour market), in the social and economic elements of public employment, and for government employees. In addition, some public corporations have distinguished themselves as 'model employers' – employee relations trendsetters for the rest of the economy. Until recently, Renault, for example, was traditionally considered to be in the vanguard as regards the introduction of a whole range of social benefits.

In the 1980s, however, the notion of the State as the 'model

Table 2.2   Government employment, year-to-year changes (per cent)

	1976	1977	1978	1979	1980	1981	1982	1983	1984
Austria	4.3	2.3	1.5	3.8	0.5	2.2	2.2	2.3	2.5
Belgium	3.4	2.0	4.8	5.3	1.1	0.9	1.0	−1.0	1.2
Denmark	3.3	4.5	4.7	5.8	4.6	4.1	3.7	1.0	−0.8
Finland	6.4	3.6	3.9	3.5	3.3	4.5	3.3	3.2	2.0
France	–	–	–	–	1.6	2.0	2.6	2.3	1.5
Germany	1.7	0.9	2.3	2.6	1.7	1.6	0.9	0.7	0.3
Ireland	3.9	3.2	3.1	3.4	3.2	3.0	4.9	−2.1	−1.5
Italy	3.5	3.4	1.6	2.1	1.0	2.1	1.3	0.6	2.0
Luxembourg	2.6	2.6	1.2	2.5	2.7	0.9	0.9	1.2	1.7
Netherlands	3.3	2.7	2.1	1.9	1.6	2.0	0.8	−0.1	−0.4
Norway	8.0	4.8	5.9	4.3	4.4	4.2	2.0	2.5	1.0
Portugal	1.2	–	5.7	6.3	4.3	4.1	4.0	3.8	2.1
Spain	7.7	0.9	–	0.3	4.5	−1.4	4.3	3.9	−1.9
Sweden	4.8	4.1	5.1	4.5	3.9	2.4	1.0	1.0	2.9
Switzerland	2.3	3.0	2.2	2.9	2.7	1.5	0.8	1.1	0.8
UK	2.0	−0.8	0.3	1.7	−0.7	−0.6	−1.0	0.5	0.2
Total EEC	2.6	1.7	1.3	2.1	1.3	1.1	1.2	1.2	0.6

Source: Organization for Economic Co-operation and Development, 1991a

Table 2.3   Private and public sector unionism (1985), density rates (per cent)

Country	Private sector	Public sector
Austria	52	71
Denmark[1]	81	82
France[2]	13	42
Germany (FR)	28	58
Great Britain[3]	44	82
Italy	39	49
Netherlands	17	46
Norway[4]	50	95
Switzerland	25	61

[1] = 1984; [2] = 1975; [3] = 1979; [4] = 1980

Source: Visser, J. (1990), p. 50

Table 2.2   (Cont.)

1985	1986	1987	1988	1989	Average 1960–68	1968–73	1973–79	1979–89	1960–89
1.7	2.8	1.6	1.7	1.7	1.8	3.3	3.4	1.9	2.4
1.7	2.7	-2.9	1.6	0.1	2.4	1.9	3.9	0.6	2.0
0.7	0.9	0.6	0.9	0.9	–	8.9	4.8	1.6	4.3
2.6	1.8	2.8	2.3	1.4	4.5	4.7	4.7	2.7	4.0
2.6	1.5	0.3	0.4	0.4	–	–	–	1.5	–
1.3	1.6	1.1	0.5	0.6	3.7	3.8	2.3	1.0	2.5
-2.2	0.2	-0.5	-3.9	–	–	–	3.7	–	–
1.4	0.9	2.1	1.7	0.3	–	–	2.7	1.4	–
3.1	2.4	2.0	3.3	4.0	–	–	2.4	2.2	–
0.8	0.8	0.5	-0.4	-0.4	1.3	2.4	2.3	0.5	1.4
2.7	1.6	3.4	1.5	1.7	–	5.1	5.4	2.5	4.1
2.0	2.2	–	–	–	4.0	5.8	–	–	–
6.0	7.6	–	3.9	7.8	–	–	–	–	–
1.0	-0.5	-1.3	0.8	2.0	5.2	6.3	4.9	1.3	4.0
0.8	1.2	–	–	–	3.3	4.5	2.8	–	–
0.3	0.5	0.5	0.5	-3.1	2.5	2.5	1.5	-0.3	1.3
1.6	1.6	0.4	0.9	0.1	2.1	3.4	2.2	1.0	2.0

employer' changed considerably. Here again, the United Kingdom led the way. The Conservative government saw trade unions as a hindrance to the operation of the market-place and an obstacle to economic efficiency. It placed no importance on the right to join a trade union and, indeed, trade union membership was banned in 1984 at the Government Communications Headquarters (GCHQ) in Cheltenham. By then, the Conservatives had already started to undermine the position of trade unions with laws which made it unlawful to require contractors to employ union labour only or to recognize unions. In addition, the Local Government Act 1988 made it unlawful for local authorities and other public bodies, including the fire and police authorities and education committees, to consider 'non-commercial matters' (such as union membership) in their choice of contractors. The institutions of collective bargaining have also been undermined in parts of the public sector. The long-standing collective bargaining machinery for secondary school teachers was abolished in 1987 by the Teachers Pay and Conditions Act, which made it possible for the Secretary of State for Education to determine the whole range of teachers' employment terms and conditions. The British government has also encouraged the introduction of differential pay schemes, either as a function of location, skill, or individual performance. In the Civil Service, for instance, recent pay agreements have made some allowance for flexibility as regards location, skill and individual performance (Fredman and Morris, 1989, pp. 25–9).

In other Western European countries no other government has led such a concerted campaign against trade unionism. Moreover, it would be difficult to imagine an incident such as the banning of trade unions at GCHQ in many Western European countries, since the right to join a trade union is enshrined in the constitution. Indeed, in France, for example, the government attempted in the early 1980s to shore up the position of the trade unions. There is, however, some evidence of the introduction of differential pay schemes. Although performance-related pay only accounts for a fraction of the overall pay bill in Scandinavian countries, individualized pay increases have featured as part of national agreements. In Denmark the first steps towards more flexible job and salary structures were taken with the so-called 'modernization' of the public sector by the Danish Conservative-led government in 1983, and this subsequently led in 1987 to the introduction of flexible pay with the aim of improving recruitment and retention, rewarding outstanding performance and enhancing job structure flexibility through reclassification awards. However, the agreement allocated a mere 0.1 per cent of the total annual pay bill to individual rises (20 per cent of this was allotted to recruitment and retention and 40 per cent each to the two other aims). In Sweden, an element of individualized pay was introduced by local authorities in 1986. The criteria for individual pay increases were level of responsibility, degree of difficulty, supplementary job demands, performance (but not recruitment as in Denmark). The general pay increase for local authorities stood at 4.5 per cent for 1988 and 2 per cent for 1989, with an additional 2.0 per cent and 1.5 per cent respectively for individualized pay increases. A one-year agreement for central government employees in 1988 also contained an element of pay individualization (*IDS European Report*, June 1989, pp. 14–5).

The European Dimension

Clearly within the framework of employee relations there is no international equivalent of the State. No international body can expect to play the role of an arbitrator, mediator or conciliator. No international organization is important enough to exercise any influence as an employer. In spite of the regular complaints in the British press about 'the army of Eurocrats in Brussels', the Commission of the European Community only employs approximately 10,000 civil servants (less than many local authorities in the United Kingdom) and so is hardly in a position to serve as a significant example to employers in other parts of the EC, whether at the national level or in the private sector. While there are some moves towards the Europeanization of the economy, particularly within the framework of the Single European Market and Economic and Monetary Union, no international body is yet making a significant contribution in terms of macro-economic policy making.

Where the international community can play a role, however, is in the establishment of rules regulating employee–employer relations. While important influence is now being exercised by the EC, it must not be forgotten that other bodies, notably the International Labour Organization (ILO), the Organization for Economic Co-operation and Development (OECD) and the Council of Europe, have also aimed to establish international employment standards.

Founded in 1919, the ILO now has a membership of more than 150 countries throughout the world. It aims to establish 'standards concerning employment and working conditions found acceptable by labour and management through collective bargaining and by the legislator through labour laws and regulations', by introducing Conventions, which, when ratified, create binding international obligations for the countries concerned, or Recommendations, which are not binding. The ILO has adopted over 150 Conventions and over 160 Recommendations relating to issues, such as freedom of association, forced labour, the protection of women and young workers, the search for employment, safety and hygiene at work, hours of work and paid vacations. States may choose not to ratify certain Conventions or, once ratified, to denounce them. As a result, the impact of this international body may be somewhat undermined.

The Organization for European Economic Co-operation (OEEC) was founded by 16 European countries in 1948 to establish 'a sound European economy through the co-operation of its members', largely by managing the Marshall Aid funds which were provided by the USA to rebuild the war-torn economies of Europe. In 1961 it changed its membership by adding non-European countries, modified its goals, and changed its name to the Organization for Economic Co-operation and Development (OECD). The major contribution made by the OECD to the establishment of rules regulating employee–employer relations is to be found in the guidelines for multinational companies which were adopted in 1976. These guidelines cover seven different areas, one of which is industrial relations. They recommend that multinational companies should respect the right of employees to be represented by trade unions and to engage in constructive negotiations with a view to reaching agreements on working conditions; observe standards of employment and industrial relations which are not inferior to those operating in the host country; use local labour; provide information about the activities of the company; and implement non-discriminatory employment policies. In its own evaluation, the OECD described the guidelines as 'a successful instrument'. 'They have provided guidance on a series of difficult problems arising from the novel character of MNE (multinational enterprise) operation. In such areas as the disclosure of information by MNEs, relationships between their parent and affiliate companies, their relations and bargaining with labour unions, and in several others, they have established advanced standards of proper conduct, which at the same time are reasonably specific, thoughtful and responsive to real problems' (Organization for Economic Co-operation and Development, 1991b, p. 9). However, the OECD's own assessment needs to be tempered by the fact that its guidelines, like ILO decisions, remain voluntary and rely very much on the willingness of the parties involved to carry them out.

While there is much talk these days of the Social Charter, the shorthand name for the Community Charter of Fundamental Social Rights for Workers, it must not be forgotten that 13 of the Member States of the Council of Europe signed the first European Social Charter in Turin on 18 October 1961, and undertook to ensure that the following social rights would be effectively exercised; *inter alia*, to work, to safe and healthy working conditions, to fair remuneration; to organize and to engage in collective bargaining; to the protection of the interests of young persons, women, physically disabled persons, mentally disabled, migrant workers; to vocational guidance and training; to benefit from social welfare schemes. This Social Charter is not binding and these are no sanctions for refusing to carry out these recommendations.

Although the EC does not have at its disposal the same range of powers which are exercised by national governments, it has been able to have a growing impact on industrial relations in Western Europe. Community law refers to the body of legal norms that exist within the framework of the European Communities, and is divided into two parts, primary and secondary law. The former consists of the legal norms that are contained in the Treaties and accessory documents, and the latter contains the legal norms which derive from primary law and which are contained in the decisions taken by the European institutions, namely Regulations, Directives, Decisions, Recommendations and Opinions. Regulations have general application, are binding in their entirety and directly applicable in all Member States without any specific legal intervention from the latter. This means that Regulations supersede national law, and that national law which is contrary to Regulations is null and void. Directives are also binding upon each Member State to which they are addressed, but not in their entirety, being only goals to be achieved. This means that Directives need to be translated into national law in the most appropriate way. Like Regulations, Decisions are binding upon those natural and legal persons to whom they are addressed, (i.e. individuals as well as Member States). On the other hand, Recommendations and Opinions are not binding. They have a moral rather than legal authority, which is also the case for Resolutions and Solemn Declarations, as is the case, for example, with the Community Charter of Fundamental Social Rights for Workers.

Before examining the law-making process of the EC, it is worth describing briefly the composition and functions of the institutions of the European Community established by the original Treaty of Rome, namely, the European Parliament, the Council of Ministers, the Commission, the Court of Justice, the Economic and Social Committee, and also the European Council, which was formally created in 1974 and which has subsequently become the supreme policy-making body within the Community.

The European Parliament

The European Parliament meets in Strasbourg and Brussels and is made up of 518 representatives who have been elected for a period of five years by direct universal suffrage, with the following number of representatives per Member State.

Belgium	25
Denmark	16
Germany	99
France	87
Greece	24
Ireland	15
Italy	87
Luxembourg	6
Netherlands	31
Portugal	24
Spain	64
United Kingdom	87

these figures will be in place following the European Parliament elections in 1994

The European Parliament is not like national parliaments since it does not provide political support for a government; nor does it have the same array of legislative powers, which at the European level are the prerogative of the Council of Ministers. The European Parliament has a consultative role, which means that it must be consulted by the Council of Ministers on all aspects of EC legislation. Secondly, it has a supervisory role. The European Parliament can dismiss the Commission, if it is capable of passing a vote of no confidence, which requires a two-thirds majority of votes cast (such action has not yet been taken successfully). Thirdly, it has certain co-decision-making powers in budgetary affairs. Acting on the majority of its members and two-thirds of votes cast, it may reject the entire draft budget of the European Community, which will then allow for certain individual modifications to be negotiated.

Following the adoption of the Single European Act in 1986, the powers of the European Parliament were increased slightly, as part of a process which has become known as the Co-operation Procedure. In those policy areas which can be decided upon within the Council of Ministers by qualified majority voting (e.g. the establishment and functioning of the Single European Market), the European Parliament can reject or amend a decision. In the former case the Council of Ministers can proceed only if it is able to agree unanimously on the proposal: in the latter, if the Commission in corporates the amendments, the Council of Ministers can adopt them by a qualified majority but needs unanimity to reject them.

The Council of Ministers

The Council of Ministers is the most important law-making institution and the embodiment of the national interest at the European level. It is not one single organization, but a variety of different bodies, depending upon the subject at issue. Thus, for example, when the Social Affairs Council meets, the one which is responsible for all employee relations issues, it is made up of Ministers of Employment and/or Social Affairs from the 12 Member States. Its major function is to make decisions on draft proposals which have been put forward by the Commission.

Much has been written about the way in which decisions within the Council of Ministers are taken. It was initially expected that the Council would gradually move towards qualified majority voting but in the mid-1960s the French insisted upon safeguarding their national sovereignty and forced on the other Member States the so-called Luxembourg Compromise which required unanimous voting. However, the Single European Act re-introduced the notion of qualified majority voting and, in the area of employee relations, a qualified majority only is needed for the following issues: free movement of workers, the mutual recognition of diplomas, certificates and other evidence of formal qualifications, the establishment of the internal market, the improvement of the working environment, health and safety of workers, economic and social cohesion, issues relating to the environment. Unanimity is still required for decisions regarding the rights and interests of workers and the European Social Fund.

When the Council of Ministers acts by a qualified majority, the votes of its members are weighted as follows:

Belgium	5
Denmark	3
Germany	10
France	10
Greece	5
Ireland	3
Italy	10
Luxembourg	2

Netherlands	5
Portugal	5
Spain	8
United Kingdom	10

Fifty-four votes in favour of a proposal are sufficient for a decision to be taken, which means that it is possible to outvote one large Member state and also to protect the interests of the smaller Member States. In practice, proposals are not normally put to a vote in the Council of Ministers, even in the cases where it would be constitutional to do so. Usually further negotiations ensue, and draft proposals are watered down.

The Commission

The Commission consists of 17 members, one from each of the smaller Member States and two from the larger. The members of the Commission are appointed by the common accord of the governments of the Member States. Their term of office is four years and is renewable. Whereas the Council of Ministers represents the national interest, the Commission is entirely European in its outlook. In the general interest of the European Community, its members should be completely independent in the performance of their work and should not seek or take instructions from any government or from any other body. Each Commissioner has responsibility for one administrative department, known as a Directorate-General (DG), and therefore for one set of issues. The present Commissioner for Social Affairs is responsible for 'employment, industrial relations and social affairs'. Commissioners responsible for social affairs over the years have been as follows.

Padraig Flynn (IRL)	(1993–199)
Vasso Papandreou (GR)	(1989–1992)
Peter Sutherland (IRL)	(1985–1989)
Ivor Richards (GB)	(1981–1985)
Henk Vredeling (NL)	(1977–1981)
Patrick Hillary (IRL)	(1973–1977)
Albert Coppé (B)	(1970–1973)
Lionello Levi Sandri (I)	(1967–1970)
Henri Rocherau (F)	(1962–1967)
Sicco Mansholt (NL)	(1958–1962)

The most important power of the Commission is the right of initiative it enjoys for European legislation, which clearly gives it a significant role in shaping the agenda of the European Community. Secondly, in the event of disagreement between Member States within the Council of Ministers, the Commission has the authority to amend its proposal in order to reach a compromise, which gives the Commission a key position as a power broker. Another task is to ensure that the provisions of the Treaty of Rome and the measures taken by the institutions are applied. If the Commission considers that a Member State has failed to fulfil an obligation under the Treaty, it may bring the matter before the Court of Justice. The Commission also has a decision-making power of its own, particularly concerning the management and implementation of EC programmes. Moreover, it is competent to conduct the negotiations that may lead to the conclusion of international agreements and to maintain such relations as are appropriate with all international organizations.

The Court of Justice

The Court of Justice is based in Luxembourg and should not be confused with the International Court of Justice in the Hague, or the European Court of Human Rights in Strasbourg. It consists of 13 judges who are appointed by the governments of the Member States for a period of six years. It decides whether Member States have complied with their duties under the Treaties and monitors the legality of the acts of the Council of Ministers and of the Commission. The Court is also competent as regards preliminary rulings concerning the interpretation of Community law at the request of courts or judges of Member States. The Court of Justice makes a preliminary ruling which is binding for the judges in Member States. The judgements of the Court of Justice are made in last resort and are enforceable in all Member States of the Community.

Economic and Social Committee

Of particular relevance for employee relations within the EC is the Economic and Social Committee, which consists of representatives of the various categories of economic and social activity, in particular, manufacturers, farmers, workers, professional occupations and the general public. The members of the Committee are appointed by the Council of Ministers for a period of four years. Their appointments are renewable. From the four larger Member States, twenty-four members are appointed; then there are twenty-one from Spain, twelve from Belgium, Greece, the Netherlands and Portugal, nine from Denmark and Ireland and six from Luxembourg. The Economic and Social Committee has the right to be consulted and since 1972 may give advice on certain issues on its own initiative.

European Council

In the 1960s and early 1970s, heads of government and State came together at a number of *ad hoc* summit conferences in order to resolve conflicts over issues which had languished in the Council of Ministers and to give a new *élan* to Community development. The meetings at the Hague in 1969 and Paris in 1972 were particularly important in this respect. In 1974 it was decided to institutionalize these meetings within a body which became known as the European Council (not to be confused with the Council of Europe) These meetings had no formal constitutional status until the adoption of the Single European Act in 1986. The European Council has no precise legal obligations and so has a relatively free hand to decide what it wishes to discuss.

The Decision-making Process of the EC

The decision-making process of the European Community has changed somewhat over the years but, at the beginning of the 1990s, it functioned as shown in figure 2.1.

The Commission has a monopoly over initiating Community legislation. This right of initiative has been somewhat eroded over the years by the simple fact that the Commission needs the Council of Ministers to adopt its proposals, and so has to bear in mind the positions of the members of the Council of Ministers before exercising this right. It is in its interest to make a proposal which is likely to be adopted by the Member States. The Commission forwards its proposal to the Council of Ministers which refers it to the European Parliament and the Economic and Social Committee for their opinions. At this stage the Commission may amend its proposal to take the advice of the European Parliament and the

Figure 2.1   Decision making in the EC (post-Single European Act, pre-Treaty on Political Union)

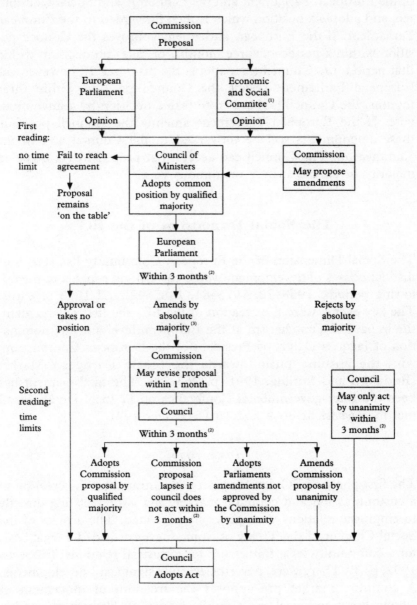

[1] Must be consulted on agriculture, movement of labour, right of establishment, transport, approximation of laws, social policy, European Social Fund, vocational training
[2] Maximum 4 months
[3] May only restore parliament's position as expressed in first reading or deal with passages not considered in first reading

Economic and Social Committee into account. The Council discusses the proposal from the Commission, as well as the opinions of the European Parliament and the Economic and Social Committee, and adopts a position which is then forwarded to the European Parliament. If the European Parliament approves the Council position within a period of three months, or takes no decision within that period, the Council then adopts the proposal. If, however, the European Parliament rejects the Council position within three months, the Council is required to take a decision by a unanimous vote. If the European Parliament amends the Council position, these amendments will be forwarded to the Council and to the Commission. The Council can accept that proposal by a qualified majority or amend it by a unanimous vote.

The Social Dimension of the EC

The Social Dimension of the European Community has seen four distinct phases of development which correspond roughly to the following periods: 1958–72, 1973–84, 1985–92, and 1993 onwards. The key events were the creation of the EC, the first enlargement, the impact of Thatcherism at the European level and the nomination of Jacques Delors as President of the European Commission, with the ensuing push towards the Single European Market (Bridgford and Stirling, 1991, p. 263–72). The final element has been the Inter-governmental Conference on Political Union which met in Maastricht on 9 and 10 December 1991.

1958–1972

The first phase of EC development concentrated on the creation of a customs union and common market, and issues relating directly to employee relations were generally neglected. The articles of the Social Chapter of the Treaty of Rome 'never provided a legal basis for a community legal framework for industrial relations' (Roberts, 1992, p. 3). There were, nevertheless, two significant developments. A common market presupposes the freedom of movement of labour, but in practical terms employees are less likely to move from one country to another in search of work if they lose their entitlement to social security benefits. As the harmonization of the different social welfare systems was out of the question for technical, financial and political reasons, it was decided to move gradually towards the co-ordination of the different systems in line with article 51 of the Treaty of Rome, thus ensuring that migrant workers could aggregate their entitlement to benefits. The other issue was that of equal pay, whose significance we discuss in more detail in chapter 5. However, it should be noted here that the establishment of the principle of equal pay had more to do with economic than social policy. As Quintin (1988) notes, France 'already had legislation establishing the principle of equal pay and it considered that it would be at a competitive disadvantage unless all Member States adopted the same principle' (p. 71).

1973–1984

The second period coincided with a more interventionist phase during which the provisions of European Community law were used to improve and harmonize living and working conditions. The summit conferences held in the Hague and Paris paved the way for the completion, further development and enlargement of the EC. In the wake of this the Council of Ministers agreed to a number of Directives on workers' rights in relation to redundancies and equal opportunities. In addition, in the mid-1970s, the Council of Ministers agreed to an action programme for safety, hygiene and health, as a result of which other Directives were introduced.

The Council of Ministers was however unable to agree on a number of other issues, particularly those relating to employee participation and information. The most famous was the so-called Fifth Directive on the structure of public limited companies which was initially proposed in 1972 and which aimed, in certain circumstances, to encourage employee participation. Later on, there was the so-called Vredeling Directive, which would have required public limited companies with more than 100 employees (in the first version) to provide employees with information on matters such as the company's economic and financial situation, its employment outlook, production and investment plans, rationalization activities and the introduction of new working methods. Opposition to both sets of proposals was widespread both within and outside the institutions of the EC, and so no decisions were reached. Unanimity was required within the Council of Ministers for a proposal to be adopted, and this process only worked when consensus prevailed. In the United Kingdom the 1979 elections returned a government which was committed to liberalizing the economy and reducing the power of trade unions and which was not prepared to see this crusade nullified by restrictive employee relations policies at the EC level. Consequently any further proposals, such as the Directive granting full time status to part time workers or allowing parental leave, were systematically blocked by the British government, thus effectively bringing the second stage of Community development to an end.

1985–1992

Stage three coincided with the appointment in 1985 of Jacques Delors, a former French Socialist Minister of Economic and Financial Affairs, as President of the European Commission. The EC claimed that it was formally abandoning any pretension of being the 'overseer' of European employee relations. The adviser to Jacques Delors on social affairs has claimed that the Commission was moving from a strictly 'normative' approach which 'aims at applying a single harmonizing framework to the Community as a whole' to a 'decentralized' approach which 'rejects as counterproductive any kind of social legislation at the Community level' (Venturini, 1989, p. 62). While it is clear that the EC may have eschewed a strictly normative approach, it is not the case that it abandoned attempts to introduce social legislation. According to Goetschy (1991), 'a definite acceleration of European social codification and norm setting can be observed. This is due to the shift from a harmonization logic to a mutual recognition logic, to the impetus inherent in the implementation of the action programme and, more generally, to on-going progress with the EMU, institutional reforms and political unification' (p. 272). This acceleration resulted from four significant initiatives: the Single European Act, the Single European Market, the Social Dimension and the Social Dialogue, all of which have important consequences for employee relations in Europe.

As previously explained, in an attempt to speed up decision making in the Council of Ministers, the Single European Act introduced qualified majority voting for certain measures 'which have as their object the establishment and functioning of the internal market' (article 100 A i) and which encourage improvements 'especially in the working environment, as regards the health and safety of workers' (article 118 A ii). While there is still some confusion over these precise definitions and ultimate decisions from the European Court of Justice will still be necessary, it is no longer possible for one particular Member State to block certain decisions within the Council of Ministers, as has been the case with the Directive on the adjustment of working hours, for example, which is based on article 118 A ii. The British government has, however, indicated its intention to challenge the Directive's legal base.

Linked to the Single European Act were further proposals for the Single European Market. The Commission published a White Paper entitled *Completing the Internal Market* which was approved by the Council of Ministers in June 1985. It contained approximately 300 proposals designed to remove physical barriers to trade between countries within the EC and to establish the Single European Market by the end of 1992. The consequences for employee relations in Europe are still not completely clear, not least because States have been slow to apply EC Directives to national legal provisions. The Cecchini Report predicted a rise in unemployment for the first two years of the Single European Market. Evidence would suggest that competition will intensify and, in response, employers will aim to reduce labour costs either by putting a brake on wage increases, shedding labour and worsening working conditions in countries with high labour costs or, where appropriate, by engaging in 'social dumping', that is, moving investment to countries with low labour costs. It is precisely because of the fear of a deterioration of employee relations conditions that the Social Dimension was proposed.

The European Commission published a Community Charter of Fundamental Social Rights for Workers which was to act as a partial counterweight to the Single European Market and was described in its introduction by Jacques Delors as 'a keystone of the social dimension in the construction of Europe'. It calls for minimum standards in major areas of labour law and was agreed by eleven Heads of State and governments at a European Council meeting held in Strasbourg in December 1989 (the United Kingdom was alone in voting against it). It addresses such issues as working conditions; freedom of movement of labour; minimum pay; social welfare schemes; freedom to join a trade union, to engage in collective bargaining and to participate in strike action; vocational training; equal opportunities; information, consultation and participation; health and safety; child labour; pensioners; and the disabled. This so-called Social Charter is not legally binding on Member States but is supported by a legislative Action Programme with 47 proposals. Of these, 17 are draft Directives, ten of which are in the field of health and safety. Some of the more sensitive issues such as pay are only the subject of Opinions and are not, therefore, binding on Member States. Indeed, the impact of the Social Charter has been considerably reduced in scope through redrafting and the limitations of the Social Action Programme. Furthermore, the Commission has refrained from making any proposal on a number of issues, notably, the right to strike, which may have posed difficulties for a British government, and anti-discrimination measures on grounds of race, colour or religion (*European Industrial Relations Review* 1991). Its long-term effect should prove to be more significant if it is able to act 'as a catalyst, bringing political pressure to bear on national governments and employers to approximate upwards social provisions and working standards' (Tsoukalis, 1991, p. 152).

1993 onwards

At the Maastricht conference, the twelve Heads of the EC Member States agreed on a set of issues critical to the future development of the European Community. They signed a Treaty on European Union which put forward new policies on areas such as education and training and foreign and security policy, as well as a Treaty on Economic and Monetary Union.

In terms of employee relations, the Treaty on European Union gave out contradictory signals. On the one hand it contained explicit reference to the principle of subsidiarity (Article 3 b), which was previously defined by Jacques Delors 'as the decentralized organization of responsibilities so as to ensure that nothing that could be done by a smaller entity is handed over to a large one' (quoted in Guéry, 1991, p. 91). For many observers this was seen as an attempt to put a brake on moves towards the centralization of policy making within the EC. From a British perspective this had previously been interpreted as follows: the Community should act only where objectives can be attained better at Community level than at the level of the individual Member States. On the other hand the Member States agreed nevertheless to create the conditions for a Social Dimension which would be achieved by legalist and voluntarist means.

The European Council unanimously approved a Social Chapter to the Treaty on Political Union which will make it possible to legislate on a number of issues emanating from the Social Charter which have been held up in the Council of Ministers. The Social Chapter empowers 11 Member States (i.e. all except the United Kingdom), using European Community institutions, to take decisions by qualified majority, on:

- improvements, in particular, of the working environment to protect workers' health and safety;
- working conditions;
- information and consultation of workers;
- equality between men and women; and
- integration of persons excluded from the labour market.

The Council of Ministers will still take decisions unanimously in the following areas:

- social security and social protection for workers;
- protection of workers when their employment contracts are terminated;
- representation and collective defence of the interests of workers and employers, including co-determination;
- conditions of employment for third-country nationals legally residing in Community territory; and
- financial contribution for promotion of employment and job creation.

The provisions of the new Social Chapter specifically exclude issues such as pay, the right of association and the right to strike.

While the legal position remains a little confused and some categories appear to overlap, it would seem that it will now be easier for a number of decisions to be taken in the field of employee relations within the EC. It appears that the British government representatives will not participate in any of the deliberations on Commission proposals covering areas in the agreement; nor will they be able to participate in the adoption of these issues. Because of this, the qualified majority within the Council of Ministers will be reduced to 44 (out of 66) from 54 (out of 76). The resulting measures will not apply to the United Kingdom, nor will any of the financial consequences of these measures. Nevertheless, it remains to be seen whether the United Kingdom can seal itself off from some of these developments. In the case of information and consultation rights leading to the creation of Europe-wide works councils, it would seem that any European company operating in the United Kingdom, and Japanese or American company operating in the United Kingdom and Western

Europe and any British company operating in Western Europe will be required to implement any Directive upon which the eleven agree. It is no doubt the case that British trade unions will try to ensure that the United Kingdom is not excluded from the provisions of this Social Chapter. As John Edmonds (1992, p. 7), General Secretary of the GMB, clearly stated, 'every time a social directive relating to employment conditions or anything else covered by the Social Chapter is passed in Europe, we will submit a claim to every employer with which we have bargaining rights in Britain for comparable terms'. British employers will be less enthusiastic, but there are clear indications that the United Kingdom cannot realistically opt out. 'Mr Herwig Kressler, personnel manager at Unilever, says he will probably ignore the 'opt-out' altogether rather than have one set of rules for the United Kingdom and another for other EC countries. Other personnel managers say they would probably include the United Kingdom in works councils but try to opt out of more costly measures' (Goodhart, 1992, p. 10).

In addition to these changes, the position of the 'social partners' is reinforced within the decision-making process of the European Community. The Commission is given the task of consulting management and labour on the possible direction of Community action, which may lead in the medium term to a diluted form of European neo-corporatism. If, on the other hand, management and labour should so desire, the dialogue between them at Community level may lead to contractual relations including agreements, thus reinforcing moves towards collective bargaining at the European level.

Conclusions

There are considerable differences in the relationship between public authorities and employee relations in the countries of Western Europe. The obvious differences exist between the United Kingdom and the other countries of continental Europe. Legalism and voluntarism make uneasy bedfellows, as can be seen from the divergent positions taken during negotiations concerning employee relations issues at the level of the EC. However, there are some signs of convergence. Employee relations in the United Kingdom are becoming more legalistic, certainly as far as the activities of trade unions are concerned. There is some evidence to suggest that some of the countries with a legalist tradition are becoming slightly more voluntaristic, so as to introduce an element of flexibility into employee relations. Neo-corporatism is nowhere to be found in the United Kingdom of the 1980s and 1990s, but it still provides an accurate description of government–union relations in many countries, particularly in Austria and Scandinavia. Moreover, governments in many Western European countries were sorely tempted to attack wage inflation by means of neo-corporatist arrangements which require some form of incomes policy.

The State still plays a role as a mediator, although this is being transposed by the changes in the pattern of collective bargaining, employee participation and industrial conflict which will be considered in chapter 4. The State is still a major employer in all Western European countries in spite of moves towards privatization. (These moves have been more pronounced in the United Kingdom than in other Western European countries.) There is some evidence to show, however, that the State is taking the role of 'model employer' much less seriously than has traditionally been the case, or, at least, that it has adopted a new model.

The major change in the impact of the public authorities on employee relations in Western Europe is to found at the European level. The EC is setting in place a significant body of social legislation and informal rules, thus reinforcing the view that a Europeanization of employee relations is slowly taking place, an issue which will be considered in greater detail in the Conclusion.

3

Management and the Unions

The three key actors in employee relations are management, workers and the State, although using these terms can be problematic because our understanding of them is laden with cultural, social and political values. We dealt with the State in the previous chapter and we now turn our attention to the role of management and workers within European employee relations systems.

The term 'workers' carries with it the ideological baggage of the class struggle and 'employees' has often been adopted as a more neutral term. Many workers are self-employed and others have the ambiguous employment relationship of a government sponsored training scheme. We also have divisions between 'staff' and 'manuals', and trade unions regard employees as their 'members'. Our focus in this chapter is on employees as members of trade unions.

The term trade union is one that has generally crossed cultural boundaries and although there may be many differences in organizational forms there is a common understanding of their role as a collective organization of workers. Trade unions are an invariable feature of industrialization in any country in the world. They may be politically suppressed or turned into toothless adjuncts of the State but they inevitably re-emerge. Their precise organizational forms and their methods will depend on both their history and the effectiveness of different bargaining strategies. In essence, trade unions are democratic organizations whose purpose is to protect and improve the terms and conditions of employment of their members. However, there are different types of unions, different ways of organizing, different strategies and different ideologies. It is often difficult to talk of a 'trade union movement' within any one nation and the problems are magnified in any attempts to define a European one. The concept of 'management' can also conceal more than it reveals. Owners or employers may also be managers but the development of joint stock companies and the decline of nineteenth century entrepreneurial capitalism has made this much less common in larger organizations. Managers may or may not be employees. Shareholders participate in the running of private businesses without being employees as do elected representatives in the public and voluntary sectors. Management as an occupation may be distributed both vertically and horizontally within an organization. Thus, an individual with a high grade or professional status may have little or no 'managerial' function compared with a relatively low status supervisor. The issue is further complicated by systems of employee involvement or participation. How do worker directors or team leaders fit into management structures? The concept of management also carries with it social and political connotations. Managers are the owners, the bosses or just plain 'them'. They are a part of a system of authority and control that is opposed to the workers.

This complexity and diversity provides the context for the rest of this chapter. However, we shall also find common themes in terms of historical development, political policies and organization. We begin our discussion with the emergence of European trade unionism and deal with employers and managers in the second half of the chapter.

The Development of European Trade Unions

Trade unions exist to protect and improve the living and working conditions of their members. They may try to achieve this through collective bargaining at the workplace (or a combination of workplaces) or through influencing the policies of the State. These two potential approaches have provided the basis for a broad distinction to be made between those European unions with a political or ideological base and those that have relied on collective bargaining.

Clegg (1976) has used collective bargaining as the basis of his analysis of the differences between European unions. He suggests that 'variations from one country to another in union density, structure, government, workplace organization, strikes and approaches to industrial democracy can be explained largely by differences in the structure of collective bargaining' (p. 99). It could be argued equally that the structure of collective bargaining is determined by the nature of the trade union movement within the nation. In this respect, the 'political' nature of many continental European unions may have led to a clearer relationship to the State and this may have been one factor that pre-empted the emergence of workplace collective bargaining on the British model.

As we have already suggested, the development of workers' organizations in Europe is neither a uniform nor a unilinear process. While trade unions are a product of industrial capitalism they are not passive agents to be shaped into the same form in all historical circumstances. Trade unions are also the product of the active participation of their members. Thus, while some common themes link European unions together we should be surprised by neither diversity nor change. The post-war trade union movement in the Federal Republic of Germany, for example, has little in common with the same movement before the onset of fascism and may change again as the new German State develops following unification.

However, this is not to argue that past events do not shape current practices and there are a number of historical features that have shaped the trade union movement in Europe. The most significant have been national boundaries, the process of industrialization, political ideology, and the activities of employers and the State.

The contemporary focus on the European Community as a shorthand for Europe as a whole is misleading both now and, even more so, historically. Continental Europe has been the stage for a continuous process of empire building, revolutions and national boundary changes. The collapse of the Soviet bloc is another stage in that development. These developments have necessarily had an impact on European labour movements. At one end of the spectrum might be the United Kingdom – relatively isolated geographically, immune to modern boundary changes and with its own predominant language, its trade unions were also the product of the first development of industrial capitalism. It is not surprising in these circumstances to find an insular and distinctive trade union movement. Kendall's (1975) analysis of European trade unionism, for example, counterposes Britain with the rest of Europe and links the movement more closely with that in the United States.

By contrast, systems of employee relations in Scandinavia, for example, show common characteristics that reflect cultural links and cut across national boundaries. In Europe national boundaries have never had the permanence of those in the United Kingdom so that, for example, laws which had their origins in one State might also carry their effect into others. The Le Chapelier Law, which effectively banned trade unions in France following the revolution, was also implemented in what are now Belgium and the Netherlands. In Finland, the development of the labour movement was shaped by the geographical proximity of the Soviet Union and the revolutionary upheavals of 1917.

In situations where national boundaries are prone to change, religions and ideologies – which know no such frontiers – have a greater opportunity to become a binding force. Thus, national trade union organizations based on, say, Catholicism may find more in common with similar movements in other countries than they do with, say, communist trade union centres in their own. These relationships may be highly complex and links between individual trade union confederations are often fluid, particularly now that communist ideology is being challenged by the break-up of the former Eastern European bloc.

A further significant feature shaping the historical development of European trade unionism has been the emergence of industrial capitalism. This occurred at different times in Europe and the pace of development also varied. Given that trade unions are a product of this process, their growth is clearly closely related. In general terms, Hobsbawm (1975) has described the 20 years from the early 1850s to the early 1870s as 'the period when the world became capitalist' (p. 29). More particularly, it was a time of economic transformation for Europe and the base on which the emergent trade unions rested.

It is clear that many European trade unions can trace long historical antecedents in friendly societies and other working class organizations but by the 1870s they had consolidated themselves into recognizable organisations. They did so on the back of a wave of industrial militancy which

> ... gripped Germany and France in 1868, Belgium in 1869 (retaining its force for some years), Austria-Hungary shortly after, finally reaching Italy in 1871 (where it was to peak in 1872–4) and Spain in the same year. Meanwhile the strike wave was also at its height in Britain in 1871–3. (Hobsbawm, 1975, p. 112)

By the end of this period European trade unionism had become generally established although one of the exceptions illustrates the links between economic development and trade union development. The process of industrialization was slower in politically divided and agrarian Italy. The 1901 census indicated that still only 15 per cent of the employed population worked in the industrial sector. It was only in 1906 that the first national trade union confederation was formed although stable individual organizations had existed since the 1890s, and agricultural and co-operative organizations from before then.

If the relationship with economic development is relatively clear cut in this respect, the interplay between unions and politics is at least as decisive but infinitely more complex. There is an inevitable link between trade unions as organizations seeking to improve living and working conditions and political action towards the same end. In the United Kingdom, where the distinction between industrial and political has been clearly made, the early trade unionists were, nevertheless, also often involved in Chartism, co-operation and a variety of forms of political agitation. However, what is often seen as distinctive about the United Kingdom is the growth of a socialist political party from the trade unions rather than the other way around.

It is neither possible nor appropriate to limit the relationship between European trade unions and politics to one restricted to political parties. A whole variety of political and religious ideologies have affected the development of trade unions. These have ranged from anarchism in Spain, syndicalism in France and the Netherlands, communism in France, Italy and Portugal, social democracy in Scandinavia, socialism of one sort or another in most of Europe, fascism in Germany, Spain and Portugal, and Catholicism in Belgium, France, Italy and the Netherlands to Stalinism in the Eastern European bloc. However, the eventual emergence of social democratic and labour parties committed to reform rather than revolution became the base of the relationship between trade unionism and politics. Within this dominant framework, communist-led trade union centres remained as a focus in countries such as France, Italy and Portugal, and Christian confederations continue to exist in Belgium and the Netherlands, for example.

As well as shaping their own political existence the trade unions were shaped by the political practices of employers and the State. In the absence of universal suffrage and political power in their formative years the trade unions received a uniformly hostile response. They found themselves legally outlawed throughout Europe. In France, Belgium and the Netherlands the French Le Chapelier Law of 1791 banned organizations of workers. In France itself, 'laws against strikes were enforced with some severity; over 13,000 persons were prosecuted in the four decades before their repeal' (Kendall, 1975, p. 13). In the United Kingdom, trade unions were unlawful until the repeal of the Combination Acts in 1825 and it was not until the 1871 Trade Union Act that they gained a proper legal status. In other European countries similar legislation prevailed or the State simply banned or repressed nascent trade union movements. However, in the years following the revolutions of 1848 trade unions gained legal status in countries such as Austria, Germany and Sweden. There were further attempts to ban unions in the 1870s in Germany and Denmark, and in Luxembourg the anti-union legislation introduced in 1879 was not officially repealed until 1936. However, by now trade unionism was well established and the State was only able to halt its further development through the brutality of fascism and military dictatorship, as in Germany, Spain, Portugal and Greece. In part the repressive activities of the State reflected a fear of the revolutionary potential of trade unions through their association with socialist politics. They were also a response to the fears of employers that the activities of trade unions, through effective collective bargaining and industrial action, would eat into profitability.

The ultimate political accommodation of trade unions followed two paths. On the one hand there was the adoption of rights of association and the withdrawal of labour as fundamental human rights which were sometimes enshrined in written constitutions. This approach gives rise to the positive rights often enjoyed by continental European trade unionists in contrast to the negative immunities typical of the United Kingdom. On the other hand, such immunities provided the basis for the protection of trade unions from the actions of employers (rather than the State itself) attempting to limit the effectiveness of collective bargaining.

This brief overview of trade union development clearly illustrates the hostile climate which they endured during their formative years. This generally encouraged political action although its form was different in the different nation States. There are also common features in the development of collective bargaining as the most significant method of improving terms and conditions of employment.

Differences in historical development mean that there remain important differences in national movements which inhibit cross-country collaboration. However, a number of factors have more recently encouraged a convergence in trade union practice. These include the development of transnational enterprises with global human resource strategies, the Europe-wide experiment with neo-corporatism which drew trade unions into government, the current developments in EC social policy and the decline in importance of ideological differences based on cold war politics.

The Growth of Internationalism

Alongside the development of national trade union movements has been the growth of international organizations. As we have seen, the fluidity of national boundaries in nineteenth century Europe made some 'international' activity inevitable. British labour history also records a spectacular example of international solidarity when a donation of over £30,000 from Australia ensured the success of the 1889 dock strike (McCarthy, 1988, p. 149). However, it was ideology rather than instrumentalism that was the basis for the earliest international organization. The First International Workingmens' Association was founded in 1864 in London and brought together a mix of socialists and trade unionists. Its influence, and that of Karl Marx within it, lasted for about a decade. Its activities were followed by the development of international trade union organizations on an industrial basis. The 1890s saw the foundation of international associations of dockers, garment workers, engineers, iron and steel workers and miners. 'Twenty-eight trade based internationals (or International Trade Secretariats, ITSs, as they later became known) were in operation by 1914' (Kendall, 1975, p. 19). The early years of the twentieth century saw the further development of international organizations based on national trade union confederations, many of which had their origins in the 1890s, and the International Federation of Trade Unions was established in 1901. In 1919 the tripartite International Labour Organization was established as part of the League of Nations. This body became a part of the United Nations after the Second World War and remains significant in setting world standards in industrial relations and health and safety matters.

The contemporary development of trade union organization on an international level can be looked at in terms of the growth of transnational bargaining arrangements and political ideology. Historically, the former has been insignificant while the latter has bedevilled successful organization and undermined international credibility. However, the most recent developments suggest that European collective bargaining may slowly be emerging and that political differences are fast disappearing.

On a global level, international trade union organization has been dominated by the ideological divisions characteristic of cold war politics. A brief period of global unity following the end of the Second World War was brought to an end in 1949 when the trade unions of the western capitalist economies founded the International Confederation of Free Trade Unions (ICFTU), leaving the Soviet bloc movements to dominate the World Federation of Trade Unions (WFTU). In addition to these two dominant organizations there is the smaller, Christian-based, World Confederation of Labour (WCL). In Western European terms, the ICFTU was the most significant organization but some communist-led confederations, such as those in Italy and France, affiliated to the WFTU.

Neither of the world federations has any collective bargaining role and so their activities have been dominated by political action. This is expressed through pressure group activity and solidarity action. The ICFTU has given particular attention to human rights in relation to trade union activists in countries dominated by dictatorships. The world federations also provide information and advice to affiliates as well as developing trade union education programmes. It has been claimed that their activities in Third World nations have most tarnished their reputations, as they have appeared to serve the interests of national foreign policies rather than emergent trade union movements (Munck, 1988, pp. 190–1). However, the radical upheavals in the European command economies have led to the effective demise of the WFTU and the ICFTU now dominates the international arena. The ICFTU has grown in affiliated membership from 47 million in 1947 to 99 million in 1991. It now has 144 affiliates in 102 countries and territories compared to 66 in 50 countries on its foundation.

At a European level, the most significant organization is the European Trade Union Confederation (ETUC). As with the world organizations, the ETUC has had no collective bargaining role although developments in the European Social Dimension following the Maastricht summit in 1991 may lead to change in this area. Its main function has been to act primarily as a political pressure group on behalf of its constituents. In this respect the EC is becoming an increasingly important focus of attention.

The ETUC has its base in the European affiliates of the ICFTU but since its formal foundation as a separate entity in 1973 it has accepted membership from confederations which previously had been associated with national communist parties. It has specifically sought to avoid the ideological divisions that beset the world federations. By 1990 the ETUC had 39 affiliated confederations from 21 Western European countries. This represented some 45 million trade unionists or around 95 per cent of organized workers (European Trade Union Institute, 1990a, p. 12). By 1993, the ETUC had 46 members and two confederations, from Poland and the Czech and Slovak Republics, as observers.

Alongside these global organizations have grown the industry-based International Trade Secretariats (ITSs) whose European links are the European Industry Committees which became formal members of the ETUC in 1991. The Trade Secretariats have close links with the ICFTU and have also a political, informational and educational role as well as providing support for affiliated unions in dispute. The Secretariats have been particularly concerned with the growth of multinational companies and have sought to use them as a base for involvement in collective bargaining. Bendiner (1987, p. 23) has noted the role of the International Metalworkers Federation in the discussions over the location of a new Ford motor plant in Europe when it acted as an intermediary between national trade union movements.

Finally, there have been attempts to build links between trade unionists working in the different branch plants of transnational companies. As capital is globally organized and controlled, labour has sought to develop ways of influencing decisions made beyond national boundaries. There are formidable obstacles to the development of cross-national collective bargaining and trade unionists have generally confined themselves to the more limited aims of exchanging information and, occasionally, organizing industrial action in solidarity disputes. Attempts by the ITSs to become the basis for international collective bargaining have so far been unsuccessful although they have established 'some 60' world company councils to link together trade unionists in different branches of transnational companies (Munck, 1988, p. 191). The European Community may encourage these developments through its proposed Directives on European works councils. However, as Milne (1991) indicates in his interview with the German IG Metall leader at Ford, Wilfred Kuckelkorn, there are still significant difficulties facing joint union action.

> Kuckelkorn says: 'We want the British unions to win a 35 hour week and they will get practical solidarity from Germany, including overtime bans and working to rule.' But with another breath Kuckelkorn rejects out of hand any thought of joint European collective bargaining with Ford: 'the national unions cannot accept European negotiations. If you take away the power of the national unions they will go down.'

Kuckelkorn's views are not necessarily shared by those who argue that European collective bargaining would increase the power of national unions.

Trade Union Organization

There are several traditional categories used to distinguish between trade unions. They are based on union membership patterns: craft unions have recruited skilled workers across industries; industrial unions have sought to recruit all workers in an industry whatever their occupation; general unions have had open recruitment policies but have generally been dominated by semi- and unskilled workers; and white collar unions have restricted themselves to clerical, professional supervisory and managerial grades. British trade unionism is a complex patchwork of each of these features whereas much of the rest of Europe has a more coherent structure based on industrial unionism. However, political and confessional divisions are more characteristic of these movements and the analytical value of this traditional typology has declined. Indeed, to try to impose such a typology onto European unions with their wide variety of historical traditions could mislead more than it illuminates. Poole (1986) has suggested that in Europe the 'most common single pattern is for industrial unions' (p. 78) but he adds craft, conglomerate, general, enterprise, public sector, white collar and professional and ethical or religious. This list could be extended by subdividing the ethical and religious categories and identifying Catholic or Protestant federations, communist and socialist groupings of various persuasions, as well as liberals, conservatives and independents. In addition, comparisons might be made in terms of union government and organizational structures. In this context,

European trade unionism ranges from the comparative simplicity of the Austrian or Swedish movements to the almost Byzantine complexities of those in Greece or France.

In view of this diversity it becomes difficult to categorize European trade unions according to a single criterion. Our approach is to adopt three broad features common to all trade unions and to suggest that individual national movements exist along a continuum. The first feature is that of collective bargaining. Clegg (1976) has suggested that collective bargaining is the key feature differentiating European trade unions. Most obviously, a high degree of centralization in bargaining is linked with the same feature in trade union organization. The second important comparative feature is the political development of the trade union movement and the links that are made with political parties. A trade union movement can be divided and fragmented by such political divisions, as in Italy, or united in support of a single party, as in the United Kingdom. The final feature is the membership base that we have discussed as the traditional method for categorizing trade unions. Thus we have a three-part characterization based on bargaining arrangements, political differences and the membership base. This leads us to identify trade union movements on a range from highly centralized or cohesive through to decentralized and fragmented. As 'ideal types' we have trade union movements at one end of the spectrum with an industrial union structure, a single confederation linked to one political party and a centralized bargaining system. At the other end of the spectrum are trade union movements with a diverse membership base, political divisions and fragmented bargaining arrangements. Inevitably, national trade union movements do not fit neatly into categories and there are cases of centralized bargaining existing alongside political divisions or fragmented bargaining with political unity. Nevertheless, linking these three factors together gives us a more realistic picture of European trade unionism than one that relies on a single feature. This can be illustrated with one or two examples.

The trade union movements in both Austria and the Federal Republic of Germany have strong features of a centralized movement. They were both reformed after the Second World War and were able to leave old traditional methods of organization behind and develop movements based on industrial unionism. In Austria there are 15 unions affiliated to the dominant confederation, the Österreichischer Gewerkschaftsbund (ÖGB), and in the Federal

Republic of Germany, there are 16 unions affiliated to the major confederation, the Deutsche Gewerkschaftsbund (DGB). Thus both movements are organizationally centralized although in the Federal Republic of Germany there is an important confederation for salaried staff – the Deutsche Angestalltengewerkschaft – with around 500,000 members. Neither of the confederations in Austria or Germany conduct negotiations directly although in Austria the individual unions act as 'authorized agents' and it is the ÖGB which signs agreements. In this particular sense, bargaining cannot be described as completely centralized. However, it generally takes place within a restricted framework which is heavily influenced by regional agreements and individual workplace bargaining over pay is uncommon. In terms of political links, both trade union confederations are formally neutral but have developed close relationships with their respective social democratic parties. Each of these three features taken together gives a picture of a cohesive and relatively centralized trade union movement.

A different range of factors has led to the generally centralized trade union movements in the Nordic countries. Organizationally, there are two significant trade confederations in most countries. In Sweden, there are 24 industry-based unions affiliated to the Landsorganisationen (LO), the major confederation. The Tjänstemännens Centralorganisation (TCO) is about half the size of the LO and is a federation of white collar and professional employees. The TCO has 20 affiliates largely organized on 'industrial' lines (e.g. the civil service and the banks) but with some occupational unions such as the Association of Supervisors and Foremen (SALF). Collective bargaining in Sweden has been part of the centralized Nordic tradition with negotiations taking place within three sectors: private, central State and local government. In terms of political affiliations, the LO has a long-standing and stable relationship with the Social Democratic Party (SAP) which has governed Sweden for long periods of time. The TCO takes a more politically neutral stance. As with Austria and Germany, this gives us a relatively cohesive and centralized trade union movement.

At the decentralized or fragmented end of the European trade union spectrum are the movements in France and Greece. There are five significant trade union confederations in France and within them a range of organizational structures (European Trade Union Institute, 1987). National unions based on industries are the most important but local and regional organizations are also significant.

There is not the tight industrial union structure characteristic of Austria and Germany. Politically, the confederations maintain an officially neutral stance. However, the Confédération Générale du Travail (CGT) has traditionally had close links with the Communist Party and the Confédération Française Démocratique du Travail (CFDT) has more recently had some links with the Socialist Party, or at least parts of it. As Bridgford (1990) notes, these political differences between all five confederations 'were further exacerbated by factionalism within the differing confederations' (p. 133). Collective bargaining arrangements in France have been in a fluid state in recent years but, in general:

> The law provides for agreements at different levels, with the most general issues pertaining to each sector or industry being settled at national level and regional or local adjustments being effected by means of separate agreements or additional clauses. Finally, detailed provisions may be added at the level of the individual workplace, and also by means of separate agreement or additional clauses, in order to take account of its own specific situation. (European Trade Union Institute, 1987, p. 64)

In all, the French trade union movement is fragmented and this may be one of the factors explaining a relatively low membership density figure (Bridgford, 1990, p. 126).

A further example of a fragmented trade union movement is that in Greece which has recently emerged from years of repression. New union laws have been introduced but the fresh start has not led to the sort of clarity in organization that developed after the Second World War elsewhere in Europe. Greek law allows 21 workers in a company to form a trade union and around 5,000 local unions have grown on this basis. Most unions are affiliated to the major national confederation but they remain small and range from the larger unions for construction and banking workers down to those with memberships in the hundreds representing, for example, bottled drinks employees or undertakers. Organizationally, then, the Greek trade unions show no single discernible pattern which is likely to lead to a small number of centralized unions. In terms of collective bargaining, the major negotiations on minimum rates are carried out by the national confederation with separate agreements for the public and private sectors (European Trade Union Institute, 1984). However, these are supplemented by agreements at industry, company or local level, thereby moving away from a centralized pattern. In terms of the Greek unions' politics, the position would appear more straightforward given that there is one major confederation. However, the civil service union is not a member and there are also four smaller central organizations. Within the dominant body, the GSEE, there are five main organized political factions and the confederation maintains links with a number of political parties (ibid., p. 26).

These examples illustrate extreme ends of the spectrum and it is difficult to categorize European trade union movements into discrete pigeon holes. The United Kingdom, for example, has a predominantly decentralized private sector bargaining system and a range of union types. On the other hand, public sector bargaining has been largely centralized and there is a single confederation, the TUC, which supports a single political party. However, the three categories of organization, political affiliation and collective bargaining do provide a framework within which to compare European trade unions.

Workplace Organization

The development of workplace representation is a consistent feature of trade unionism in any country. It is a necessary adjunct to collective bargaining (even when highly centralized) and it has its own role to play in protecting employees from arbitrary or unfair management decisions. The protection of workers' health and safety is another important focus for workplace representatives. Politically, the workplace representative has been asked to fulfil a mission far beyond the prosaic role of dealing with grievances or disciplinary cases. Some variants of Marxism have seen them as the vanguard of working class activity. Syndicalism based its approach to action on the revolutionary power of industrial unionism and the concept of workers' control. In countries such as Italy, Spain and France with their politically divided trade unions such ideas were a significant current in their historical development. However, it is pragmatic rather than political issues that have come to dominate workplace representation in Western Europe.

The role of what we have simply called the 'workplace representative' differs between European countries. There are, however, three distinct general functional groups that can be identified at a European level. The first includes representatives of the employees, elected by the whole workforce, often to serve in some sort of worker participation system. This reflects a general political will for establishing a mechanism that enables workers to participate in the decision-making process of their organization. Thus, representation is on the basis of all employees, though not necessarily all managers. The second group of representatives are union officials elected or appointed by the members alone. Their function is to act as agents of their trade union at the workplace and their role will be circumscribed by legal arrangements and collective agreements. The final group of representatives are concerned with health and safety matters. Again, the function is common throughout Europe although the specific arrangements will vary.

The three functions identified as discrete categories above inevitably overlap in reality. For example, a union representative is also likely to be elected to the employee participation body and may serve on a health and safety committee as well. In Belgium, for example, the union representative (*délégué syndical*) has distinct legal rights to engage in collective bargaining; the representative on the *conseil d'enterprise* has separate rights but is often the same person and, in smaller companies where formal health and safety committees do not exist, the function is again taken on by the union representative (European Trade Union Institute, 1990b, p. 10). This multiplicity of functions is most clearly illustrated in countries which often have low levels of formal trade union membership where the strength of organization is reflected in voting levels for trade unionists to bodies that represent all employees. For example, in Spain and France 'works councils' are often dominated by trade union representatives.

We deal in detail with employee participation systems in chapter 4 so our focus in the rest of this section is on the trade union rights and roles of workplace representatives. In this respect there are two important areas to consider: firstly, the legal rights of union representatives in such areas as time off work, facilities and protection from dismissal and, secondly, their bargaining role.

It is clear from table 3.1 that there is a widespread network of trade union rights in the workplace across Western Europe. In some cases these are derived from those extended to 'works councillors' but, as we have noted, these are often trade union members. Many of the basic rights of workplace representatives have been long established by custom and practice but it is interesting to note the extent of legal codification in the 1970s and 1980s. Such legislation was introduced in Italy (1970), Austria (1974), Sweden

Table 3.1 Union representatives' rights and activities in selected European countries

	Legal right to recognition	Recognition through collective agreement	Rights to time off and facilities	Protection from dismissal	Workplace bargaining role
Austria	•				
Belgium		•	•	•	•
Denmark		•	•	•	
Finland	•			•	
France	•		•	•	•
Greece	•		•	•	•
Italy	•		•	•	
Netherlands		•			
Norway		•	•		•
Portugal	•		•	•	•
Spain	•		•	•	
Sweden	•		•		
UK		•	•	•	•

(1974), the United Kingdom (1975), Spain (1980 and 1985), Greece (1982), and France (1984). In other European countries the collective agreement is the basis for representatives' rights and there is an inevitable overlap between the two arrangements with custom and practice still putting the 'flesh on the bones'. In Austria and Germany, the system of employee representation formally predominates over trade union organization so direct statutory protections are less prevalent. There is a similarly restricted role for trade union workplace organization in the Netherlands.

Representational rights would have little impact if they were not supported with rights to paid time off and the facilities to carry out union duties. Again, table 3.1 indicates the spread of such legislation. However, there is no uniformity in the approach as examples will indicate. Paid time off for union activities is often tied to the role of 'works councillor' and we treat these two areas together here. In Italy, delegates are entitled to a legal minimum of eight hours time off a month on full pay and an additional eight days a year without pay. In Portugal, they are allowed five paid hours a month and in France the system is based on the size of the workforce, with a maximum allowance of 20 hours a month. In Denmark and the United Kingdom, specific times have not been legally established but local arrangements ensure 'reasonable' time off. In Italy, some time off rights have been extended to employees as well as their representatives. They have the right to hold meetings during working hours for a maximum of ten hours a year. A right to unpaid time off for union members also exists in the United Kingdom but it is rarely utilized.

Rights to time off for representatives also extends to training, which can include trade union training, the training of 'works councillors' or more general educational leave. Actual practice varies widely between countries. In France, educational provisions are extended to all employees and there is actually a minimum period of two days. The maximum is 12 working days or 18 in the case of trade union lay tutors. There is, finally, 'a global limit on trade union education leave per firm, which is calculated in terms of the size of the firm and in terms of [total] days' leave' (Bridgford and Stirling, 1988, p. 236). Legal entitlement to time off for training is widespread as is the alternative, namely arrangements established primarily through collective agreements.

The right of access to facilities is a broad phrase in itself and it is broadly interpreted in Europe. Rights to call meetings, have access to rooms and notice boards are commonplace. In Portugal, for example:

> The law requires that delegates be allowed to carry out their official business of liaising between the union and its members without hindrance provided that does not interfere with the usual activities of the firm. Trade union delegates may distribute and display information in the workplace and may convene meetings of all workers in the workplace, including during working hours, for a total period not exceeding 15 hours per year. (European Trade Union Institute, 1990b, p. 86)

A final protection for trade union workplace representatives is not to be dismissed for their activities. We discuss the general provisions on dismissal in chapter 5 but it is important to note here that extra provisions normally apply to trade union activists. Table 3.1 indicates the spread of such legislation. One example is the Finnish system under which, except in cases of serious misconduct or redundancy, termination of a union agent's employment requires the consent of the majority of employees he or she represents. In

Belgium, legislation was updated in 1991 to provide protection for trade unionists on works councils and their deputies, and also those standing for election to them. British law protects all employees from dismissal for trade union activities.

Having discussed the rights of union representatives it is important to turn to their role. In the United Kingdom, shop stewards are often regarded as both negotiators of collective agreements and representatives of individual members. Their role as national union delegates is much less significant. In much of the rest of Western Europe, employee participation systems or centralized bargaining arrangements can significantly reduce the role of the union representative as a workplace bargainer. On the other hand, political differences between confederations highlight the role of the workplace representatives in relation to their unions. For example, at times of works council elections, representatives may take on an advocacy role that is unfamiliar in the British arena. Thus, workplace representatives will carry out different functions in accordance with the employee relations system in each country.

Table 3.1 indicates that there are still a number of countries in which workplace representatives are involved in collective bargaining. However, in some countries trade unions as such are specifically excluded from a local wage bargaining role. In the Federal Republic of Germany, for instance, pay negotiations are generally carried out by trade unions above plant level and local agreements are limited. There are similar restrictions in the Netherlands.

Finally, workplace trade unionists are involved in health and safety arrangements. In many cases, health and safety committees have statutory power which is conferred when organizations reach a particular size. The committees normally comprise management and employee representatives and sometimes technical experts. The United Kingdom is unusual in operating its health and safety system through the election of trade union delegates. The European practice is to extend participation to all employees or even to use the works council as the forum for health and safety matters.

Workplace organization is a key feature of trade unionism in general. However, the pervasiveness of shop steward organization in the British system represents one end of a European continuum. This makes it difficult to talk about exact counterparts to the shop steward, particularly where some form of employee participation system is operating. Many European countries make a distinction between the role of union representatives and the role of employee representatives whereas in Britain the two are normally combined.

Trade Union Membership

Having discussed the historical development of European unions and their methods of organization, it is now necessary to locate this discussion within the overall pattern of trade union membership across Europe. However, cross-national comparisons in this field are fraught with difficulties (Walsh, 1985). Firstly, there is the problem of compiling the statistics themselves. When done by the trade unions, there may be difficulties in the compilation of accurate records and a tendency to overestimate, particularly where there are competing confederations. Official agencies and records do not always exist and data may be collected only at long time intervals. Secondly, there may be differences in the definition of the term 'trade union', particularly in relation to professional associations. Thirdly, there is the question of the different types of membership which arises because, in some countries, the unemployed, pensioners or even students may belong to a union. For example, in Italy as much as one-quarter of the membership may be retired. Fourthly, the basis for calculations may change over time making historical comparisons more difficult. Fifthly, once membership figures are generated there remains the question of which are the most accurate indicators. Absolute figures, percentage growth figures or density figures may all be used but give a different impression. For example, on calculations based on Visser's (1988) figures, the Dutch trade union movement experienced a 30 per cent growth between 1950 and 1970 but saw a decline in density from 42.3 to 36.5 per cent. Density is a notoriously difficult figure given the potentially different definitions of the workforce and the variations in its composition across Europe. Finally, we should not take membership as the sole indicator of trade union strength. For example, in countries with low membership levels the unions may still dominate the elections to employee representative bodies and also be politically influential.

With these important caveats in mind we can, nevertheless, provide a general picture of membership patterns in Europe. At the broadest level, the membership density levels in the 1980s were:

Finland	80–90%
Sweden	80–90%
Belgium	70–80%

Denmark	70–80%
Austria	60–70%
Luxembourg	60–70%
Norway	60–70%
Ireland	40–60%
Italy	40–60%
United Kingdom	40–60%
Germany	40–60%
Spain	20–40%
Greece	20–40%
Portugal	20–40%
Netherlands	20–40%
France	< 20%

The situation in that decade reflects the overall pattern that has developed since the end of the Second World War and, in some cases, earlier. As is clear, membership levels are highest in Northern Europe and, particularly, Scandinavia. There are lower levels and more confused situations in the three Southern European countries that emerged from dictatorships in the 1970s, namely, Greece, Portugal and Spain. They also retain significant agricultural sectors where trade union membership is traditionally low, in contrast to the nations of the north which are more industrial. France has a long-standing tradition of low membership levels and even at the peak in 1970, less than one-quarter of the workforce was organized.

In general, the period from 1945 onwards was one of widespread growth for European trade unions. In Visser's (1988) analysis of ten European countries, eight had experienced absolute increases in membership, and seven in terms of union density, between 1950 and 1970. Taking the longer period to 1980, nine had membership increases, the major gainers being Denmark, Norway and Sweden whose movements more than doubled in size. There were increases of over 50 per cent for Italy and Germany and of over 40 per cent for the Netherlands and Switzerland. Trade union membership in the United Kingdom expanded by 39 per cent and even Austria, which saw the lowest growth rate within Visser's ten, expanded by 29 per cent. The reasons for this growth in union membership have been well rehearsed.

- A labour market based on full and expanding employment which was completing a shift from agriculture to manufacturing industry;

- The growth of the public sector and white collar employment;
- The political climate of consensus or social democracy in much of Europe and the drawing of the trade unions into 'neo-corporate' policy making;
- The positive attitude of many employers to union recognition;
- A favourable legal climate.

The bargaining strength and visible success of trade unions in many countries made them attractive organizations to join.

These different features are illustrated by changes in national trade union movements. For instance, in Finland, a period of separatism in the trade union movement was ended by a merger of two of the central confederations in 1969 to form the Suomen Ammattiliitojen Keskusjärjestö (SAK). This led to an increased role for the trade unions in Finnish political policy making. At the same time the Finnish economy was changing and the trade unions were able to develop a high level of organization among white collar workers and women. In 1987, 43.9 per cent of the SAK's membership was female and the first and third largest affiliated unions were of municipal workers and civil servants. In the United Kingdom, trade unions benefited from an expanding public sector and favourable recognition policies. The trade union movement itself was able to organize and bargain successfully, particularly at local level while at national level unions were invited into both Downing Street and Whitehall. Less successful movements were those whose ideological pluralism impeded both political co-operation and successful collective bargaining. In Italy, the period of greatest membership growth occurred during the 1970s and it is no surprise to find that this coincides with a period of rapid growth in workplace organization following a period of industrial conflict known as the 'hot autumn' of 1969 and the increased co-operation between the three separate trade union confederations.

From the 1980s onwards, trade union membership has generally gone into decline in most of the European countries. However, the picture is not uniform between nations and at the beginning of the 1990s there was some evidence of stability or at least a more restricted rate of decline, and even of increase, for example in Sweden. The causal factors remain those associated with trade union growth but these have now either gone into reverse or changed significantly. The consensual politics of neo-corporatism have become less central to European policy making. The United Kingdom's return to free market economic policies during the Thatcher administration were at the forefront of these developments but similar challenges grew in, for example, the Netherlands and even Sweden where the social democratic government lost the 1991 election. Alongside this have grown changes in employer attitudes that we shall discuss in more detail later in this chapter but they are less receptive to the institutionalized role of organized labour, particularly at the workplace level. Finally, changes in the labour market have favoured the growth of low union density occupations and sectors (see chapter 1).

Again, these general changes can be illustrated by particular examples. The situation in the Republic of Ireland illustrates both the role of employers and the labour market:

> Irish companies seem to be showing a greater interest in strategic human resource and industrial relations policies which call into question the traditional – for Ireland – adversarial style of collective bargaining and the associated systems of employment and work regulation. Such new approaches also countenance making greater use of various types of non-standard working arrangements such as higher levels of part time and contract employment. This compounds the problems faced by the unions in that it represents a reversal of the trend towards standardisation and bureaucratisation which had underpinned the growth in unionisation in the 1960s and 1970s.
> (*European Industrial Relations Review*, September 1988)

Further examples could be drawn from a number of other nations but it is important to bear in mind what we said at the outset in relation to the dangers of generalizations that fail to take into account the particular historical circumstances of the development of national labour movements.

The development of trade unions is, of course, inextricably linked with the organization and policies of employers and managers. These have also been subject to considerable pressure and change in the post-war years.

Employers' Organizations

Employers and managers have, like workers, found it necessary to combine. However, their organizations are unlike trade unions in many ways although some serve similar purposes. A superficial survey of organizations reveals a wide variety of bodies. Firstly, there are organizations that can generally be described as 'professional associations'. These have individual membership and function to protect and improve the status of a particular profession, encourage communication between practitioners and act as pressure groups within their areas of expertise. But they generally have little direct influence on industrial relations except where they move towards the status of a trade union. However, there are some organizations, such as the British Medical Association and the Royal College of Nursing within the British National Health Service, that have effectively adopted the dual functions of a professional body and a collective bargaining agency.

The second type of organization is related to employers rather than managers, and companies rather than individuals. These are generally called 'trade associations' and are organized on an industry basis to promote the interests of affiliates. They seek to protect and advance a particular industry in a variety of ways including public relations and publicity, political pressure, information collection and dissemination and the encouragement of research and development. In general, their activities have little direct bearing on industrial relations and need not detain us here. However, in some European countries, such as Belgium, France and Italy, they adopt the additional functions of employers' associations (Oechslin, 1985, p. 237).

It is the third type of organization, namely the employers' associations, that is central to the development of industrial relations in many Western European countries. They are commonly referred to as the employers' equivalent of the trade unions but, while the development of both is inevitably interlinked, there are important differences between them. In particular, membership is open to organizations rather than individuals and employers' associations rarely have the ideology of a 'movement' characteristic of the trade unions.

Employers' associations are, in essence, organizations which represent the interests of their affiliates in matters relating to the employment contract. They may do this directly through collective bargaining or indirectly by offering advice to members or seeking to influence government policy making. Inevitably this central focus of attention has become blurred at the edges as related functions are developed in areas such as labour market policy but the central role of employers' associations remains in industrial relations.

This point is clear from even a brief analysis of their historical development. Oechslin (1985, p. 229) has suggested a link between employers' associations today and 'the guilds of the Middle Ages and Classical times'. Since similar claims have been made regarding the lineage of trade unions (Pelling, 1971, p. 17) the links must be regarded as tenuous. Contemporary associations trace their origins to the turn of the century, such as those formed on a sectoral basis in Denmark in 1896 and in Sweden in 1901. In the United Kingdom some organizations existed before then but in most of the rest of Europe the associations were formed in the first two decades of the twentieth century. The commonest sequence of growth for the associations was to move from local to national bodies and from industry-based associations to multi-sector organizations. The main reasons for their growth at this time have been succinctly recorded by Bean (1985):

> The objectives were first to counter the rapid growth of trade unionism which was taking place with the acceleration of the industrialisation process. Secondly, to stimulate employer alliances for purposes of market regulation, especially in those industries with competitive product markets, as a means of regulating wages and thereby helping to stabilise market conditions. And thirdly the inducement in some countries for employers to federate was a result of actual or threatened state intervention in the employment relationship. (p. 51)

As we shall see, these historical functions have remained central to the work of employers' associations.

Contemporary employers' organizations

Bearing in mind our definition of national employers' associations and their three functions of counterbalancing trade union strength, collective bargaining and pressure group politics, various types of organization have emerged. Employers' associations can be distinguished both in terms of their horizontal coverage across and between industries or sectors and their vertical organization from local to national level. Sisson (1987, p. 54) also suggests a distinction between 'primary' and 'secondary' organizations. The former allow direct affiliation at national level from individual employers while the latter are essentially federations of local employers' organizations. The latter type is more common in the European countries in Sisson's survey but the Confederation of British Industry (CBI) in the United Kingdom is an example of a primary national organization.

Surveys by Sisson (1987), and Windmuller and Gladstone (1984), reveal the variety and complexity of the horizontal and vertical organization. However, 'peak' or multi-industry organizations have emerged across Europe. In some cases there are divisions based loosely on distinctions between agriculture, manufacturing industry, commerce and the public sector. For example, in Italy the three central organizations are Confindustria, Confcommercio and Confagricoltura. In addition, there are often central confederations representing small and medium-size enterprises as a distinct category. Sisson's five country survey found these central bodies to be highly representative with membership densities between 80 and 90 per cent of those employers eligible to join.

Alongside the central confederations the most common employers' associations are based on industries or sectors. Indeed, these often pre-date the central confederations and generally have more immediate employee relations functions for their affiliates. They are commonly organized on a national basis with local offices based on national geographical and administrative structures. However, the location of industries in particular areas can often lead to the domination of associations by particular 'branches'. It is also the case that many associations are effectively controlled by a small number of major employers. On the other hand some such employers have withdrawn from these organizations to give themselves the freedom to conduct their own negotiations. For example, Volkswagen is outside the German association and Ford has never participated in the appropriate British body.

The potential variety in structure nevertheless encompasses some common characteristics in terms of function. Firstly, the associations have not generally linked themselves to a specific political party in the way that many trade unions have done. This is not to deny their undoubted political activities and preferences which have often led to tacit support for 'conservative' parties and governments. This is hardly surprising as employers are unlikely to challenge a status quo that has generally served their interests. Only in the Netherlands has a division in employers' associations developed along the same lines as the confessional differences within that country's trade union movement. However, the general political commitment to free enterprise has led some confederations to exclude public sector industries. This is true in the Federal Republic of Germany, for example, where, in particular, the iron and steel producers are excluded because their legal status puts them in a position where their delegate to the employers' body could be a worker director. The German central confederation also very clearly illustrated the political role of employers' associations when it challenged in the courts the extension of the co-determination system by the Social Democrat government in the mid-1970s. In Sweden, the employers' political challenge to the 'wage earners' fund' led to an unprecedented protest march. However, while political pressure group activity in the field of employee relations legislation can be seen as a common function of employers' associations they are more often to be found in the corridors of power than on the streets.

A second common feature is the provision of various services to their member organizations. Gladstone (1984) describes this as their 'key function' and goes on to list the most important ones as

> . . . research and data collection and the dissemination of the results of such activities, advisory services in legal, legislative, and related matters, the representation of, or assistance to, individual members in collective bargaining and dispute settlement procedures, and education and training activities. (p. 30)

The increasing complexity of industrial relations issues in Europe since the Second World War and the general increase in statutory intervention makes these functions of growing importance. It is particularly significant for smaller enterprises which may not have the resources to employ staff with the appropriate expertise.

A third potentially common area is that of collective bargaining. However, as we discuss in chapter 4, there are widely different traditions in Europe which create a variety of roles for central employers' associations. These range from the key role played by national confederations in the centralized bargaining arrangements of the Nordic countries to the complete non-involvement of organizations like the British CBI. At an intermediate level, the German BDA is not directly involved but it issues recommendations which are normally observed. The industry-based employers' associations are much more commonly involved in collective bargaining and, in much of Europe where sectoral agreements are the dominant pattern, it is their primary purpose.

The final common characteristic that we consider here is related to the development of employers' associations in response to trade union growth. More specifically, it relates to 'mutual insurance policies' in the event of an industrial dispute. Sisson (1987) has suggested that such support can take many forms, such as

> ... an agreement not to offer employment to strikers or trade union members; an understanding that in the event of industrial action there will be no poaching of customers from members or that raw materials or other supplies will be pooled or that the payment of bills will be postponed; and a scheme, either *ad hoc* or permanent, for the provision of financial assistance to the members who are involved in industrial action. (1987, p. 73)

Such policies are not characteristic of all employers' associations and their existence is clearly related to the nature of the collective bargaining system. For example, the British CBI has effectively failed to establish such a scheme in the United Kingdom where enterprise bargaining is a major feature of negotiations in manufacturing industry and the unions in general are disinclined to coordinate wage claims. So employers may therefore regard strikes as individual failures rather than common problems. However, sectoral or industry-wide bargaining poses different issues elsewhere in Europe and mutual support and even lock-outs are more common practice. Such a situation exists in Germany, for example.

> The unions have over recent years favoured the use of the selective strike or *schwerpunktstreiks* in preference to comprehensive strikes. With this approach, key firms are targeted under a strategic 'master plan' with a view to causing the greatest degree of industrial disruption with the minimum of cost. In order to counter this strategy employers' organisations have often responded with the use of selected lock outs by firms ... In 1984, for example, the year of a major dispute in the engineering industry over a shorter working week, over one and a half million more working days were lost as a result of lock outs than as a result of strike action. (*European Industrial Relations Review*, September 1989, p. 26)

Sweden is another example of a country where employers have been prepared to resort to lock-outs but, in general, employer solidarity there is confined to mutual financial support and a refusal to take competitive advantage of companies engaged in dispute.

National employers' associations are sometimes regarded as the counterpoint to trade union organizations. However, there is rarely the same variety of organizational structures or the same expressly ideological commitments. They are also federations of other organizations rather than bodies of individual members. In much of Western Europe they exert a considerable influence on industrial relations both through collective bargaining and their pressure group activities. In this respect they are likely to play a significant role for the foreseeable future although, as Windmuller (1984) suggests, their exact functions will be shaped by the paradoxical trends towards both centralization, for example, at the EC level, and decentralization, for example, in wage bargaining. We complete this overview by focusing on the centralization process through a consideration of international employers' organizations.

International employers' organizations

International employers' organizations have not developed to the extent or the complexity of their trade union counterparts. They have not been divided by cold war politics and have found less need for global organization both at multi-industry and sectoral level. However, some organizations do exist at world and European level.

There are a number of industry-based world employers' organizations but, unlike their national counterparts, they have little or no industrial relations functions. The most significant multi-industry employers' body is the International Organization of Employers (IOE). This has its origins in an organization founded in 1912 (Oechslin, 1985) but the real stimulus to its growth was the first International Labour Organization (ILO) conference in 1919. The IOE had a membership of 92 national federations in 88 countries by the mid-1980s and its major function is to act as the secretariat of the employers' group at the ILO. This is not insignificant given the ILO's role in establishing labour standards but the IOE has few of the pretensions of the global trade union organizations in terms of organizing international solidarity.

Of increasing significance is the major employers' organization in Europe, the Union of Industrial and Employers' Confederations of Europe (UNICE). There is an equivalent public sector body called the European Centre of Public Enterprises commonly known by its French initials as CEEP. These are both 'secondary' organizations in Sisson's categorization as membership is through affiliated national confederations.

UNICE and CEEP both have Europe-wide membership but their focus of attention is primarily at EC level, and UNICE's foundation year of 1958 is significant in this respect. CEEP began in 1961 and was reorganized to create its present structure in 1965. UNICE comprises 32 member federations from 22 European countries. It describes its own principal functions as maintaining effective communications between member organizations, influencing European policies and Directives and promoting its own policies and opinions at national level. It does not list collective bargaining as one of its activities but its political lobbying has the potential to shade into bargaining in the EC where both itself and the ETUC have an institutionalized role. The development of the Social Dialogue opens up the potential for bargaining, particularly following the Maastricht summit. UNICE has firmly resisted the idea of any role in company bargaining but it has accepted the principle of voluntary agreements as an alternative to the extension of employment law through EC Directives. UNICE has also been prepared to issue 'joint opinions' with the ETUC and there have been significant statements on new technology (1987) and education and training (1990). CEEP has been prepared to go somewhat further and in 1990 signed a framework agreement with the ETUC for the public sector (initially railways and energy) on vocational training.

It is clear that the role of employers' associations at the EC level has expanded considerably in recent years and the action programmes related to the Social Charter are only likely to increase that involvement. In this respect, UNICE and CEEP's political roles are likely to become increasingly significant and international employer's organizations may become central to the Europeanization of employee relations. However, managerial strategies in employee relations are also developed at the organizational level and it is this area that we now discuss.

Convergence or Divergence?

There are a number of factors currently internationalizing management strategies.

- Firstly, their is the increasing significance of the global market-place.
- Secondly, there is the domination of those market-places by transnational companies.
- Thirdly, there are technological changes and developments that cannot be constrained by national boundaries.

- Fourthly, there is the international dissemination of management theory and practice through management consultants, business schools and a variety of other educational activities.
- Finally, there is the increased geographical mobility of managers themselves.

Each of these pressures might suggest a convergence in management styles in a variety of areas including human resource management. The apparently logical outcome is clearly identified by Hanaoka (quoted in Kidger, 1991):

> There is an international drive towards convergency for 'good management' or 'excellent management'. In the excellently managed company personnel management is influenced only slightly by national culture. (p. 154)

The ideas of convergence in management strategies are not new and have been consistently linked with the 'logic of industrialism' (Kerr et al., 1962). The development of mass-production technologies and the growth of 'scientific management' was influential on a global scale and associated with the identification of 'one best way'. Technological 'logic' was necessarily complemented by inescapable managerial methods in the 'Fordist' model. Latter-day proponents of convergence in management styles use models of 'excellence' or flexible specialization as examples of successful approaches for others to adopt.

At the other end of the spectrum are those who suggest that successful management strategies are those adapted to the particularities of individual national cultures – that is, 'when in Rome do as the Romans do'. As Poole (1986, p. 11) argues, in an industrial relations context, 'to presuppose that societies with diverse political economies and at varying stages of development are becoming increasingly convergent in employee relations structure and process is to strain credibility. *Ceteris paribus*, it is the obverse case that is persuasive.'

The implications of Poole's argument are that the factors which are crucial to the convergence thesis are not the key ones influencing organizational development and managerial strategies. Instead, there are equally significant factors working in the other direction. In general, these derive from influences outside the organization itself whereas much of the convergence argument is based on internal influences. The significant external constraints include almost indefinable national (or even regional) cultures, the economic development of a country and the related patterns of employment, the pattern of education and training and its availability, the political structure and policies, and the social structure, of particular nations. The 'convergence' and 'divergence' arguments are each persuasive in their own terms. On the one hand we have a picture of global transnationals dominated by their own corporate cultures, exporting headquarters' policy and training their own management clones, all at the expense of nations in general and trade unionists in particular. On the other hand we can be persuaded that corporate management practice cannot be transposed from an American burger bar to a bank in a Third World country or a car factory in a former command economy. Indeed, even exporting managerial approaches across the common national borders of Germany and France might seem an impossible task.

In reality, these polar opposites reflect theoretical constructs rather than management practice. The pragmatic adaptation of global strategies to national circumstances provides a less coherent model but a better guide to practice. The rest of this chapter is devoted to assessing how that management practice operates within a European framework.

Transnational Companies

A key actor in the development of management policies on a global scale has been the transnational company. As we have suggested already, the picture of managerial omniscience is overdrawn although corporate power remains of considerable significance. Discussing the development of management strategies in the Dutch transnational, Philips, board member George van Houten suggests that his company has the 'goal of internationalizing management'. In human resource management terms this requires sophisticated data collection and policy making.

> [Philips' developed] a human resources data bank so that we had information about human resource needs and availability. The data bank profile provided then, as it does now, an analysis of current manpower, anticipated needs at all levels of management and the time required to have people available to fill top level positions . . . The entire workforce worldwide is ranked into twelve hierarchical levels

and each employee knows where he stands. Management levels begin at level 60 (levels 10 through 50 are covered by bargaining agreements subject to national labour policies). (van Houten 1989, pp. 108–9)

There are many other transnational companies that place great value on a corporate culture and the management strategies that go with it. Evans and Lorange (1989) have suggested a number of typical human resource policies associated with the 'global enterprise'.

Examples of such procedures are worldwide policies regarding recruitment and promotion criteria; 'single status' policies; a uniform stance towards unions; standardized procedures for performance evaluation; global compensation policies; uniform monitoring of human resource management through opinion surveys; a code of corporate values guiding the indoctrination of newly hired recruits. (p. 152)

These policies are now the commonplace of human resource management textbooks. This, in its turn, helps to strengthen and universalize the particular approaches. In this way the strategies are extended beyond the transnational companies into national private sector businesses and into the public sector. Thus the industrial relations director becomes the personnel officer who is, in turn, transformed into the human resource manager. There is, of course, considerable debate as to whether changing the nameplate on the door has led to genuine policy change (Storey, 1989). However, our point is the importance of the spread of style as well as content.

Room for Manoeuvre?

As we have already suggested, the image of monolithic transnational policy making is one that can be challenged from a number of directions. Firstly, there is the question of diversity of management styles in different transnationals which challenges the notion of a holy grail that will reveal the 'one best way'. Secondly, there is the issue of the policy process itself within the organization and, finally, there is the empirical question of implementation.

To some extent we have dealt with the first point but Tomlinson (1982) sums up the argument succinctly.

The diversity of managerial strategies pursued by capitalist firms is apparent. Some have been very 'liberal', some very 'authoritarian' in their industrial relations policies. Some have stressed sales maximisation and small profits per item sold, some large profits on small quantities. Some have focused on technological developments as the way to long-run profits while others have focused on selling techniques as the way to success. The variations can be almost infinitely multiplied. (p. 35)

The second point is a related one and argues that the policy-making process within transnationals is neither necessarily coherent nor monolithic. Pluralists' perspectives on organizations and employee relations have long stressed the potential for conflict between competing managerial interest groups in the formulation of policy. Add to that the potential power of institutional shareholders and the role of the workforce, particularly through the trade unions, and the image of a centrally planned and co-ordinated management policy becomes increasingly blurred. As Ramsay (1990, p. 7) suggests, 'these diverse and competing interests tend to generate various localised (organizationally and spatially) strategies which may distort or subvert policy intentions laid down at the top'. This leads us into our third point and takes us from policy generation to implementation.

It is clear that large organizations need to be able to transmit policy decisions successfully from the top-tier decision-making bodies to lower levels of management and the workforce. It is also evident that decisions will need to be made about the level of autonomy available to local managers. To some extent this is determined by the product mix and markets in which the business operates. It is potentially easier for a single product company operating solely in, say, Western Europe to develop consistent corporate management policies than for a multi-product company operating on a global scale. However, there are other factors affecting the development of corporate industrial relations policies. Bean (1985) notes the significance of different national cultures on decision making between American and European transnationals.

US-based M(ulti) N(ational) E(nterprise)s concentrate authority at corporate headquarters, with greater emphasis on formal management controls and a close reporting system. In contrast, for European-based MNEs there was found to be a looser relationship between head office and local subsidiaries as well as a greater willingness to accept the judgement of local managers. The reasons for this more pronounced emphasis in US MNEs for close and systematic managerial control may be partly related to the organisational structure of US firms. They display a greater tendency than do European firms to operate rigidly hierarchical decision making at the corporate level. (p. 193)

Another factor which needs to be taken into account in determining the strength of corporate policy over local decision making is the importance attached to the particular policy area. In this respect, employee relations issues in particular, and human resource matters in general, have often had less significance in the past than areas such as finance, production and marketing. However, human resource management policies are increasingly gaining a higher profile and there are a number of reasons for this. Firstly, there is the general desire of transnationals to improve their tarnished reputation as 'good employers'. Secondly, there is the stimulus of demographic changes which emphasizes the recruitment and retention of good staff. Thirdly, there is the related issue of retaining a flexible labour force that might have required considerable investment in training. Fourthly, a number of successful transnationals, particularly from Japan, have become 'market leaders' in their human resource management policies. Fifthly, nations and the EC have given a high profile to personnel policies through legislation and directives in such areas as equal opportunities and works councils. Finally, there remains the simple and most potent point that, for most organizations, employees are their most significant operating cost.

An indication of the growing importance of human resource management as a corporate policy area is the expanding role of personnel managers or their equivalents on the main boards. One major European survey has concluded that:

In most countries, a substantial majority of organisations employing more than 200 people have the person responsible for human resources or personnel issues on the main Board of Directors or an equivalent body. (Price Waterhouse/Cranfield, 1990, p. 11)

The picture is not so clear cut in the United Kingdom, the evidence showing that anywhere between one-third and a half of British companies have personnel directors (Marginson et al., 1988, pp. 60–2). The European evidence must also be discussed in relation to the question of whether being a member of a Board necessarily implies influence. The Price Waterhouse/Cranfield survey suggests that 'a significant minority of Board level personnel specialists have no say in shaping corporate policy and only become involved at the point where the plan is implemented' (p. 12).

Nevertheless, however it is shaped, corporate policy making is assuming increasing significance in the development of industrial relations policies. Marginson et al.'s study of decision making in this area indicated that over one-third of British companies in their survey 'instructed' their local managers on a range of industrial relations issues, a further third 'advise', 11 per cent give 'broad guidelines' and only 8 per cent offer 'complete autonomy' (p. 189).

What is developing in the human resource field is the equivalent of the 'tight–loose' general management model, an attempt to balance central control of strategic decisions with local autonomy to allow individual initiative and flexible responses. Thus, the discussion of human resource management decision making returns us to our starting point on the relationship between convergence in policy and divergence in practice.

The European Manager?

A key factor in implementing a human resource policy is having the appropriate staff to carry it out. On a European scale, organizations have the extreme options of 'parachuting in' expatriates steeped in the corporate culture of the home country or opting for local managers with a thorough understanding of host country conditions. In reality the approach adopted is likely to be a mixture of these options and the likelihood of senior managers in transnational companies spending their whole career at corporate headquarters is diminishing. There is pressure to internationalize management both from above and below. Corporations regard internationally mobile managers as both disseminators of corporate policy and gatherers of skills from local practice. The managers themselves regard international assignments as potentially interesting in themselves and as part of their own career development both within the organization and beyond it. Thus, the strategy for the employment of managers outside of headquarters has shifted from that of 'fire fighting' on issues that could not be handled locally to one of corporate management development.

In Western Europe, these developments are likely to be further stimulated by the developments in the Single European Market and the associated Social Dimension. In some areas of business, such as technical standards, there will be greater uniformity in practice and a reduced need for specialized local knowledge. In addition, some markets will open up and lead the way to cross-border mergers, with some organizations taking the opportunity to register as European companies. Even in sectors such as local government the policies on public procurement and regional aid will require a greater knowledge and experience of Europe. Furthermore, social provisions on the free movement of labour and the measures that go with it, such as the mutual recognition of qualifications, will encourage the mobility of European managers. One survey of European personnel management suggests that

> In the largest companies mobility is inbuilt. The whole Unilever system is geared towards international transfers . . . while in Philips it has become a key concern to get managers from different countries together in working parties on a divisional basis. It is also a policy in the product divisions to ensure that each manager has at least one international assignment as a career development opportunity. (Incomes Data Services, 1988, p. 31)

As such mobility increases and the pressure for international expertise grows can a European management style be said to be emerging? Thurley and Wirdenius (1989, p. 11) argue that 'there is as yet no generally accepted ideology or model of European management which can be set against that of Japanese or American management'. They go on to suggest that this is a result of the historical development of Europe and its industry which has resulted in the lack of a clearly identifiable management group.

Lane (1989) has suggested that there are also structural differences in the organization of management in different European countries. For example, she notes that French business has a more rigid and hierarchical structure than the 'flatter' organizational model common in the Federal Republic of Germany. We are again faced with the problem of teasing out general trends from national diversity. Looking at this issue in terms of management development, Evans, Lank and Farquhar (1989) argue that if no single European model can be identified there are at least broad approaches. They suggest a Latin Europe model which focuses on the recruitment of graduates from a few elite educational institutions and their 'competitive' career progression. The Germanic tradition focuses on a period of 'apprenticeship' followed by progress along a formal career path. In the Anglo-Dutch model there is less elite recruitment and a period of on the job learning before high-flyers are identified. These different approaches to management development have implications for the more general organization of management and the development of managerial styles but how do they translate into the specific areas of human resource management and employee relations?

In this respect there is a need to draw on influences from outside Europe in order to identify common themes in European human resource management. It is also important to note the increasing significance of human resources to general management theory. Taking these last two points together it is possible to begin to discuss common themes on a European basis. In particular, we can identify three areas of policy development that are becoming increasingly widespread and will have important implications for the conduct of employee relations. Firstly, there is the general area of employee recruitment and retention policies; secondly, there is the growth of employee involvement programmes; and, thirdly, there is the 'individualization' of employment practices.

We have discussed changes in the labour market in chapter 1 and the emergence of the flexible firm model with its core and peripheral employees. We also noted the significance of demographic changes in relation to recruitment. While bearing in mind the critical analysis of these developments it is clear that European companies are adopting recruitment and retention policies designed to attract and develop a stable core workforce. These policies have reached their greatest sophistication in relation to senior management staff with the scarcest skills but they are significant in all areas of an organization. The key elements in recruitment and retention practice are flexible employment practices, equal opportunities, training and remuneration.

As we saw earlier, there has been some change in the patterns of work with an increase in part time and temporary employment. In addition, some organizations are developing home-working for managerial and professional staff although it remains a source of low paid labour for the unskilled. Annual hours packages are becoming more common as are nil hours or on-call contracts. In general, traditional practices in terms of working times are being reviewed and subjected to challenge and change.

In this context, equal opportunities must be broadly interpreted. As well as the more common target groups for recruitment – women, ethnic minority groups and the disabled – employers are also relaxing traditional attitudes in relation to age. The development of equal opportunity policies also has significant implications for retention by giving the organization a positive image and unblocking promotion paths.

Training and retraining policies are an essential component in the development of a flexible workforce and they also add to staff development opportunities and relate to career prospects. The increasing significance of training across Europe is indicated in the Price Waterhouse/Cranfield (1990) study which concluded that

> The use of training to overcome skill shortages is reflected in the substantial increase in money spent on training all categories of staff in every country we surveyed. The biggest increase in investment has been on the training provided to managers and professional staff. (p. 34)

National government policies and EC decisions are serving to reinforce best practice in training and there is every likelihood that it will continue to expand.

Remuneration packages have always been the key to recruiting and retaining staff. However, as we discuss below, the 'cash nexus' is being reconstituted.

Employee Participation and Pay

At the heart of the human resource approach is a commitment to the employees as individuals in return for their loyalty to the organization.

> HRM values are essentially individualistic in that they emphasise the individual–organisation linkage in preference to operating through group or representative systems. (Guest, 1989, p. 43)

Linked to this individualism are the development of payment methods and employee involvement schemes.

Employee participation will be discussed in detail in chapter 4 but we should note here the broad range of policies that fall within this category and which range from State sponsored policies of co-determination through financial participation to work related group schemes such as quality circles. Again it is clear that EC policy is reinforcing developments that are already taking place at organizational level. Lane (1989) has noted the importance of formal industrial democracy systems in the three countries that she studied.

> Both the degree and the form of participation achieved varies markedly between our three societies. Managerial prerogative has been reduced more strongly in Britain and Germany than in France. (p. 247)

Human resource management policies which adopt an essentially unitarist perspective would not follow Lane's 'zero-sum' argument in relation to management power and have focused attention on employee participation systems designed to encourage employee commitment rather than formal consultation systems through representative bodies such as trade unions. Such approaches to employee participation are not new but they have been given a significant boost by the success of Japanese companies in translating their practices to their European plants. Their approach is encapsulated in a comment about the role of management from a personnel director of the British plant of a Norwegian transnational.

> Management has the final responsibility for planning, organising and controlling the operation . . . That responsibility is *to consult* before deciding, to *involve people* before actually pressing the button and to *account for their stewardship* back to the employees. (Fox, 1986, p. 23)

In short, if employees are to be committed to the organization then its managers must be committed to them.

The final element in the human resource package that we are considering here is that of remuneration. Pay is necessarily a major factor in any employee relations policy and is central to recruitment and retention. There are clear indications that there is a European movement towards more flexible and more individually tailored pay structures, particularly for managerial staff (Price Waterhouse/ Cranfield, 1990). These schemes are likely to be related to more sophisticated employee assessment and performance schemes rather than traditional collective agreements.

It cannot be our argument here without extensive Europe-wide research that there is a new European-style human resource policy package. Nor can we yet argue for the existence of a European human resource manager. However, we have identified a number of common themes in this section and we would argue that the continued growth of European firms, reinforced by the policies of the EC and stimulated by international trade union action, is likely to encourage convergence in management practice.

Conclusion

In this chapter we have explored the variety of management and trade union organizations and styles and tried to draw out some common themes. It is clear that both European managers and trade unionists face similar problems in their different countries. These may demand similar solutions and therefore encourage convergence in organizational responses. In this respect we have seen that, for example, employers' associations and trade unions have emerged in each of the European nations and that they have broadly similar functions. However, organizational details will vary from country to country. A major influence in this respect is the role of the State in shaping the employee relations framework within which managers and trade unions operate. This is particularly significant in relation to collective bargaining and employee participation. Where collective bargaining is centralized and industrial democracy encouraged by legislation then employers' associations have a more influential role and the importance of trade union, rather than employee, involvement at workplace level may be reduced. Nevertheless, we have seen that broadly comparable rights for workplace representatives exist across Western Europe although the detail may vary substantially. Managers at organizational level are now being influenced by a raft of common ideas in the human resource management field. These policies are being reinforced by EC decisions and the increasing geographical mobility of middle and senior managers.

Managers and trade unions are responding to a period of rapid change in the environments in which they work. Shifts in the labour market, the decline of the command economies and the increased competitiveness of world markets all have their impact on employee relations. It is noteworthy that the responses of these two main parties to 'the system' are adopting increasingly international and European perspectives and adapting them to suit national circumstances.

4

From Collective Bargaining to Social Dialogue

Previous chapters have examined the background to employee relations in Western Europe and have investigated the identities and roles of the various actors. In this chapter we turn to the practice of employee relations and more specifically the various aspects of collective bargaining at the national and European levels. Collective bargaining can be defined in general terms as a process of decision making between parties representing the interests of employees and employers, and in the introduction to an ILO comparative survey, its overriding purpose is described as 'the negotiation and continuous application of an agreed set of rules to govern the substantive and procedural terms of the employment relationship, as well as to define the relationship between the parties to the process' (International Labour Organization, 1987, p. 3).

However, here again we run up against the problem of terminology. As was noted by a French observer, it should not be assumed that the expression 'negotiation' occupies the same centrality in employee relations in France as 'in other countries where it appears as the fundamental vocation of trade unions, the best means of resolving disputes between employees and employers and finally the favoured instrument of social progress' (Adam, 1978, pp. 385–91). In those countries, for example, where the State plays an important role in the employee relations system, there may be less incentive to participate in the process of collective bargaining. For example, as we shall see in chapter 6, some countries have a minimum legal wage which increases automatically as a result of changes in the retail price index, and this may discourage the low paid from participating in the process of collective bargaining.

There is, nevertheless, broad agreement that collective bargaining fulfils a series of functions – 'in addition to rule making, thereby reducing the degree of uncertainty confronting workers and management, it can also be a vehicle for resolving disputes, a power relationship, and where it takes place at enterprise or plant level, it may be regarded as a form of participation for workers or their representatives' (Bean, 1985, p. 70). In this chapter we propose to examine these related aspects. Firstly, we will investigate certain features of the rule-making function and, most notably, aspects of the structure and scope of collective bargaining. Secondly, we shall examine the various institutionalized ways in which employees and their representatives participate in the decision-making process at the level of the enterprise. As a supplementary point there will be an investigation of embryonic forms of collective bargaining and employee participation that have been established at the transnational European level. Thirdly, we shall consider the consequences of the failure of collective bargaining and employee participation for resolving disputes, as manifested by the incidence of industrial conflict in Western Europe.

Collective Bargaining in Europe

Bargaining levels

The level at which collective bargaining is conducted is determined by a number of variables which include geographical and economic circumstances. Of particular importance are the structures and goals of employers' and workers' organizations, as well as those of the government. This has meant that collective bargaining displays the characteristics of a varied and multi-form mosaic in each country. Moreover, levels are not constant, and, as will be seen later in this section, there is some evidence of a tendency towards the decentralization of collective bargaining. The complexity of the British case is instructive. 'There are negotiations between employers' associations and trade unions at the national or industry level. There is bargaining at the company level between a particular employer and the trade union he recognizes . . . At lower levels, multi-employer bargaining sometimes takes place at regional or district levels and company bargaining at divisional levels. Beyond that there is often a further stage of negotiations at the workplace . . . Frequently there remains a final level of bargaining at shopfloor level' (Daniel and Millward, 1983, p. 177). Similar degrees of complexity can be found in most other Western European countries. Nevertheless three broad categories emerge: national economy level, national sectoral level and enterprise level (including plant bargaining). Sometimes it is possible to identify one specific level with one particular national environment, but normally the bargaining structure of each country displays elements of different inter-related levels of bargaining.

National economy level bargaining has been particularly prevalent in those countries which were identified in chapter 2 as having a neo-corporatist tradition (e.g. Denmark, Norway, Sweden and, until the early 1960s, the Netherlands) – indeed national economy level bargaining is one of the characteristics of such a tradition. Representatives of central confederations of trade unions and employers' associations come together, sometimes with government representatives as well, to negotiate wages and conditions of employment, and the results of these negotiations then serve as a bench-mark for collective bargaining at other levels. (In this way governments can influence the content of negotiations and thus seek to control wage inflation, a central element of the potential success of economic policy making.) National economy level bargaining implies and requires a high level of centralization and discipline within the trade union movement and within the employers' associations in order to ensure resulting agreements stick. Recent examples of this type of bargaining can be found in Scandinavia where a two-year central agreement was signed in Norway for 1988–9, in Sweden for 1989–90 and in Finland for 1992–3. Although this type of bargaining lost favour in the Netherlands, central agreements were signed on wages in 1973 and on work-sharing in 1982.

Other countries have some experience of national economy level bargaining but recent examples are less numerous. In Belgium, for example, a central framework agreement on jobs, pay and working time for 1987–8 was signed in September 1986, (the first bipartite central agreement since 1975) and a further agreement was signed for 1991–2. (*European Industrial Relations Review*, December 1986, pp. 9–11; January 1991, pp. 3–4) In the United Kingdom the Labour government negotiated a 'social contract' with the Trades Union Congress in 1974 whereby the government agreed to introduce supportive employment legislation and to increase income tax for higher earners in exchange for a voluntary income policy. Similar negotiations took place in subsequent years. In 1978, however, a 5 per cent pay guideline advocated by the government was challenged repeatedly by the trade unions in the so-called 'winter of discontent', and this form of pay bargaining fell into disrepute and was totally rejected by subsequent Conservative governments. France could not be described as neo-corporatist, yet there have been occasions when national economy level agreements involving working conditions (but not wages) have been signed, particularly in the early 1970s. These covered job security, maternity benefits, single status, vocational training, early retirement payments, unemployment benefits and short-time working. In spite of the presence of a Socialist President (from 1981 onwards) and a Socialist government (from 1981 to 1986 and from 1988 to 1993), there was no similar attempt to draw the trade unions into a planned approach to collective bargaining, and fewer national economy level bargaining agreements were successfully concluded during the 1980s.

National sector-wide bargaining, involving trade unions on the one hand and groups of employers on the other, has been the norm in the majority of Western European countries, both in the public and private sectors. In the public sector, employees in all levels of government (central and local), in health, education, the fire service and the police have all been the subject of national sector level bargaining agreements, as have employees in industries such as the railways, water, gas, coal and electricity and the postal and telephone services. In most public sector industries this has traditionally been the only form of collective bargaining, with occasional glimpses of local bargaining. More recently, some governments, most notably in the United Kingdom, have attempted to introduce a greater element of flexibility into public sector bargaining with the introduction of merit- or performance-related pay, which clearly could have a significant impact on bargaining levels.

In the private sector the high level of national bargaining in most sectors has often suited employers and trade unions alike. On the one hand, by guarding against 'leap-frogging' (whereby trade unions play one employer off against another), employers could expect to regulate pay and labour market conditions more effectively. Moreover, in some countries, such as the Netherlands and France, employers could ensure that trade unions were excluded in this way from local management decisions. On the other hand, trade unions could expect to negotiate agreements on behalf of sections of the labour market which have traditionally been too weak to extract concessions from employers on their own and also to establish minimum terms and conditions. National sector-wide agreements have long played an important part in the Italian system of industrial relations, (Guigni, 1987, p. 233) but there has been a trend in the 1980s towards an 'articulated' form of collective bargaining combining national economy-wide bargaining and company level bargaining, thus speeding 'the waning of importance of the intermediate and industry levels' (Negrelli and Santi, 1990, pp. 18–3) This said, however, a three and a half year agreement in the Italian metalworking industry was signed in December 1990. In Belgium, on the other hand, national sector-wide agreements have traditionally been the norm, but the reinforcement of linguistic divisions between the Flemish and the Walloons 'with ever more marked social and economic overtones' has led to a consequential drift towards the regionalization of collective bargaining (International Labour Organization, 1987, p. 94) In the Federal Republic of Germany there are negotiations at the national level in a few sectors such as construction, banking and insurance, and these are often supplemented by regional agreements based on the *Länder*. In other industries, for example metalworking and chemicals, negotiations on most issues take place at regional level, but with some form of national coordination (Sisson, 1987, p. 88).

Enterprise level bargaining, with a single employer who is often dominant within a certain sector and who tends to remain outside any national bargaining framework, has not been as prevalent in Western Europe as it has, for example, in the United States of America or in Japan. This level of bargaining often complements negotiations which have taken place at a higher level. It also makes it possible to adapt to the specific circumstances of each company. In Italy 'agreements covering an entire company are common; there are others whose scope extends to a group of companies with activities in several branches or to a holding company' (Guigni, 1987, pp. 235–6). Ford in the UK, Volkswagen in the Federal Republic of Germany, and Akzo, Shell, Unilever and Philips in the Netherlands provide well-known examples of enterprise level bargaining. Linked to enterprise level bargaining is plant bargaining which is prevalent in those multi-site enterprises where the nature of work varies and therefore requires different terms and conditions of employment. Increasingly plant bargaining is seen as the locus for the negotiation of bonuses and incentives.

Table 4.1 Levels of basic pay determination in the private sector
for manual workers (percentage of organizations)

	DK	E	F	I	N	NL	S	UK
National/sector-wide collective bargaining	53	42	24	59	66	75	69	22
Regional collective bargaining	23	19	11	2	18	n.a.	6	7
Company	6	21	50	45	24	24	36	37
Establishment/site	8	17	27	12	21	8	15	40
Individual	13	8	16	9	20	9	12	8

Source: Hegewisch, 1991, p. 30

Bargaining levels vary significantly between countries, as can be
seen from the results of a Price Waterhouse/Cranfield Project undertaken by Hegewisch (table 4.1). Britain and France are alone in
having such a low level of national sector-wide pay bargaining in
the private sector for manual workers. In other countries national
sector-wide pay bargaining tends to predominate. However, regional
level bargaining is prevalent in Denmark, Spain and Norway.
Enterprise or company level bargaining is prevalent in France and
Italy and generally more so than plant (or establishment/site) bargaining. Only in the United Kingdom is there such a high level of
plant bargaining (Hegewisch, 1991, pp. 29–30). It is no easy matter
to explain this diversity. In his comparative study of the management of collective bargaining Sisson (1987, p. 107) notes that 'employers have an essentially contingent approach to the level at which
negotiations take place; their attitudes and policies towards these
levels are conditioned first and foremost by what they perceive to
be in their best interest in the particular circumstances . . . The
levels at which multi-employer bargaining take place both reflect
the relationship that exists between employers and trade unions
and are a major influence on it.'

Decentralization of collective bargaining

There has been much discussion of the decentralization of collective bargaining. This begs the question: decentralization from
what? There has certainly been movement away from national

economy-wide bargaining. As can be seen from table 4.2, it has become virtually impossible to reach agreements of this kind in Belgium, tripartite 'concerted action' no longer exists in Germany and in the United Kingdom national concertation has disappeared. In some countries there is evidence of employers refusing to abide by decisions taken by the employers' federation or refusing to allow the latter to take decisions at the national economy-wide level. For a time in the early 1980s the Swedish industrial employers' association in the private sector withheld its bargaining authorization from its own peak organization and insisted on separate negotiations (International Labour Organization, 1987, pp. 109–10).

National sectoral bargaining is still important, but losing ground in Belgium. In the United Kingdom it is declining: fifteen negotiating bodies have collapsed since 1986, including the councils for banking, multiple food retailing, commercial television and water, and ten others have been reduced in coverage and influence. For example, Blue Circle Cement left the Cement Manufacturing National Joint Industrial Council and now has a company-wide agreement and Tesco left the Multiple Food Retail Employers' Association agreement in 1988 which led to 'its subsequent break-up as a federated agreement' (*Bargaining Report*, October 1989, pp. 5–11). Moreover, some companies have decentralized bargaining within their own organizations, for example, Lucas Aerospace, Metal Box, Pilkington, Cadbury's, British Cellophane and the recently privatized British Airport Authorities.

These moves towards decentralization have occurred as a result of government policy on the one hand and attempts by employers to reduce labour costs on the other. The most obvious recent example of legislation encouraging the trend towards the decentralization of collective bargaining is to be found in France. At the beginning of the 1980s the French Socialist government introduced a series of laws, the so-called Auroux laws (after the Minister of Employment of the time), one of which created an obligation to negotiate at company level once a year on issues such as wages, working time and working conditions. Although there is no obligation to reach an agreement, there is evidence to demonstrate 'the massive revival of company-level bargaining' (Segrestin, 1990, pp. 114–15). Governments have also encouraged the decentralization of collective bargaining in the public sector, some, particularly the British government, by means of privatization. On the other hand, employers have aimed to introduce a greater element of flexibility into production methods and work organization and thus have decentralized their business strategy and consequently their bargaining structures. Employers have also striven to match wage increases to productivity, and as part of this process have attempted to individualize wage payments (i.e. to link them more closely to individual performance), thus further contributing to the decentralization of collective bargaining.

It would, however, be wrong to give the impression that this shift towards decentralization is universal – the extent of decentralization of pay determination to local level, and consequently to a direct response to local performance or local market conditions, remains limited (Hegewisch, 1991, p. 30). Indeed, as a reaction to the unpredictability of decentralized collective bargaining, employers in some countries have reverted to a more centralized approach. Within different companies a downward shift in bargaining structures has not always been accompanied by a real decentralization of power. Moreover, according to Brown and Wadhwani, there is considerable international evidence to suggest that many countries with substantial unionization avoid unacceptably high levels of inflation and/or unemployment by some degree of co-ordinated bargaining (quoted in *IRS Employment Trends*, 6 June 1990, p. 13). In addition, the Europeanization of the economy may put a further, if partial, brake on the decentralization of collective bargaining.

Bargaining scope

Quantitative demands, particularly wages, still constitute the central element of collective bargaining. However, pay has become a more diversified item for negotiation as a result of four distinct developments. Firstly, wages have increasingly been fixed on an individual basis, particularly in France, Ireland and the United Kingdom, although this is still a minority trend. Secondly, wages may be linked to company performance through profit-sharing schemes. (Such schemes are operated by Renault in France, Fiat, Olivetti and Zanussi in Italy, Baxi and John Lewis in the United Kingdom, and Akzo Chemicals in the Netherlands; in addition, German companies such as BMW and Mercedes-Benz are preparing to set up profit-sharing schemes.) Thirdly, there has been an increase in non-taxable fringe benefits ('remuneration supplements') in the form of supplementary pension schemes, as in France, Italy, the Netherlands and the Federal Republic of Germany. Finally,

Table 4.2   Changes in the level of collective bargaining

Type	Pre-1980	Post-1980
Belgium National concertation	Keystone of entire employee relations system, fostered by all governments for its economic and social regulatory and planning effect	Virtual impossibility of reaching agreements at this level after 1975 Loss of significance of substance of the new agreements reached, either because made under State compulsion or because modest in social and economic impact
Sector-wide collective bargaining	The level preferred by organized labour and employers' organizations because it enables strong sectors to lead weak ones (union advantage) and because it puts all firms in a given industry on an equal footing (employer advantage)	Still an important bargaining forum, but clearly losing ground (drastic decrease in number of contracts signed at this level) Loss of homogeneity of traditional industries Marked tendency to decentralization of bargaining
Decentralized company level bargaining	Bargaining at this level was significant, but it was viewed as designed to improve upon national and industry contracts	Failing significant agreements at higher levels, often the only way of reaching any contract at all Fostered by employers Scope for bargaining limited by government (i.e. legal wage freeze)
Germany National concertation	Tripartite 'concerted action' 1969–77, effective only during the first years	Only some verbal proclamations in favour of re-establishing tripartism
Sector-wide collective bargaining	Most important bargaining level in all industries (in some bigger industries, also regional bargaining)	Loosening by transferring some functions to negotiators at company level
Decentralized collective bargaining	Only in a few companies not affiliated to employers' associations (among them, Volkswagen)	Works councils increasingly adopting some complementary bargaining functions

Table 4.2 (Cont.)

Type	Pre-1980	Post-1980
Sweden National concertation	Tried by successive governments. Sometimes temporarily established	Tendencies in both directions
Sector-wide collective bargaining	Firmly established traditions but under strong leadership by central confederations and cartels; modifications by local bargaining	Endeavours from employers (some organizations and big companies) to promote decentralization and differentiation, partly and temporarily successful
Decentralized collective bargaining	Local modifications of national sector agreements (institutionalized wage drift)	Employers are (unilaterally) introducing additional modifications, profit-sharing, convertibles, options
UK National concertation	Encouraged by successive governments, but never stably established	Almost complete disappearance
Sector-wide collective bargaining	Widely established throughout public sector and in private manufacturing (especially manual workers), but under pressure from decentralized shop-floor movements	Declining as a result of shift from manufacturing to services, from manual to non-manual work and to some extent as result of managerial strategy; rising as result of growth of public services
Decentralized collective bargaining	Widespread in several manufacturing industries (especially engineering) at plant level; growing in public services	Continuing to grow, but now as a result of managerial preference for company level industrial relations

Source: adapted from Baglioni and Crouch, 1990, p. 60, 147, 310, 349

there has been renewed interest in employee shareholding, for example in Carrefour (France), Italgas and Valeo (Italy) and the National Freight Corporation (United Kingdom) (Vaughan-Whitehead, 1990, pp. 11–13).

There has been a slight shift in emphasis to more qualitative demands. Within the German context, this has centred on five major issues: protection against the consequences of rationalization, job security, the reduction of working time, the improvement of working conditions and skill-based pay systems (Fürstenberg, 1987, p. 217). In the Federal Republic of Germany the improvement of working conditions has focused increasingly on issues relating to the environment. The reduction of working time for manual workers, in particular, was a central bargaining issue in many Western European countries during the 1980s. The metalworking industry led the way and there are numerous examples of agreements leading to reduction in working time: 36.5 hours (from 1 November 1988) in the steel industry in the Federal Republic of Germany; 37–39 hours (from the beginning of 1990) in many firms in the engineering industry in the United Kingdom; and 37 hours (from 1 September 1990) in the Danish metalworking industry.

Collective Bargaining at the European Level

The integration of national economic systems within the European Community has not automatically led to the Europeanization of collective bargaining, and there have been very few examples of real transnational bargaining arrangements. Employers have been anxious to respond to local employment conditions and content to play one workforce off against another, and trade unions have been slow to overcome the enormous problems involved in establishing appropriate strategies for transnational bargaining. There has also been opposition, not only in the ranks of management but also on the trade union side, to the establishment of 'common expiration dates' for agreements so that they coincide in the parent multinational company and in the overseas subsidiaries (Bendiner, 1987, p. 101). However, there is evidence of some change. In an upbeat article, one of the political secretaries of the European Trade Union Confederation has posited three reasons to explain why 'European industrial relations and European collective bargaining will be here sooner rather than later'. Firstly, the actors themselves are increasingly thinking in transnational terms; secondly, legislation at EC level will encourage the move towards transnational collective bargaining; finally, European Monetary Union will not be realizable or sustainable unless collective bargaining becomes European (Coldrick, 1990, pp. 60–1). Moreover, the draft Directives on European company statutes and European works councils foresee elements of European collective bargaining in areas such as profit-sharing and information and consultation rights. In addition, the ETUC, UNICE and the CEEP reached an agreement on 31 October 1991, signalling their readiness to sign joint agreements at the European level which could, in certain circumstances, replace planned EC legislation. The spirit of this agreement was then incorporated in the Social Chapter appended to the Treaty on European Union which was negotiated in Maastricht in December 1991.

It remains to be seen what mandate will be given to the ETUC, UNICE and CEEP by their constituent national bodies since, like governments, employee relations actors are affected by perceptions of national sovereignty (Roberts, 1992, p. 8). It also remains to be seen what the scope of such agreements will be and what form they will take. In the event of an inability to conclude an agreement, what sanctions could be applied? In the first instance it may be that these agreements correspond more properly to union–management information and consultation exercises, an issue which will be considered in greater detail both at the national and transnational levels in the following section.

Employee Participation in Europe

Employee participation can be defined as some form of institutional arrangement enabling employees and their representatives to participate in the decision-making process within the workplace. It comes in different forms and has produced a wide range of different practices. According to Poole (1986, p. 172), 'the origins of this variability are to be found in the nature of strategic choices informed by wider cultural and ideological meanings, transmitted through public policies and legislative enactments, distinctive institutional practices and given "constellations" of the distribution of power in the "larger" society and among the "actors" themselves'. In the United Kingdom, employee participation has generally occurred within the process of collective bargaining, but also traditionally via the activities of joint consultative committees, and more recently via team briefings and quality circles (Marchington, 1987, pp. 162–82). In most other Western European countries (Austria, Belgium, France, the Federal Republic of Germany, Greece, Luxembourg, Netherlands, Portugal and Spain for example) employee participation is mandatory, as a result of statutory provision, and in others (in the Nordic countries for example), it is provided for by

Table 4.3　Composition of works councils in EC Member States with statutory works councils

	Employee representatives only	Joint management employee bodies
Belgium		•
Germany	•	
France		•
Greece	•	
Luxembourg		•
Netherlands	•	
Portugal	•	
Spain	•	

Source: Gold and Hall, 1990, p. 8

national collective agreements. This means that in both cases employees have rights to information and consultation and, more exceptionally, to joint decision making. In addition, in some countries, separate bodies at board level may have been set up with joint supervisory powers, a form of employee participation which has been described in Britain as 'industrial democracy'.

Works councils vary according to the composition of their members. As can be seen from table 4.3, works councils comprising solely employee representatives exist in West Germany, Greece, Portugal and Spain while in the Netherlands, a representative of the employer attends alternate meetings of the works council only for consultation purposes. In the other countries (Belgium, France and Luxembourg) works councils are joint bodies with management and employee representatives. Both types of body normally represent the interests of the entire workforce of a firm, although in Germany executives' committees (*Sprecherausschüsse*) have existed since 1989 to represent the interests of top executives.

Legislation in all countries (except Portugal) requires that a workforce size threshold be met before a works council can be established. As can be seen from table 4.4, this varies from five permanent employees in Germany to 150 in Luxembourg. The number of representatives varies according to national legislation and the size of the firm. The minimum number of works councillors ranges from one in Germany to six in Belgium, while the maximum number

Table 4.4 Workforce size thresholds/minimum and maximum numbers of works councillors in EC Member States with statutory works councils

	Workforce size threshold	Number of works councillors	
		Minimum	Maximum
Belgium	100	6	25
Germany	5	1	–
France	50	3	15
Greece	50[1]	3	7
Luxembourg	150	1	–
Netherlands	35[2]	3	25
Portugal	–	3	11
Spain	50	5	–

[1] Or 20 where there is no recognized union
[2] Works councils in undertakings with 100 or more employee acquire greater powers

Source: Gold and Hall, 1990, p. 6

varies from seven in Greece upwards to an unspecified number in countries such as Spain.

Access to information represents the lowest level of employee participation. Even in the United Kingdom, for example, employees are provided with some form of information. The Employment Protection Act 1975 places a general duty on employers to divulge information for collective bargaining purposes. However, according to Section 18 of the Act, information is restricted where it endangers national security, contravenes another law, breaches confidential sources, relates to individuals without having their agreement or, more importantly where it may cause substantial injury to the enterprise. Employers need only to give information in a form which they consider to be the most suitable. Moreover, employers can refuse to provide information 'where the compilation or assembly would involve an amount of work or expenditure out of reasonable proportion to the value of the information in the conduct of collective bargaining'. As a result, the legislation is little used.

The difference between the United Kingdom and other Western European countries lies in the fact that in other systems the provision of information is not quite so dependent on the discretion of the employer. In certain countries the right to information is relatively general. In others, Belgium and Austria for example, the right to information is spelt out in great detail. In Belgium when a works council is set up, detailed information in writing must be given as regards the legal status of the firm, its competitive position, financial structure, production and productivity levels, labour costs, budgeting and costing, current general policy and pricing, scientific research programme, State subsidies and basic organizational structure. Every year the works council must be given written information on changes in employment levels and workforce composition (by age and sex), future employment prospects, financial results for the last year and financial objectives for the next year. Every quarter the works council must be given oral information (backed up by written summaries) on current levels of employment and future prospects, changes in the general strategy of the firm as well as the reasons for these changes and their impact on employment, the way in which general management strategy has been implemented, the use being made of State subsidies, sales forecasts, stocks, orders, the company's market situation and productivity. Works councils are entitled to occasional information (followed by written comments and statistical information) when there are events that may have important consequences for the firm and its employees. All in all, employees in Belgian firms have remarkably extensive rights to detailed information as to the activities of the firm in which they work.

Consultation is the next stage of employee representation. Employees are not merely informed, but are in a position to give their opinion formally before decisions are taken. This does not of course mean that employers necessarily accept this opinion. Generally, the list of issues for consultation is shorter than that for information. In the French case, the works council has the right to be consulted on the following: any change affecting working conditions or terms of employment (when these include 'rapid and important' technological innovations, the committees must be given an 'adaptation plan' which gives details of the impact on jobs, proposals for retraining and related topics); vocational training; profit-sharing; redundancies and social plans drawn up to deal with them.

The next stage of employee representation is co-determination – joint decision making. Here employees' representatives have the right to give their opinion, and in addition the agreement of the works council is necessary before certain decisions can be taken.

In theory this allows them the power of veto, but in practice it provides an opportunity for some form of negotiation. The works councils mentioned in the previous sections also have some decision-making powers, but it is the German body, the *Betriebsrat*, which is best known internationally for its joint decision-making powers. In certain areas, it has a genuine right of co-determination. The employer cannot act without the agreement of the works council, and if an agreement cannot be reached, the matter is decided upon by a conciliation committee. Co-determination areas are as follows: the organization of working time, wage payment procedures, holiday schedules, the introduction of performance monitoring schemes, health and safety at work, administration of social services within the company, recruitment, regrading, transfers and dismissals and the implementation of vocational training measures.

Some countries have provision for industrial democracy, whereby employee representatives sit as full members on the supervisory bodies administering the firm in which they work – to all intents and purposes, workers on the board. Here again, although a measure of statutory employee representation on company boards is to be found in Denmark, France, Luxembourg and the Netherlands, it is the German case which is the best known. West German joint stock and limited liability companies have a two-tier management structure, comprising supervisory and management boards, and employee representatives are elected to the supervisory board. The supervisory board appoints and dismisses members of the management board which is responsible for the day-to-day running of the firm; it reviews the performance of the management board, and examines the company books and approves its accounts. The extent of co-determination depends on the type of scheme in operation and the composition of the supervisory board. In the mining industry and the iron- and steel-producing industries in the Federal Republic of Germany, there is genuine parity between representatives of employees and shareholders on the supervisory board (five of each, with an eleventh 'neutral' person nominated by both sides). In firms with more than 2,000 employees there is also parity between shareholders' and employee representatives but, in the event of a stalemate, the casting vote belongs to the chairperson who is elected solely by the shareholders. In firms with 500 to 2,000 employees, employees have the right to elect only one-third of the representatives to the supervisory board, leaving employee representatives in a clear minority.

In certain countries, rights to information, consultation, participation and co-determination are considerable, but, as Strauss (1979,
p. 250) has noted, two significant questions remain:

1   To what extent is prescribed (or intended or *de jure*) participation
    associated with actual (or *de facto*) participation?
2   To what extent is prescribed and/or actual participation associated
    with favourable outcomes such as higher productivity, increased worker
    satisfaction, fewer grievances, or (depending on one's values) increased
    power for the working class?

Trade unions have often criticized the effectiveness of works
councils. They have claimed that the information provided by the
employers is inadequate and of limited usefulness. It may arrive too
late, even in countries where timeliness is required by law – in
Germany, for example, information should be provided 'in good
time' to enable the works council to discharge its duties under the
Works Constitution Act. It may also be difficult to understand; in
Belgium company auditors are now required to explain the annual
accounts to the works council, and in France works councils may
ask external experts for assistance. In certain countries doubts concerning *de facto* employee participation are so manifest that legislation has been introduced in order to remedy the situation. In Belgium
for example, employers who do not observe the consultation procedures may have to pay extra compensation, in excess of normal
arrangements, if redundancies result from any changes. In France,
a law was passed in the mid-1980s stating that firms failing to
consult their works committees annually on research policy and
technological development may forfeit State research grants. In the
Federal Republic of Germany, critics of the system for employee
representation would argue that the trade unions as such are not
represented. Moreover, the *Betriebsrat* cannot discuss pay or the
introduction of new technology. The most significant weakness in
the German case is, however, the inability to use strike action, since
the Works Constitution Act specifically states that 'acts of industrial warfare between the employer and the works council shall be
unlawful'. According to Kotthoff (quoted in Berghahn and Karsten,
1987, pp. 114–15), works councils in the Federal Republic of
Germany can range from the 'respected' to the 'ignored', as the
following typology demonstrates:

1 the works council which is respected but has an ambiguous position between workers and management;
2 the works council which is firm in its representation of workers' interests and is respected by the employer;
3 the works council which is co-operative but acts as a countervailing power;
4 the works council which is an organ of management;
5 the isolated works council;
6 the ignored works council.

There is however some evidence to suggest that participation may enable employees to exercise some influence over the decision-making process within their enterprise. A transnational comparative research project examining this issue concluded that 'there is a reliable, statistical connection between Participative Structure and *de facto* Influence Sharing at the lowest levels of the organization' (Heller, 1986, p. 81). The author goes on: 'the existence of formal rules makes a substantial difference in promoting the actual participation of employees' (ibid., p. 82). Another study has shown that, where indirect forms of participation are concerned, statutory provision plays a critical role where union organization is weak at plant or company level. However, where union organization is strong the evidence for improved participation in works councils is mixed (Gold and Hall, 1990, pp. 43–5).

In answer to Strauss's second question, the link between employee participation and 'favourable outcomes' is unclear. In the Federal Republic of Germany the presence of works councillors on supervisory boards has strengthened the position of the works council. Moreover, trade unionists on the supervisory boards have obtained access to information that under normal circumstances they would not have, and this information may be used for other purposes. However, this influence may be a mixed blessing, since the loyalties of the trade union representatives on these bodies may be divided between the enterprise and their members. Paradoxically, co-determination has strengthened the position of management *vis-à-vis* the shareholders. Employees on the supervisory board have been more likely to argue for the reinvestment of profits rather than the payment of dividends, a position which would tend to reinforce the views of management. As a result, employee participation has tended to encourage more sophisticated manpower planning and more reflective decision making in the firm (Berghahn and Karsten, 1987, pp. 131–5).

Another source gives a different perspective on the German situation. When large-scale redundancies have been made, 'trade unions have often remarked that the system of participation in iron and steel, and perhaps more so in the mines, has prevented problems of redundancies, rationalization and technical change from leading to serious consequences or social tension' (International Labour Organization, 1981, p. 91) However, not all trade unions would want to participate in the messy process of economic and social restructuring. Moreover, in these particular instances of economic and social restructuring German employers have explained the dissipation of social tension during these periods by a high level of demand for labour in other industries. While *de jure* participation cannot by itself ensure *de facto* participation and/or 'favourable outcomes', since other variables (economic conditions, trade union strength and management style) also play a crucial role, it can provide a minimum level of participation which might otherwise be denied employees.

Employee Participation at the European Level

Moves to encourage employee participation met with little success in the initial stages of economic integration in Europe, but were given a fillip by calls for a Social Dimension to accompany the Single European Market. These measures are essentially of three different types – social dialogue, participation by means of legal intervention, as proposed by the Commission of the European Communities, and participation by means of voluntary collective agreement, as established by a number of multinational companies.

Article 118b of the Single European Act called for the development of dialogue between employers' and employees' representatives at the European level which could, 'if the two sides consider it desirable, lead to relations based on agreements'. Meetings between representatives of the ETUC, UNICE and CEEP took place from the 1980s onwards initially in a castle just outside Brussels, Val Duchesse, which gave its name to this type of talks. Joint working groups were set up to examine two specific issues – macro-economic policy in the EC and the social consequences of the introduction of new technology – and they both came up with joint opinions. The first group agreed on a co-operative growth for employment strategy. The second group agreed on a number of statements concerning vocational training and also on a definition of the word 'consultation' within the context of the introduction of new technology – 'the action of gathering opinions and possible suggestions concerning the implication of such changes for the firm's workforce, more particularly as regards the effects on their employment and their working conditions'. This definition leaves little opportunity for the influencing of decision making but bears witness to the mutual desire to develop some concrete form of consensus at the European level. After a short hiatus it was decided that a steering group composed of representatives from the ETUC, UNICE and CEEP should be set up in 1989 to monitor progress in the area of social affairs, and working parties were established to examine issues such as education and training and the European labour market.

> This institutionalization of social partners' relations at European level has been an important step for industrial relations in the Community, not least because labour and management organisations become accustomed to systematic and structural European level contacts and deliberations. (Roberts, 1992, p. 6)

Social dialogue has progressed in two further significant areas. Firstly, the ETUC and the CEEP (but not UNICE) signed a framework agreement in September 1990 and agreed to carry out concrete action in two sectors – rail transport and energy distribution – with an emphasis on basic vocational training, training in the new technologies and training for improved health and safety in the workplace. Secondly, social dialogue moved to the sectoral level and spawned a variety of new meetings, notably in the retail sector where an agreement on vocational training was signed.

The Commission has shown considerable perseverance in its attempts to introduce workplace employee participation in the EC. In the 1970s the Council of Ministers agreed on two measures requiring some form of employee information and consultation – the Directive on procedures to be applied in the event of collective redundancies (EC/75/129) and the Directive on employees' rights and advantages in mergers and takeovers (EC/77/187). However, within the Commission there have been two differing institutional sources of legislation related to employee participation – the Directorate-General responsible for financial institutions and company law (DG 15) and the Directorate-General covering employment, industrial relations and social affairs (DG 5) – and two different approaches – the 'company law' approach of DG 15 and the 'social affairs' approach of DG 5. (Hall, 1992, pp. 554–5). This ambiguity helps to explain why other attempts to introduce employee participation have been less successful.

In 1972 the Commission first proposed the so-called Fifth Directive on the structure of public limited companies which would have guaranteed a measure of employee participation in certain circumstances. It would have required limited companies with 500 or more employees to set up a two-tier board system with supervisory and management functions. The supervisory board with minority employee representation would have had the right to nominate and dismiss members of the management board. The latter would have been required to submit a report every three months on the state of company affairs to the supervisory board. The authorization of the supervisory board would have been needed for the closure or transfer of the company or substantial parts of it, for substantial curtailment or extension of the company's activities, for substantial changes of organization within the company and for the establishment or termination of long-term co-operation with other companies. This original proposal was watered down in 1975 and again in 1983, thus allowing for a more nebulous form of participation and a higher employment threshold level (1,000 employees or more). These latest provisions 'represent considerable relaxation as compared to the earlier proposals and leave a great deal of latitude to Member States in the choice of management systems . . .' (Vandamme, 1986, p. 143). However, the Commission's (and the European Parliament's) perseverance has not been rewarded, and, in the face of opposition from UNICE and the British government, negotiations have dragged on aimlessly. However, with the advent of the Single European Market, further proposals for employee participation were put forward in 1989 under the guise of a memorandum on the Statute for the European Company. These proposals had originally been put forward as a draft Regulation in 1970, then amended in 1975 and buried in 1982. This memorandum is even more tentative and defensive than the reconstituted Fifth Directive. At the time of writing, no further action has been taken but the British government has already expressed its opposition to such an initiative.

In 1980 the so-called Vredeling Directive (named after the member of the European Commission responsible for Social Affairs at the time) was put forward. It required public limited companies with complex structures (i.e. multinational companies) and with more than 100 employees to provide employees' representatives at the local level with regular information concerning the whole of the company on matters such as the company's economic and financial position, its employment situation, its production and investment plans, its rationalization plans, its projects for the introduction of new working methods. In addition, companies were required to consult employees' representatives when planning decisions which would have had a substantial impact on employees' interests – i.e. the closing or transfer of the whole or a major part of the firm; restriction, extensions, or substantial modifications to the activities of the firm; major organizational changes; and the establishment of long-term co-operation with other firms or the cessation of such co-operation. In the event of infringement of the requirement to disclose information, Member States could impose penalties in certain circumstances. Moreover, employees' representatives at the local level could have access to the parent company when local information was judged to be insufficient (*Official Journal* C297/80). Opposition to this proposal both within the EC and outside (particularly from the USA) was fierce. The Commission proposed an amended version in 1983, which increased the threshold for firms concerned to 1,000 employees, reduced the frequency with which information should be given, restricted the type of information to be given, proscribed the notion of a direct approach to the parent company (in the event of a deadlock within a subsidiary), and tightened up the regulations on confidentiality (*Official Journal* C217/83).

The Community Charter of Fundamental Social Rights for Workers underlined the importance of information, consultation and participation of workers in companies or groups of companies with subsidiaries in two or more Member States (Article 17) and, in December 1990, the Commission proposed a Directive on European Works Councils. In order to avoid some of the difficulties associated with the Vredeling proposal, national arrangements would remain untouched. Moreover, this proposal would only apply to transnational companies, the idea being that increasing transnationalization of the economy would lead to the establishment of appropriate European bodies (Roberts, 1992, p. 10). Any company with more than 1,000 employees within the EC and with at least two establishments in different Member States, each employing at least 100 workers, would be required to set up a

European Works Council. Workers' representatives and management should determine by written agreement the nature, composition and mode of operation of the European Works Council in terms of their own particular circumstances. During its annual meeting the European Works Council would be provided with the following information:

- the structure of the firm;
- its economic and financial situation;
- probable future developments in terms of business, production and sales; and
- the employment situation and investment prospects.

The European Works Council would also be consulted on any management proposal likely to have serious consequences for the interests of the employees, although the final decision would rest with management. Each Member State may decide, however, that management has the right to withhold information which, if divulged, would substantially damage the interests of the firm. This requirement exists alongside a general clause referring to the need to keep the confidentiality of the European Works Council meetings (Com (90) 581 final). This draft Directive and the others relating to information, consultative and participation rights have not been agreed by the Council of Ministers and therefore have not passed into law. However, there may be some movement on these issues. The Social Chapter of the Treaty on European Union stipulates that the Council of Ministers may take decisions by qualified majority voting on the information and consultation of workers.

Without waiting for legislation on employee participation from the institutions of the European Community, some transnational companies have been prepared to establish their own form of information and consultation procedures. The three best examples all come from transnational companies which have their original base in France, a country not known for its participatory tradition in employee relations. After some years of informal links with employees' representatives, the management of St-Gobain, a glass and building materials group with over 100,000 employees world-wide and subsidiaries in 11 Western European countries, met in December 1983 with trade union representatives from its glass factories. After a hiatus, they met again in 1989 and decided to meet annually. These meetings provide information about company performance, strategy and acquisitions. Secondly, the European management of BSN, a food, beverages, glass and packaging company with over 45,000 employees world-wide and plants in nine Western European countries, met in 1986 with a delegation from the European Committee of Food, Catering and Allied Workers' Union (ECF). It was decided to establish annual meetings between the management of BSN and a group of trade union-appointed representatives from the food sector. In 1988, the group signed a joint agreement with employee representatives which stated that the management and employees' representatives would study four specific industrial relations issues: information disclosure, in order to standardize information on social and economic matters; training; equal opportunities for women; and trade union rights. The third example is the Thomson Grand Public group (TGP, later known as Thomson Consumer Electronics, TCE) which has over 50,000 employees world-wide and plants in France, Germany, Italy, Spain and the United Kingdom. In October 1985 it signed a two-year agreement with the European Metalworkers' Federation (EMF) proposing to set up two specific joint bodies, an agreement which was subsequently renewed indefinitely. First a liaison committee was set up, composed of the TCE Chairman (or his representative) assisted by the appropriate directors and the EMF General Secretary accompanied by officials from EMF affiliates (three from France, three from the Federal Republic of Germany, two from Italy, two from the UK and one from Spain). Then there is the European TCE commission, which has the same representation on the management side but has employee representatives who are elected on a proportional basis from among the works councils of the company in each country. Both bodies meet at company's expense and have the same information rights. They are to be informed of the economic, industrial and commercial activities of the company, modifications in the economic and legal organization of the company, major structural and industrial changes prior to their implementation and plans for technological change (European Trade Union Institute, 1991, pp. 8–11, 25–9, 36–7). The agreement with Thomson Grand Public is important for a number of specific reasons: this was the first time that a manufacturing company recognized an International Trade Secretariat or European Industry Committee as an official representative of the workforce; it created the first example of a 'European works council'; and it incorporated the spirit of the Vredeling Directive (Northrup et al., 1988, p. 533).

In addition, one transnational company has made provisions for 'workers on the board'. Mannesman-Röhrer Werke in Germany and the French firm Usinor Sacilor and its subsidiaries merged in January 1991 to form a transnational company called Europipe. Its European supervisory board is made up of six shareholders and six workers' representatives. The following matters have to be submitted to the approval of the supervisory board: new types of production, areas of business or research; plant establishment or closure; and changes in company contracts (European Trade Union Institute, 1991, pp. 16–18). These bodies are more likely to be set up: '(a) where companies have a single ownership and management structure within Europe, produce similar products and services in different locations or integrate production across locations, or have strong business reasons (such as restructuring plans) for engaging in dialogue with unions; (b) where unions are able to create an encompassing organization covering all affiliates in the enterprise; (c) where enterprise organization within companies already exists at national level; and (d) where significant groups within the workforce are potentially mobile across borders' (Marginson, 1992, p. 540).

An evaluation by Gold and Hall of their activities has concluded that most arrangements only provide information covering corporate strategy, that consultation is rare and that negotiation is non-existent. (European Trade Union Institute, 1991, pp. 40–1) Moreover, these arrangements have done little to protect workers' employment. In October 1991 Thomson closed the last of the Ferguson plants which it owned in the United Kingdom without consulting its employees or, it seems, local management (*The Guardian*, 15 October 1991). For any transnational information and consultation procedures to remain and prosper it is doubtless necessary to heed the advice of the Social Relations Co-ordinating Manager of BSN who stressed the importance of a pragmatic step-by-step informal approach to the setting up of Europe-wide participation procedures which 'one day must be complemented by legislation at the European level' (Bergougnoux, 1990, p. 672).

Industrial Conflict

Collective bargaining and employee participation may be vehicles for resolving disputes between employees and employers, but the institutionalization of industrial conflict is, of course, not automatic. Indeed, some would argue that conflict between employers and employees is the norm; institutionalization of this conflict is an exception or a temporary truce. Industrial conflict manifests itself in many different forms: strikes, work-to-rules, go-slows, overtime bans, labour turnover, absenteeism and even sabotage on the employees' side; and lock-outs, 'investment strikes' and restructuring on the employers' side. However, strikes are the most visible forms of industrial conflict and will provide the focus of this particular section.

According to the International Labour Organization, a strike is defined as 'a temporary stoppage of work wilfully effected by a group of workers (or by a group of employers) with a view to enforcing a demand or expressing a grievance'. While the emphasis is on collective action, this definition does not include a reference to trade unions; nor do legal definitions in certain countries, for example, Belgium, France and the Federal Republic of Germany. In a number of Western European countries, the right to strike is formally incorporated in the constitution (France, Greece, Italy, Portugal and Spain), while in others the right to strike is implicitly guaranteed by law. Ireland and the United Kingdom are unusual in not guaranteeing the right to strike, whether implicitly or explicitly. Employees in these two countries have a 'negative right' to take part in strikes in furtherance of a trade dispute and be granted immunity from legal proceedings. However, the extent of this immunity was considerably reduced in the United Kingdom during the 1980s.

The right to strike is nevertheless limited on occasions by national legislation and in some countries, for example Sweden, unofficial or 'wildcat' strikes are forbidden. Secondary action is permitted in all countries, except Germany, the Netherlands and more recently the United Kingdom. Political strikes are illegal in Austria, the Federal Republic of Germany, Ireland, the Netherlands and Spain, although of course it is often difficult to decide when a strike is political, or indeed when a strike is non-political. Strikes may also be unlawful during the life of a collective agreement, for instance in Denmark, the Federal Republic of Germany, Spain and Sweden. In France employees are forbidden to strike if their activity is essential for public order (soldiers, judges, police and prison officers), and other sections of the workforce may be required to maintain a minimum service. France is unusual in that the government has the power to requisition strikers and oblige them to resume work, although this power has not been used since the miners' strike in 1963.

In the 1980s there were strident calls in some countries for further limitations on strike activity, particularly in the public sector, but in the main these calls have gone unheeded. Italy is an exception – in 1990 the Italian Parliament passed a law obliging trade unions to give ten days' notice of strike activity in a large number of different areas within the public sector (hospitals, public health, civil defence, refuse collection, customs, energy supply, courts, environmental protection, museums, public transport, banks, schools, postal service, radio and television) and requiring the provision of a minimum service. Interestingly, the three major Italian confederations (CGIL, CISL and UIL) supported the adoption of this law, because their attempts to channel the demands of the workforce had been undermined by the activities of the newly formed extra-union co-ordination groups, the Cobas (ETUI Newsletter, July 1990). The British government was also reconsidering the matter in 1993 following an industrial dispute with schoolteachers.

In all major Western European countries machinery has been set up to record strike statistics, which is not the case with other forms of industrial conflict. However, as Walsh (1982, pp. 65–72) has pointed out, there are certain methodological problems concerning the reliability of these data. The comparability of statistics is affected by three issues: the measurement base, definitional limitations and the range of measures and classifications. The collection of strike statistics is done in a relatively informal fashion. No two countries can be said to be collecting their statistics on the same basis, the major problems being the minimum threshold for recording disputes, the inclusion of indirect effects, the non-measurement of political strikes in certain countries and the exclusion of large sections of employees from the statistics. Table 4.5 demonstrates the discrepancies that exist from one country to another in terms of data collection. In the United Kingdom, for example, a strike is only recorded when it involves more than ten workers and lasts for more than one day, unless 100 or more working days are lost. Political stoppages are not included, but indirectly affected workers are. In France, on the other hand, there is no restriction on size, but public sector and agricultural workers are excluded, as are political stoppages and indirectly affected workers.

There is a second major problem inhibiting comparative analysis: 'the strike itself is not a homogeneous phenomenon' (Bean, 1985, p. 129). Strikes do not have the same function in all employee relations systems. They may be an expression of protest, political gestures, or an integral part of the process of collective bargaining, whether before negotiations begin, as a demonstration of serious bargaining intent, or afterwards, if talks break down. In addition, strikes have a particular significance in a country like Switzerland because of their scarcity value; the same cannot be said of strikes in a country like Italy.

Strikes in Western Europe

As can be seen from table 4.6, the International Labour Organization publishes three major sets of statistics for strike incidence, relating to the number of strikes and lock-outs (D/C), the number of workers involved (W/T), and the number of working days lost (D/J). The number of working days lost is the most useful indicator of strike activity since these data demonstrate the actual levels of production lost. However, they are difficult to analyse from a comparative perspective because of the variations in the size and industrial distribution of the labour force in each country. These data become more readily comparable, however, if the number of employees per country is incorporated into the figures.

Table 4.7 shows the number of working days lost through strike action per thousand employees in all industries and services between 1980 and 1989. There is considerable variation from one year to the next. Often the figures are influenced by a small number of significant stoppages, such as the miners' strike in the United Kingdom during 1984–5, the three-day strike in Finland in 1986, the Fiat strike in Italy in 1980, and the nationwide lock-out in Sweden in May 1980. Consequently it is more useful to examine trends in strike activity and averages over time. The United Kingdom is not as strike prone as is sometimes suggested. It had a lower level of strike activity during the period 1980–9 than Spain, Italy, Greece and Ireland, but considerably more than Denmark, France, the Federal Republic of Germany, the Netherlands, Norway, Portugal and Sweden, and of course Austria and Switzerland, where strikes are almost non-existent.

There is a tendency for the incidence of strikes to vary between industrial sectors. It is generally accepted that mining and quarrying, manufacturing, construction, and transport and communication are the four industrial sectors which are particularly strike prone. A comparison of the strike incidence in these sectors is instructive, as can be seen from table 4.8. The incidence of working

Table 4.5 Industrial disputes: comparisons of coverage and methodology

	Minimum criteria for inclusion in statistics	Are political stoppages included?	Are indirectly affected workers included?	Sources and notes
UK	More than ten workers involved and of more than one day's duration unless 100 or more working days lost	No	Yes	Local unemployment benefit offices make reports to Department of Employment HQ, which also checks press, unions and large employers
Austria	No restrictions on size	Yes	No	Trade unions provide information
Belgium	More than one working day's duration	Yes	No	Local police reports sent to National Conciliation Service. Follow-up questionnaires sent from National Statistical Institute
Denmark	100 or more days lost	Yes	Yes	Voluntary reports from employers' organization sent annually to Statistical Office
Finland	More than four hours' duration unless 100 or more working days lost	Yes	Yes	Returns from mail questionnaires to employers and employees
France	No restrictions on size. However, public sector and agricultural employees are excluded from statistics	No	No	Labour inspectors' reports
Germany	More than ten workers involved and more than one day's duration unless 100 or more working days lost	Yes	No	Compulsory notification by employers to Labour Offices

Country				
Ireland	Ten or more days lost or of more than one day's duration	Yes	Yes	Reports from local employment offices
Italy	No restrictions on size	Yes	No	Local police reports sent to Central Institute of Statistics
Norway	More than one day's duration	Yes	No	Questions to employees' and employers' organizations
Portugal	Up to 1985: no restrictions on size. 1986 and onwards: excludes firms with fewer than five employees. However, statistics exclude disputes which involve more than one company	not known	No	1986 and onwards: figures exclude Madeira and the Azores
Spain	No restrictions on size	Yes	No	Returns by local province delegates of Ministry of Labour and Social Security, and by some autonomous Communities. Up to 1985: figures exclude Catalonia. 1986 and onwards: figures exclude Basque country
Sweden	More than one hour's duration	Yes	No	Press reports compiled by State Conciliation Service are checked by employers' organizations and sent to Central Statistical Office
Switzerland	More than one day's duration	Yes	Yes	Federal Office for Industry, crafts, occupations and employment, collects press reports and checks with trade unions and employers

Source: Employment Gazette, June 1989, p. 312

Table 4.6 Strikes and lock-outs, workers involved and work-days lost

	1981	1982	1983	1984	1985	1986	1987	1988	1989	1990
Austria										
D/C	6	2	4	2	4	11	6	–	7	9
W/T	17.115	0.091	0.208	0.268	35.531	3.222	7.203	–	3.715	5.274
D/J	4.024	0.344	0.514	0.543	22.752	3.253	4.822	–	2.986	8.870
Denmark										
D/C	94	180	161	157	820	215	202	157	132	232
W/T	53.463	53.185	40.919	50.764	581.3	56.735	56.878	29.591	27.212	37.386
D/J	651.6	92.7	78.8	131.7	2332.7	93.2	137.3	96.5	52.9	97.6
Spain										
D/C	1,993	1,810	1,451	1,498	1,092	999	1,576	1,279	1,094	1,083
W/T	1,944.9	1,058.9	1,483.6	2,242.2	1,511.2	896.4	1,899.2	6,727.8	1,396.0	840.6
D/J	5,153.5	2,787.6	4,416.7	6,357.8	3,223.5	2,427.5	5,113.9	11,839	3,739.6	2,320.3
Finland										
D/C	1,591	1,212	1,919	1,679	833	1,236	791	1,327	606	404
W/T	488.86	165.82	419.87	558.70	170.02	589.04	98.92	172.42	157.15	199.48
D/J	659.10	207.60	719.70	1526.9	174.27	2787.5	130.89	179.82	204.21	929.02
France										
D/C	2,405	3,113	2,837	2,537	1,901	1,391	1,391	2,260	2,040	–
W/T	329.0	397.7	37.8	42.1	22.8	21.8	18.6	27.2	20.3	–
D/J	1,441.6	2,250.2	1,321.0	1,316.8	726.7	567.6	511.5	1,094.0	800.0	–
Germany										
D/C	–		–		–	–		–		–
W/T	253.33	39.98	94.07	537.26	78.19	115.52	154.97	33.48	43.93	257.16
D/J	58.40	15.11	40.84	5,617.6	34.40	27.96	33.32	41.88	100.41	363.55
Greece										
D/C	466	968	675	486	453	213	381	532	–	–
W/T	401.76	352.74	224.31	159.13	785.72	1,106.3	1,270.6	449.5	–	–
D/J	813	1,431.4	554.55	562.43	1,094.4	1,262.8	1,732.9	6,667.4	–	–

Ireland										
D/C	117	131	154	192	116	102	80	65	38	–
W/T	31.958	29.952	30.482	30.992	168.67	50.227	26.221	10.218	3.692	–
D/J	433.98	434.25	319.01	386.42	417.73	309.18	264.34	143.39	50.358	–
Italy										
D/C	2,204	1,747	1,565	1,816	1,341	1,469	1,149	1,769	1,297	–
W/T	8,226.6	10,483	6,844.2	7,356.5	4,842.8	3,606.7	4,272.7	2,712.1	4,451.8	–
D/J	10,527	18,563	98,021	60,923	26,815	39,506	32,240	23,206	31,053	–
Netherlands										
D/C	11	12	9	16	45	35	28	38	27	29
W/T	8.600	69.766	20.307	16.158	22.570	17.029	12.562	5.234	15.356	24.978
D/J	24.114	215.44	118.16	29.181	89.390	38.858	58.276	8.922	23.819	206.72
Norway										
D/C	17	12	9	21	11	16	10	15	14	15
W/T	4.294	24.581	1.018	30.635	6.557	165.74	2.462	8.332	11.287	60.674
D/J	28.257	281.18	5.897	104.35	66.473	1,030.9	12.905	83.254	16.880	139.05
Switzerland										
D/C	1	1	5	2	3	1	–	4	2	2
W/T	0.015	0.055	0.985	0.050	0.366	0.036	–	0.131	0.022	0.578
D/J	0.015	0.550	4.438	0.662	0.662	0.072	–	0.870	0.265	4.090
Sweden										
D/C	68	46	92	206	160	75	72	144	139	126
W/T	99.211	5.136	14.372	23.676	124.51	66.304	10.517	95.150	34.102	73.159
D/J	209.14	1.761	36.923	31.293	504.21	682.65	14.726	797.42	409.71	770.36
United Kingdom										
D/C	1,338	1,528	1,352	1,206	903	1,074	1,016	781	701	598
W/T	1,512.5	2,102.9	573.8	1,464.3	791.3	720.2	887.4	790.3	727.0	290.5
D/J	4,266	5,313	3,754	27,135	6,402	1,920	3,546	3,702	4,128	1,890

D/C = number of strikes and lock-outs
W/T = number of workers (thousands)
D/J = work-days lost (thousands)

Source: International Labour Organization, *Yearbook of Labour Statistics*, 1991, pp. 1045–7

Table 4.7 Industrial disputes: working days lost per thousand employees[1] in all industries and services 1980–1989

	1980	1981	1982	1983	1984	1985	1986	1987	1988	1989	Average[2] 1980–84	Average[2] 1985–89	Average[2] 1980–89
UK	520	200	250	180	1,280	300	90	160	170	180	480	180	330
Denmark	90	320	50	40	60	1,060	40	60	40	20	110	240	180
France[3]	90	80	130	80	80	50	60	50	70	50	90	60	80
Germany	10	–	–	–	260	–	–	–	–	–	50	–	30
Greece	1,740	480	830	320	320	620	710	970	3,610	–	740	(1,480)	(1,070)
Ireland	480	500	500	380	470	520	380	320	180	60	470	290	380
Italy	1,140	730	1,280	980	610	270	390	320	220	300	950	300	620
Netherlands	10	10	50	30	10	20	10	10	–	–	20	10	10
Portugal	200	280	170	230	100	100[4]	140	40	n.a.	n.a.	200	(90)	(160)
Spain	770	670	360	580	870	440[4]	320	630	1,400	420	650	650	650
Austria	10	–	–	–	–	10	–	–	–	–	–	–	–
Finland	840	340	100	360	750	80	1,350	60	90	100	480	340	410
Norway	60	20	170	–	60	40	570	10	50	10	60	140	100
Sweden	1,150	50	–	10	10	130	170	–	200	100	240	120	180
Switzerland	–	–	–	–	–	–	–	–	–	–	–	–	–

(1) Employees in employment: some figures have been estimated
(2) Annual averages for those years within each period for which data are available, weighted for employment
(3) Note the significant coverage differences referred to in the text
(4) Break in the series
( ) Brackets indicate averages based on incomplete data
– Less than five days lost per thousand

Source: adapted from *Employment Gazette*, December 1991, p. 654

Table 4.8 Industrial disputes: working days lost per thousand employees[1] in selected industries (mining and quarrying, manufacturing, construction, and transport and communication) 1980–1989

	1980	1981	1982	1983	1984	1985	1986	1987	1988	1989	Average[2] 1980–84	Average[2] 1985–89	Average[2] 1980–89
UK	1,160	330	460	330	3,230	660	180	330	430	200	1,070	360	740
Denmark	210	720	100	80	160	2,380	90	120	100	60	250	540	400
France[3]	170	160	260	150	160	90	70	70	n.a.	n.a.	180	(80)	(150)
Germany	10	-	-	-	260	-	-	-	-	10	100	-	50
Greece	1,280	720	n.a.	n.a.	n.a.	n.a.	n.a.	n.a.	n.a.	n.a.	(970)	n.a.	(970)
Ireland	650	930	630	560	670	450	270	630	220	130	690	340	530
Italy	230	930	280	210	110	420	400	490	310	370	200	400	290
Netherlands	30	10	60	40	20	50	20	30	-	10	30	20	30
Portugal	350	490	300	450	190	200[4]	240	70	n.a.	n.a.	360	(170)	(290)
Spain	n.a.	n.a.	460	530	870	290[4]	480	870	1,060	800	(610)	710	(670)
Austria	10	-	-	-	-	-	-	-	-	-	-	-	-
Finland	1,270	560	220	390	720	160	2,310	130	200	140	640	600	620
Norway	140	40	410	10	60	100	940	-	-	10	130	220	170
Sweden	2,240	60	-	10	20	10	-	10	790	40	490	170	330
Switzerland	-	-	-	-	-	-	-	-	-	-	-	-	-

(1) Employees in employment: some figures have been estimated
(2) Annual averages for those years within each period for which data are available, weighted for employment
(3) Note the significant coverage differences referred to in the text
(4) Break in the series
   ( ) Brackets indicate averages based on incomplete data
   − Less than five days lost per thousand

Source: adapted from *Employment Gazette*, December 1991, p. 656

days lost in these industries is about twice as high as in all industries and services taken together, except in Spain and Italy which
have different industrial structures. The United Kingdom has a
particularly high figure, but this can in part be explained by the
major dispute in the coal industry in 1984–5.

Why is there a relatively high level of strike activity in countries
such as Spain, Italy, Greece and Ireland, and such a low level in
Denmark, France, the Federal Republic of Germany, the Netherlands, Norway, Portugal and Sweden? Three sets of different explanations have been suggested – institutional, political and economic.

Explanations based on institutional factors stress the importance
of the 'withering away of the strike' and the institutionalization
of industrial conflict. This was most famously argued in Ross and
Hartman's classic comparative study (1960). In the first instance
strike activity is at a high level at the beginning of the process of
industrialization because of the problems of adjusting to new employee relations practices; thereafter, as employees become accus-
tomed to the rigours of the new industrial regime, the strike withers
away. It is the case that strike-prone countries like Spain, Greece
and Ireland are relatively less industrialized, whereas Italy, particularly its northern regions, has developed a modern and sophisticated industrial sector and yet still has a high level of strike activity.
The United Kingdom, the birthplace of the industrial revolution,
has also clearly undergone its industrialization process without
experiencing the withering away of the strike. On the other hand,
there is a relatively low level of strike activity in Portugal, a country
which is currently adjusting to the rigours of industrialization as
directly as any Western European country.

In the second instance, the institutionalization of industrial conflict
may be achieved by the integration of strong well-disciplined trade
unions into the process of collective bargaining. While the low level
of industrial conflict in the Scandinavian countries can be explained
by the high level of unionization and the stable and relatively
centralized form of collective bargaining, this approach does not
explain the low level of strike activity in countries, such as the
Netherlands and Switzerland, where union density is relatively low,
and above all in France where union density is low and where in
addition there is a relatively unstable and fragmented pattern of
collective bargaining. As has been explained, there has been a partial but gradual reduction in union density in Western Europe and
a partial but gradual decentralization of collective bargaining, factors

which, according to the institutional thesis, would normally lead to an increase in strike activity, but this has clearly not been the case in the 1980s. As Bean (1985, p. 140) has noted 'institutional arrangements for conflict resolution should be seen more as *intervening* [his italics], than as independent, variables affecting the level of conflicts'.

Others have underlined the importance of the political significance of strike activities. It is suggested that a higher propensity for strike action exists in countries where political parties which represent workers' interests are unable to gain political power in national governments. The argument runs as follows: with a left-of-centre government, workers' representatives are less likely to strike to affect the political decision-making process since the left-of-centre party, or parties, are more likely to respond faithfully to the demands of trade unions. For instance, Ireland and Italy, two strike-prone countries, have not had a left-of-centre government during the period at issue. However, on the other hand, both Greece and Spain have had left-of-centre governments for long periods during the 1980s, and this has not apparently inhibited strike action. (Pasok was in power in Greece from 1981 to 1989, and the Spanish Socialist Workers Party (PSOE) has been in power in Spain since 1982.) Of the strike-free countries, Austria, Norway and Sweden have had left-of-centre governments during the same period. However, there was a right-of-centre government coalition in Denmark, West Germany and the Netherlands during the major part of the 1980s. The British case would cast further doubt on this theory. The 'winter of discontent' and the concomitant wave of strike activity in 1979 was in part a reaction to the policy of a Labour government. With the possible exception of the 1984–5 miners' strike, the period of Conservative government has not been met with an upsurge of industrial conflict. This theory of the political action of industrial conflict implies a strong and disciplined labour movement, close party–union links and a clear programmatic choice between political parties, conditions which are becoming rarer and rarer.

A number of observers have noted the link between different economic factors and industrial conflict, and the significance of nominal wage increases as an indicator of strike activity – the higher the nominal wage increases, the higher the level of strike activity (Paldam and Pedersen, 1982). The data on nominal wage increases for the 1980s is a little patchy, but some data on hourly earnings in manufacturing are available (Organization for Economic

Co-operation and Development, 1991a, p. 94) For the period 1979–88, nominal wages increased the most in countries such as Greece, Ireland, Italy and Spain, which, as has been seen, have a high level of strike activity. Moreover the level of nominal wage increases was relatively low in countries such as Austria, the Federal Republic of Germany, the Netherlands and Switzerland, where there was a low level of strike activity. Paldam and Pedersen were of the opinion that nominal wage increases were more significant than real wages as indicators of strike activity, and data from the 1980s would bear this out. Real wages, as expressed by real hourly earnings in manufacturing, increased most during this period in the United Kingdom, Italy and Spain, countries with relatively high levels of strike activity. However, real wages increased marginally more in the Federal Republic of Germany and Austria (countries with a low level of strike activity) than for example in Greece (a country with a high level of strike activity).

There is also a possible link between strike incidence and inflation (Davies, 1979). It is claimed that a period of inflation is likely to engender a mood of instability in the collective bargaining process which in turn is likely to lead to industrial conflict. This theory fits most countries during this period but not all. Those countries with a relatively high level of strike activity (Greece, Ireland, Italy and Spain) also had relatively high increases in their consumer price indices for the period 1979–88. However, Portugal had a relatively high level of consumer price increases and a low level of strike activity. Moreover, strike-free countries such as Norway and Sweden were following close on the heels of Ireland in terms of relatively high levels of inflation and were ahead of the United Kingdom (Organization for Economic Co-operation and Development, 1991a, p. 87).

Others have tried to link unemployment to strike activity. On the one hand it is argued that high unemployment leads to high levels of strike activity, since during these periods employers can afford to be intransigent. On the other, it is argued that there is a link between low levels of unemployment and high levels of strike activity – workers are more likely to strike in a tighter labour market because they can realistically expect to be successful whereas during times of high unemployment there is less likelihood of winning (Hibbs, 1978, pp. 153–175). Data on unemployment for the period 1979–1988 do not make it possible to clear up this confusion. (Organization for Economic Co-operation and Development, 1991a,

p. 43) Of the strike-prone countries, Ireland and Spain had high unemployment rates while the rate of unemployment in Italy was marginally lower than the EC average, and unemployment in Greece was considerably lower still. Of the 'strike-free' countries, the Federal Republic of Germany had a consistently low level of unemployment, unlike, for example, Denmark.

While it would seem that the economic theory based on the importance of nominal real wages seems to be the most persuasive, it is difficult not to agree with Jackson: 'Studies from a variety of disciplines have tried to identify causes of patterns and variations. While some successes can be claimed, they are limited. No one explanation can be put forward which claims respect even within its own discipline' (Jackson, 1987, p. 211).

Conclusions

Collective bargaining in Western Europe forms a multi-form mosaic reflecting the different social, economic and political conditions existing in each country. The structure of collective bargaining has over the years demonstrated a remarkable level of stability, although in the 1980s a significant but partial decentralization has taken place. At the European level there has been a reluctance to match the process of collective bargaining to the forces at play in the broader economy, and the Europeanization of the economy has not yet been accompanied by the Europeanization of the process of collective bargaining. There are signs, however, at the beginning of the 1990s, that employers and trade unions are starting to contemplate a change in their behaviour and strategies.

There is an overall consensus in most countries of Western Europe (the United Kingdom being the exception that proves the rule) of the appropriateness of some form of mandatory employee representation. It comes in different shapes and offers employees a variety of different potential rights to information, consultation or participation. Evidence suggests that *de jure* participation does not by itself guarantee *de facto* participation, but it does nevertheless in certain circumstances help to reinforce the position of employees and their representatives, if only because it ensures the right to some form of representation and information about the firm's activities. It is less certain whether employee participation leads to 'favourable outcomes', however defined, and more research will be needed to establish the putative link between the two. Attempts to extend these national statutory participation systems to the European level have foundered, and even the watered-down employee participation schemes which were put before the Council of Ministers at the end of the 1980s and the beginning of the 1990s have met with stiff opposition. Now that the British Conservative government has opted out of the Social Chapter of the Treaty on European Union there may be some movement on this issue. There are a few examples of voluntary participation schemes at the European level, but they are in their infancy, and it remains to be seen whether they will be able to engender meaningful forms of employee participation in the medium and long term.

Patterns of industrial conflict in Western Europe differ considerably. In some countries strikes are extremely rare while in others conflict is still rife, and was so even in the 1980s, a decade which saw an overall reduction in strike activity. No single academic explanation for the variation in strike activity from one country to another can be proposed although it would seem that, in the 1980s at least, one of the economic theories is more convincing than some of the institutional and political interpretations. However, the correlation between high levels of nominal wage increases and high levels of strike activity does not by itself prove there is causal relationship and further research will be needed to provide a convincing comparative explanation for the differing patterns of strike activity in Western Europe.

5

The Individual at Work

From the early 1970s, individual labour law in Europe has been transformed and a framework of rights created, often where little existed before. Since the mid-1980s this legislation has been subject to the contradictory challenges of deregulation in employment markets in many countries and increased intervention in social affairs by the EC. It is always difficult to generalize within a European context that contains radically different employment structures, labour movements and approaches to legal intervention in collective bargaining, but the developing legislation is becoming broadly applicable throughout the Community.

The underlying reasons for these developments in individual labour law are clear enough. In Spain, Portugal and Greece, political dictatorships were being replaced by new democracies which were committed to long-suppressed rights at work. Less traumatically, many northern European states found themselves with strong trade union movements founded on full employment and social democratic governments. Trade unionists were, directly or indirectly, part of government. Not surprisingly, the outcome of this was the establishment of collective agreements or labour laws that created or strengthened a framework of individual employment protection. A third factor was the expansion of the EC and the gradual development of its social (as opposed to economic) functions. This occurred most significantly in the field of equal opportunities from the time of the Directives in this area in the mid-1970s.

The retreat from this high-point of individual labour law has been uneven and sometimes contradictory. The intended deregulation of employment relationships has sometimes only been achieved by an increase in government intervention. Furthermore, as individual nations have sought to remove controls in areas such as atypical employment, the EC has introduced measures to increase them. Both the approaches are justified by the argument that they will encourage the expansion of employment.

In this chapter we will look at four distinctive areas of the individual employment relationship which have been significantly affected by the changes in labour law and which are important areas of human resource management. The development of a framework of equal opportunities legislation has been common in Western European nations and it has been particularly stimulated by the EC's interventions. In no other area of employment law has Community policy been as important or as effective. However, its actions have been largely confined to differences in sex. Disability has been the subject of action programmes rather than legal intervention and the question of race has been largely ignored.

Retirement policy has also been affected by equal opportunity legislation but significant differences remain between European countries on such basic issues as retirement ages, the level of pensions and flexible retirement practices.

Individual job security provisions also vary considerably between European states and these are becoming increasingly challenged through the expansion of atypical employment contracts. Constraints on employers' ability to dismiss have been reduced in the belief, as Vranken (1986, p. 146) succinctly puts it, 'that hiring can somehow be stimulated by facilitating the process of firing'.

Finally, the issue of part time and temporary employment that we discussed in the first chapter is returned to in relation to labour law. Again we find a wide variety of European practice, particularly in relation to temporary contracts. The United Kingdoms's longstanding lack of regulation in this field is in marked contrast to many other Community States and will be most powerfully challenged by increased EC intervention.

In this and the next chapter we will look broadly at the developments in each of these areas in Europe generally before proceeding to review the role of the EC and developments in the United Kingdom.

Equal Opportunities in Europe

The area of equal opportunities has been one of considerable significance for Europe and especially the Community States. Broadly construed, the term can be used to cover a wide range of disadvantaged groups including black and disabled workers, and those from particular religious denominations or with particular sexual orientations. The list could go on to include different regions and different sections of the unemployed as well as the young and old. In practice, the concept of equal opportunity has been most widely and significantly applied in relation to gender. Even more specifically, policy development has focused on the intertwined issues of equal pay and sex discrimination in employment. It is therefore on these two issues that we focus in this section of the chapter and we will deal with other aspects of sex inequalities elsewhere (for example, in the section on retirement). However, we begin with brief discussions on the areas of disability and racism.

Disability

The problems of definition and different, or non-existent, systems of registration make calculations about the numbers of disabled people in Europe very difficult. However, a conservative estimate would seem to suggest a figure of 30 million in the EC alone (*European Industrial Relations Review*, October 1987, p. 15). Most European States have a framework of law which covers the employment of disabled people although it must be recognized that their employment prospects cannot be divorced from their other conditions of life and, particularly, their integration into local communities. It is also important to note that the law in this area requires enforcement. Thus, in 1988, France reduced its system of employment quotas from 10 per cent to 6 per cent in order to try to increase compliance (*European Industrial Relations Review*, August 1988, p. 18). In the United Kingdom, if all organizations were to attempt to fulfil their quotas there would not be enough registered disabled people available.

Quotas are a significant aspect of the law on disability with a number of Western European States setting legally enforceable target figures. These range from 2 per cent in Spain to as high as 15 per cent in Italy (*European Industrial Relations Review*, August 1988, p. 17). Attempts have also been made by the EC to establish a Community-wide figure of 5 per cent but so far without success. In some countries organizations may be allowed to withdraw from quota schemes but this often requires them to pay equivalent sums of money into State support programmes for the disabled. The 'stick' of the quota legislation is often supported by the 'carrot' of government grants to support the employment of the disabled. These may include payments for training, the adaptation of workplaces, wage subsidies or, even, in Denmark, income support for a disabled person's helper. In addition, free advisory services are often available.

Perhaps more controversially, a small number of EC States have legal restrictions specifically related to the dismissal of disabled workers. In the Federal Republic of Germany, for example, dismissal cannot take place without the consent of the agency responsible for the disabled and no less than four weeks' notice must be given. 'It is often argued that employers would rather pay the fine for not complying with their recruitment quota than recruit workers whom it will be very difficult to dismiss' (ibid., p. 18). This again highlights the point about the importance of enforcement and it could be argued that success is more likely to stem from positive action than punitive legislation.

Racism

At first sight it might appear odd that racism has not received the same attention in Europe as sex discrimination. As we saw in chapter 1, there are significant non-European populations in many European States, particularly those with colonial histories. However, unlike in the United Kingdom, many non-European nationals are working on a 'guest worker' basis rather than as settled immigrants. This has commonly led to an effectively second class legal status, as such workers fall outside legislation covering permanent residents. The development of the Single Market in the EC, while encouraging the free movement of the citizens of Member States, may also further restrict the rights of the remaining 'guest workers' as well as reduce migrant entry into the Community.

The United Kingdom's past policies on citizenship for members of the Commonwealth have led to the development of settled immigrant populations and the growth of ethnic minority group populations with full British citizenship. This in turn has led to the introduction of a comprehensive legal framework covering race relations which is like no other in Europe. However, some countries do have much wider general provisions on discrimination than exist in the United Kingdom.

These broader statements either implicitly or explicitly refer to race and are often based on international conventions established by the United Nations and the International Labour Organization (ILO). Thus, Article Five of the United Nations' Declaration of Human Rights instructs governments to 'prohibit and to eliminate racial discrimination in all its forms and to guarantee the right of everyone, without distinction as to race, colour, or national or ethnic origin, to equality before the law'. ILO Convention 111 broadens the scope of discrimination to include 'religion, political opinion, national extraction or social origin'. Similar formulations are to be found in the Council of Europe's Social Charter although the Social Charter of the European Community confines itself to sex discrimination and has no specific formulation on anti-racism.

These basic international rights not to be discriminated against may already be incorporated into national constitutions or statute law. For example, in Spain, the 1980 Workers' Statute explicitly forbids discrimination on the basis of 'social origin, marital status, race, social condition, religious or political ideas, relationships to other employees in the enterprise or language' (Olea and Rodriguez-Sanduo, 1985, p. 99). The major area in which these rights become operational in many EC countries is in the area of dismissal where termination of employment solely on discriminatory grounds will invariably be unlawful.

In spite of the clear anti-racist intent of legislation in many European States, the absence of a detailed framework of law on the model of sex discrimination will inevitably restrict the opportunity of ethnic minority groups to gain redress for discriminatory employment practices. In addition, the legislation will be more effective if support agencies are created, as they have been in relation to sex discrimination in most of Western Europe. Finally, there is a need to create positive employment policies such as are growing in relation to sex discrimination. One example of such practice is in the Netherlands where an agreement between the Central Employment Board and the Labour Foundation has set a five-year target for the creation of 60,000 new jobs in industry for workers from minority groups (*MISEP*, Summer 1991, p. 12).

Equal treatment

For some European countries such as Italy and the Federal Republic of Germany, the concept of equal rights and, hence, equal pay has been a long standing, if little used, part of their constitutions. However, since the Second World War, the concept of sex equality has become enshrined in international law and this has provided the basis for legislation in Europe. The most significant developments in EC States have been since the mid-1970s when national laws were brought into line with Community Directives. In general, the EC States have followed the Community initiative and introduced or strengthened equal treatment legislation. For instance, Denmark introduced an Equal Treatment Act in 1978; Spain incorporated the issue into its 1980 Workers' Statute; Ireland introduced an Employment Equality Act in 1977 and the Federal Republic of Germany incorporated European Directives into its own law in 1980. In some nations where collective agreements are legally enforceable, such as in Belgium, equality clauses have been included in them. Thus, sex discrimination legislation stemming from EC Directives is pervasive throughout the Community countries.

There is, however, a difference between the law and its implementation. The framing of the legislation generally makes action under it an essentially individual act. However, equal opportunities agencies have now been established in all of the EC nations and they can assist individuals in making complaints. In addition, a number of countries have a well-established system of labour inspectors who may take up discrimination cases.

> Both in Belgium and Greece the inspectors may take action even though no individual has complained . . . This system of inspectors receiving and investigating complaints with the possibility of a criminal prosecution to which the complainant may join her action for compensation, has much to commend it. It removes the burden from the individual of having to face her employer alone and leaves it to experts with adequate powers to collect the evidence. (Corcoran, 1988, p. 60)

Having said that, difficulties remain. The inspectors' normal workload is more likely to be in the areas of pay and health and safety than equal opportunities. This lack of expertise can be a significant constraining factor and Ireland has adopted a system of equality officers. There also needs to be adequate numbers of inspectors but even this is no guarantee of success. Corcoran notes that no cases had been initiated by labour inspectors in Greece for example.

A further problem is the remedy available to claimants even if they are successful in pursuing claims. Redmond (1985, p. 135) has suggested that, for example in the case of Ireland, 'where a claimant succeeds in proving discrimination she/he is likely to receive little more than a nominal amount'. These awards may be higher if the discrimination is related to dismissal but this must be weighed against the potential costs of bringing a case.

It is clear that the range of legal constraints has neither eliminated discrimination nor introduced equal pay. Perhaps the major difficulties are summed up by Treu's (1985) comments on Italy.

> The formal equalisation of job evaluation between men and women does not prevent women from being in fact under evaluated or classified mostly in the lowest paid jobs, also due to their lower average professional qualification. Discrimination is even more serious taking into account the fact that homework and other forms of peripheral work (are) under paid and under protected (and) are mainly done by women. Equality of treatment is also impaired by the substantial inequality of professional, educational, and occupational opportunities for women ... The well known difficulty of counteracting and proving discrimination ... is increased by the fact that Italian law (including Act No. 903) and jurisprudence still seems to ignore the concept of indirect discrimination and appear reluctant to admit 'objective' evidence of discrimination (e.g. based on statistical data). Indeed, the application of Act 903 in its entirety has so far been tested minimally in the courts and probably has not been pushed by the unions. (p. 71)

Current developments in equal opportunities in many European countries focus on the development of positive programmes and policies sometimes promoted by further legislation. In March 1991 the Italian Parliament adopted new laws on positive action which established a national commission for implementing equal opportunity. Positive action programmes can be initiated by employers, or trade unions, or on a joint basis and particular attention is focused on vocational training, reducing occupational segregation and eliminating differences in working conditions (*European Industrial Relations Review*, May 1991). At the organizational level there are positive action programmes being developed in the Federal Republic of Germany (*European Industrial Relations Review*, November and December 1987) and in the United Kingdom where the emphasis is on equal opportunities policies. In Switzerland, often noted for its quiescence in industrial relations, a one-day strike was held to highlight sex discrimination in Swiss society (*European Industrial Relations Review*, April 1991).

Equal opportunities at the European level

As we have suggested, much of the law in Europe in the area of discrimination is based on international conventions, EC Directives or European Court rulings.

In relation to disability, the Commission of the EC has seen its proposal for a 5 per cent quota rejected but it has established three Action Programmes for the disabled, one which ran from 1983–7, a second from 1988–91 and a third running from 1992–6. These have been concerned with a number of issues which relate to employment. They include the raising and harmonization of standards across the Community and the development of training programmes to encourage vocational integration. In addition, a Disabled Bureau has been established to monitor developments and encourage action (Brewster and Teague, 1989, p. 73).

In respect of racism, there has been a growing awareness in the EC States of the dangers of a re-emerging fascist movement and this led to a declaration on racism and xenophobia in 1985. This statement noted the particular difficulties of migrant communities, such as high unemployment levels, and condemned all forms of racism. Little real progress was made and in 1990 a Resolution of the Council of the European Communities was issued which, among other things, called for the 'resolute application of laws aimed at preventing or curbing discrimination or xenophobic acts and the preparation of such laws by those member states which have not yet done so' (Council of the EC, 1990).

In terms of equal pay between men and women, the United Nations and the ILO have well-established conventions in this area. For example, ILO convention 100 establishes 'equal remuneration for men and women workers for work of equal value'.

At the foundation of the EC, Article 119 of the Treaty of Rome established that 'men and women should receive equal pay for equal work'. However, this was as much a matter of political expediency as social principle. Byre (1988, p. 21) suggests that 'the equal pay provisions were originally prompted by economic factors and, in particular, a concern to ensure that competition in the Member States was not distorted by the employment of women at lower rates than men'. Furthermore, according to Hoskyns (1988, p. 38), 'in response to the French demand for a broad range of social issues to be included in the Treaty, the German delegation agreed to equal pay (and a small number of other provisions) presumably on the understanding that the Articles in the Treaty were not likely to be directly applicable and that equal pay was in any case covered by the German constitution'. The Germans were later to find themselves mistaken on the point of 'direct applicability'.

As well as these political reservations, it is also important to note that Article 119 does not, unlike its international predecessors, refer to equal value. This omission eventually led, in 1975, to a Directive on equal pay which was guaranteed 'for the same work or for work to which equal value is attributed'. This Directive became part of a process by which most Member States reformed or introduced laws on equal pay in line with the Community principles. However, the existence of laws does not guarantee their effectiveness and while Community legislation has clearly eliminated such obvious anomalies as womens' rates in collective agreements, it has not abolished inequalities in pay (see chapter 6). There are several reasons for this, some of which are inherent in the legislation itself and some that are beyond its current scope. Particular problems are the individualistic nature of the law, its complexity, and the time and cost it takes to bring a case. This means that the law is often little used in the Member States. However, of greater significance than the inadequacies of the law is the wider position of women in society – impaired access to education and training, their role in the family and a position in the labour market which offers them part time low status employment in occupational ghettos are all inimical to equal pay.

In order to tackle these much broader issues of discrimination, most Western European countries have introduced legislation on equal opportunities. Again, the foundation for this has been through international law. As we saw in relation to equal pay, United Nations charters and ILO conventions have been important sources of equality legislation. In the case of discrimination they take in elements such as race, religion and political opinion that go beyond gender. These general principles have been adopted by EC States but in the case of sex discrimination they have been expanded by the Community's 1976 Equal Treatment Directive. This requires countries to eliminate 'all discrimination whatsoever on grounds of sex either directly or indirectly by reference in particular to marital and family status' (Article 2). They had also to ensure that judicial remedies were available to anyone who thought themselves discriminated against on these grounds.

The remedies available have not always been adequate enough to encourage claims. However, there may be an improvement following a recent European Court decision in a German case. Awards in the former Federal Repubic had been derisory and effectively restricted to the costs of bringing a case (Weiss, 1985). An action was referred to the European Court which decided that 'although Member States had discretion as to what kind of sanctions they applied, these should ensure real and effective legal protection and have a genuine deterrent effect on the employer' (Hoskyns, 1988, p. 44). This had the effect of stimulating the German court to award damages amounting to six months' pay plus interest at 4 per cent.

The whole area of proof can add to the difficulties of winning claims and different legal traditions place the burden on different parties. The area of indirect discrimination is particularly notorious in this respect. Byre is co-ordinator of a European working party on this issue and she notes that 'no generally agreed definition has yet emerged' (Byre, 1988a, p. 29). However, she adds that there are a range of areas where indirect discrimination can occur including recruitment, promotion, working conditions, training and so on. The EC has now indicated that the burden of proof should be shifted clearly to the employer and it is likely that it will continue to take a proactive role in the whole area of discrimination.

Equal opportunities and the British perspective

If any area of European Community labour law has had a significant impact on British employee relations then it is the area of equal opportunities. Indeed, it is the most significant area of individual labour legislation in the EC. However, it is important to place this in context. The greatest impact has come in the field of terms and conditions of employment and, in particular, in relation to equal pay for equal value and pensions (which we discuss later). In the field of race relations, the Community has developed little in respect of employment policy and Britain's own legislation remains the most significant in Europe. On the other hand, the United Kingdom has not followed other European countries in developing legal constraints on discrimination covering areas such as religion and political opinion except, in the former case, in Northern Ireland. Britain's unwritten constitution and range of civil liberties, developed through the courts, distinguishes it from the more formally constitutional approach of other European countries.

In the area of disability the British framework has again been relatively immune from European influence. The Disabled Persons (Employment) Act 1944 which established the employment quota system in the UK and was clearly a response to the problem of injured war veterans. Since then, the EC has developed its two action programmes on disability in which the UK has, necessarily, participated. The impact of this is difficult to judge, but the Commission has criticized the failure of Community States to adopt a universal 5 per cent quota system.

As we have seen, it is in relation to gender issues that the EC itself has been most active and this inevitably has had the most impact on the UK. However, the start was not a particularly auspicious one. Britain's Equal Pay Act of 1970 was introduced before entry into the EC. As Brewster and Teague (1989, p. 164) observe, 'European Community legislation had little impact on this decision to legislate, or on the substance of individual clauses of the Act. If any extra-national influence was present it came from the United States, where general anti-discrimination legislation and programmes had been in operation for some time'. In 1970, European law in this area was itself restricted and it was not until the 1975 Equal Pay Directive that the concept of equal value was unambiguously introduced. This, more than any other Directive, has had a direct impact on British equality law.

In 1981, the Commission of the European Communities began proceedings against the British government for being in breach of the Treaty of Rome on equal pay by not implementing Article 1 of the 1975 Directive. The UK's defence rested on an interpretation of the 1970 Act that 'work rated as equivalent' covered claims of equal value. In 1982, the European Court of Justice ruled against the UK and the government was required to introduce amending legislation to its Equal Pay Act. The Equal Pay (Amendment) Regulations came into force from the beginning of 1984. However, the change was still not without controversy and the House of Lords' approval was subject to what Redmond (1986, p. 492) describes as 'to say the least, an unusual reservation'. It accepted the regulations subject to an amendment indicating that the regulations did 'not adequately reflect' the European Court ruling.

In spite of this, the equal value amendment has provided the basis for a significant number of claims in the UK. By June 1991, 185 claims had been brought, many against large employers such as the NHS, the electricity supply industry and British Aerospace (*Bargaining Report*, June 1991).

The impact of the EC on Britain's sex discrimination legislation has been more limited. The European Court has, however, ruled that the Sex Discrimination Act was out of line with the European Equal Treatment Directive in relation to small businesses and private households. The 1986 Sex Discrimination Act was a direct response to this, and private households and companies with less than five people are now included within the terms of the anti-discrimination laws (with some minor exceptions). The Act also declared null and void any discriminatory clauses in collective agreements.

In practical terms, the impact of European equal pay and rights legislation may have been as much in the climate they have created than simply in the legal cases. As Byre (1988a, p. 163) indicates, 'it seems clear that the external influence of EEC legislation and cases, as well as the more direct influence of UK law, have contributed to establishing a new climate for equality initiatives'. In this respect, the positive action programmes being adopted by many British companies and public authorities are likely to provide the most significant road forward.

Retirement in Europe

As we discussed in the first chapter, there is a growing elderly population in Europe. This means a growing retired population making increased demands on State welfare services. It is not our intention here to make a detailed examination of social security systems related to pensioners but there are a number of retirement issues that impinge on the employment relationship. In particular, there is the question of retirement age and the growing flexibility in this connection. In the recent past, countries have used early retirement as a means of reducing workforces. The future is likely to see a decline in young people entering the labour market and increased opportunities for older workers. However, there is no certainty that the demand and supply of skills will necessarily match. Early retirees from industries such as steel and shipbuilding will not have work experience that translates directly into commerce or the personal services sector of the economy.

Another retirement issue which has direct implications for the development of human resource management policies is that of equal opportunities in pensions and there have been significant decisions at EC level affecting this area.

Finally, we consider the financial aspects of pensions. While much of this is beyond our scope, the level at which pensions are set and the support which employers provide for pensioners will have a significant impact on retirement decisions. Each of these areas is becoming increasingly important for negotiators. In 1988, the ETUC established a Pensioners' Committee to campaign for increased rights, including a minimum pension level and the ability to maintain a decent standard of living. The European Community Social Charter recognizes these demands and adds that, 'any person who has reached retirement age but who is not entitled to a pension or who does not have other means of subsistence must be entitled to sufficient resources and to medical and social assistance specifically suited to his needs' (Clause 25).

Retirement ages

As can be seen from table 5.1, there is a broad range of retirement ages in Europe although the statutory or collectively agreed age is by no means necessarily the effective age. The lowest age is 55 for women in private sector employment in Italy, and the highest is 67 both for men and women in Norway and Denmark, and 70 for private sector workers in Iceland. The Italian position is likely to change because pensions absorb a high proportion of social security payments and government austerity measures in 1992 proposed a staged increase in the pensionable age of women to 65. The variation in age between the European countries is higher for women than it is for men although 60 remains the most common, being adopted by eight of the twenty countries in the table. The most common retirement age for men is clearly 65, being adopted in thirteen of the twenty countries. It is interesting to note that only half of the countries adopt the same model as the United Kingdom and have a differential retirement age for men and women although, apart from Switzerland, they are all EC members.

In general, these statutory ages set maxima for entitlement to State benefits and leave discretion to occupational schemes. There will be employees who work beyond the State pension ages, particularly where self-employment gives them the flexibility to do so, and those whose working lives effectively end before then. There appears to be considerable variation in the economic activity of the elderly across Europe and it is not straightforwardly related to retirement age. Tables 5.2 and 5.3 indicate the range of activity in

Table 5.1　Retirement age in public pension schemes

	Pensionable age Men (Women)	Retirement Late	Retirement Early
Austria	65 (60)	–	After 35 years of service; 60 (55) unemployed; 59 (54) long-term unemployed.
Belgium	65 (60)	70 (65)	After 45 years of service; 60 (55) reduced pension.
Denmark	67	Up to 70	50–60 unemployed.
Finland	65	Possible	60 reduced pension.
France	60	Possible	55 solidarity contract after $37\frac{1}{2}$ years' contributions.
Germany	65	Up to 67	After 35 years' contributions; 60 unemployed; 58 reduced pension.
Greece	65 (60)	Possible	62 (57) after 30 years' contributions; 60 (55) arduous work, women or reduced pension.
Ireland	65	Possible	–
Italy	60 (55)	Up to 65	After 35 years' contributions; 55 (50) redundant workers.
Luxembourg	65	Possible	After 40 years' contributions, less for miners; 57 redundant and shiftworkers or reduced pension.
Netherlands	65	Possible	–
Norway	67	Up to 70	60–63 seafarers, fishermen, forestry workers.
Portugal	65 (62)	Up to 70	60 reduced pension.
Spain	65	–	64 solidarity contract; 62 part-time, arduous work.
Sweden	65	Possible	60 reduced pension, part-time.
Switzerland	65 (62)	Possible	–
UK	65 (60)	Up to 75 (65)	64 (59) job release programme.

Source: adapted from International Labour Organization, 1988b

Table 5.2 Labour force participation of older workers

	Year	Men		Women		Total	
		55–64	65 or over	55–64	65 or over	55–64	65 or over
Finland	1962	83.2	19.8	53.6	5.2	66.7	10.7
	1975	62.3	10.3	44.4	2.8	52.0	5.8
	1985	57.8	10.6	52.9	4.8	55.1	7.0
France	1962	80.3	31.1	40.2	12.0	59.3	19.1
	1975	68.9	13.9	35.9	5.8	51.5	9.0
	1985	50.1	5.3	31.0	2.2	40.1	3.4
Germany	1962	83.0	23.2	28.2	7.9	52.9	14.0
	1975	68.1	10.8	24.8	4.5	42.4	6.9
	1985	57.5	5.2	23.9	2.5	38.4	3.4
Italy	1960	60.5	30.0	17.9	8.5	37.4	18.1
	1975	42.4	10.4	8.5	2.1	24.7	5.7
	1984	38.2	8.9	10.5	2.1	23.5	5.0
Netherlands	1975	73.0	8.0	14.3	1.8	42.2	4.5
	1984	56.5	4.2	15.8	1.0	35.2	2.3
Sweden	1963	89.6	43.3	39.9	10.9	64.1	25.7
	1975	82.0	19.9	49.1	6.1	65.6	12.6
	1985	76.0	11.0	59.9	3.2	67.7	6.8
UK	1960	94.2	25.1	28.6	5.6	58.8	12.9
	1975	87.8	15.8	40.3	4.9	62.8	9.1
	1985	66.4	7.6	34.1	3.2	49.7	4.9

Source: Euzeby, 1989, p. 14

Europe and beyond. It is notable that in all countries (with the exception of Sweden) the extent of older workers' participation in economic activity has been declining. However, there remain significant differences between nations. For example, the labour force activity rates in 1989 clearly show the Danes to have the highest level of older workers. The United Kingdom also has employment levels for these age groups that are significantly above the EC figure. Belgium and Luxembourg clearly have low levels of activity and it is significant that the EC figure as a whole only just crosses the 50 per cent level for those aged 55 or above. The general European

Table 5.3   Activity rates by age (1989)

	Years		
	55–59	*60–64*	*65–69*
Belgium	34.2	12.1	2.0
Denmark	72.6	37.5	16.5
France	51.4	16.3	4.5
Germany	58.9	21.3	4.6
Greece	51.2	33.8	14.4
Ireland	49.5	35.4	15.5
Italy	42.2	21.2	8.0
Luxembourg	35.4	13.0	–
Netherlands	44.1	15.4	6.4
Portugal	55.2	38.0	23.5
Spain	48.7	31.2	6.5
UK	67.0	38.0	10.8
EC 12	52.7	25.2	7.7

Source: Labour Force Survey, 1989, EC Commission

trend is for the effective retirement age to be less than the statutory age as employees take early retirement options, become unemployed or suffer from long-term sickness or disability.

Early retirement

Overall, a considerable amount of flexibility is becoming characteristic of retirement in Europe. Some of this is of a voluntary nature and relates to personal choices about early or late retirement. However, in other cases, organizations have chosen early retirement as a mechanism for reducing the workforce. It is important to note that these schemes may not reflect permanent changes in human resource management policies. They may, rather, be short-term expedients to deal with particular economic requirements. Thus, they might be a specific response to the need to shed labour and be restricted to specific groups of workers over relatively short time-scales. In some industries such as European shipbuilding, these schemes may be enhanced by State support for redundancy payments and income support (Stirling and Bridgford, 1985, p. 13).

The general decline in economic activity for Europe's elderly has been paralleled by the expansion of State supported early or partial retirement policies. There are a number of underlying reasons for these developments. Firstly, they may be part of a social response to the growing pressure for a shorter working lifetime. Trade unions in Europe have developed similar campaigns for the shorter working week as well as making claims for longer holidays and even sabbatical leave or career breaks schemes. Secondly, early retirement schemes may simply be a short-term measure to alleviate unemployment problems in specific industrial communities where plant closures have had a disproportionate effect on job loss. Thirdly, schemes may be designed to influence the labour market by the creation of jobs through retirement. Fourthly, EC Directives, particularly on equality, may encourage Member States to review their pension provisions. Finally, some schemes which allow for phased retirement can be regarded as attempts to ease the process of moving from full time employment to complete retirement.

Numerous options on early retirement have been developed in European States for one or other of the above reasons or combination of a number of them. One of the earliest attempts to introduce some flexibility into State schemes came in Sweden in 1976. This allowed men and women within five years of retirement to move on to part time work and to receive a pension of 65 per cent of the earnings that they lost (*European Industrial Relations Review*, April 1987). This initially popular scheme lost much of its momentum when the level of payments was reduced to 50 per cent and employment opportunities declined. However, it provided an important initial impetus for other schemes and, by the middle of the 1980s, the United Kingdom, the Federal Republic of Germany, France and Belgium were among countries that had schemes that allowed early retirement where workers were replaced by someone on the unemployed register. However, the schemes never had more than a minimal impact on the then historically high levels of unemployment and they have since been abandoned or significantly changed. In France, for example, new laws from January 1988 allowed workers to opt for phased retirement through part time employment without a replacement being employed (*European Industrial Relations Review*, May 1988).

Many other countries now have early retirement provisions established either through State schemes or collective agreements. These schemes are increasingly making statutory retirement ages irrelevant for many workers. In some countries there are special provisions for workers in particular industries or occupations – for instance, in iron and steel (Austria and Luxembourg), the police, prison and fire services (the United Kingdom), fishing, mining and the merchant navy (Portugal) and dangerous and unhealthy work (Greece). However, the tendency is to extend these provisions into other sectors and general schemes are now becoming more common. There are legal provisions on early retirement in such countries as Austria, Belgium, France, West Germany, Greece, Spain and Sweden. In a number of other countries these matters are normally settled through collective bargaining and there are a range of agreements in the Netherlands, Italy, Ireland and the UK.

The level of pensions

Making accurate comparisons across Europe about the level of pension payments is fraught with difficulties. Changing exchange rates, even within the European Monetary System, can distort figures and there are inevitable differences in purchasing power (see chapter 6). Furthermore, the overall package of benefits for the retired may be made up differently in different countries. There are also different systems for financing schemes and a variety of mechanisms for calculating payments. Thus, in what follows, we can only give broad guidelines as to general European practice.

The first thing to be considered is the coverage of State pension arrangements. The most significant point in this respect is that eligibility is related to contributions made during a working lifetime. For the majority of workers on traditional open ended full time work contracts with an employer this is a straightforward process. Contributions are simply deducted at source and commonly increased by employers' payments. However, many employees will be on atypical contracts for all or part of their working lives, many will be self-employed and some may never work, at least in the 'official' economy. All this can lead to special provisions for dependants, and those with no contributions or reduced ones. Nevertheless, most States run what would be generally regarded as 'open' schemes with universal applicability based on contributions, although in many cases a minimum contribution period is established ranging from three years in Denmark and Norway to 15 years in Austria and Spain.

The pensions themselves are often a combination of a minimum payment coupled with additional payments related to past earnings. It is these figures that are most often cited in pension campaigns but which are also the most susceptible to distortion. To make only the most obvious point, higher pensions may simply be related to higher contributions. In other words they have been paid for by deferred income. There are also considerable complexities involved in calculating pensions when schemes relate to both contributions and past pay in order to calculate earnings related benefits. However, in most European countries there is provision in State pension schemes for a guaranteed minimum payment. Even where this is not the case, social security systems are normally there to catch those who fall through the net.

In addition to this basic amount it is common for there to be earnings related payments. These can vary widely across the EC and the statistics must be treated with caution. In particular, some of the poorer Community States have high percentage figures for pension payments but these must be related to the generally lower levels of pay when making comparisons in cash terms. It also needs to be borne in mind that these are generally maximum payments in return for complete contribution records. In Spain, the national scheme offers the opportunity for certain former employees to match their previous average earnings at the 100 per cent level. In Portugal the figure is 75 per cent and in Greece it may be as high as 70 per cent for low paid workers. In the northern European States the percentages are usually lower but the standards of living are generally higher. The French scheme offers payments at the level of 50 per cent of national average earnings. In most other countries payments are related to the past earnings of the individual pension recipient although the earnings reference period used can make a considerable difference to the amount received. Calculations may be based on the best years of earnings (Portugal and Sweden), average earnings (Belgium and Finland) or earnings during a fixed final period of employment (the last two years in Greece and the last ten years in Austria).

Bearing in mind the reservations we have made about comparisons, table 5.4 is indicative of both the increase in pensions between 1984 and 1990 (with the exception of Greece) and the differences in payments. Thus, even with the high link with past earnings, Portugal's pension payments are the lowest in the EC and Greece is only one place higher. The United Kingdom stands at the mid-point but it is clearly some distance behind the 'market

Table 5.4   Old age and survivors's benefits: amounts per person in 1984 purchasing power standards

	1984	1990
Denmark	10.446	11.195
France	7.976	8.979
Germany	10.512	11.148
Greece	5.967	5.695
Ireland	5.366	5.920
Italy	5.655	6.781
Luxembourg	12.293	14.286
Netherlands	10.534	10.643
Portugal	2.333	2.456
Spain	5.513	6.189
UK	6.675	6.856
EC	7.269	8.008

[1] The base for these computations is the total population above the legal retirement age.
[2] Purchasing power standard is a number against which each national currency has an exchange value that takes into account the purchasing power of that currency. One PPS equals one ECU adjusted by purchasing power.

Source: Hutsebaut, 1989, p. 15

leaders' in Luxembourg, Denmark and the Federal Republic of Germany.

The final point to be made about pension levels is the arrangements countries make to adjust the payments. There are two significant factors in this respect: whether pensions are raised in line with earnings or prices and how often the adjustments are made. The Federal Republic of Germany and the Netherlands have made a link with wage changes but a link to prices is the more common approach. In the United Kingdom the Conservative government controversially shifted the link from earnings to prices and reduced payments as a consequence. It also has the longest period between regular adjustments with its annual changes. Six-monthly adjustments are made in France, Denmark and the Netherlands, and in Greece there are three annual alterations.

The comparisons of basic pensions arrangements is complex enough but further difficulties arise when account is taken of other benefits that are either exclusively available to pensioners or most likely to be claimed by them. Health care, home heating and travel benefits are perhaps the most commonplace but there are a variety of other arrangements often provided by local authorities rather than national governments. In Denmark, for example, there are systems of holiday and house removal grants, free installation and telephone charges and a 50 per cent reduction in the television licence fee. France offers free television licences. Ireland and Greece offer reduced charge or free access to further education and in the Netherlands an 'over 65' card gives reductions on public transport, and cultural, educational and leisure facilities. Many of these facilities are also available in the United Kingdom although they are often funded by local authorities so that their distribution is uneven. It is clearly impossible to quantify accurately such provision at a European level when it must be doubtful whether nations themselves can provide reliable data. This makes the development of uniformity in EC pension provision a particularly difficult process and it is not surprising to discover that the Community's involvement has been largely confined to equal opportunities issues.

Retirement and the British perspective

It is clear from what we have said that, in general terms, Western European countries have developed their pension provisions in isolation from each other and in line with their own historical traditions. However, in one important respect, the EC has played a decisive role, particularly in Britain, and we treat the role of the Community and its impact on the United Kingdom together in this section.

As we have seen, the area of equal opportunities has been a significant one for the Community in relation to equal pay and sex discrimination. Occupational pensions have now been brought within the scope of EC law and important judgements have been specifically related to British cases. The most significant have been in relation to the retirement ages of both men and women and have led to changes in United Kingdom legislation.

The importance of EC law rested on the crucial question of whether references to equal pay in the Treaty of Rome and the subsequent equal pay Directive could cover the 'deferred pay' of a pension. In the earliest cases, while there was some success for those supporting this view, the interpretation was not significantly clarified. In a case against British Rail the European Court of Justice held that providing free travel for retired male employees but not for females was discriminatory. However, of greater importance was the case brought by Marshall against the Southampton and South West Hampshire Health Authority. The woman involved claimed that her dismissal from employment was discriminatory because, although she had reached the statutory retirement age for women, men could remain at work until the higher age of 65. Although State social security provisions remain outside the European Court's jurisdiction, the matter was dealt with as an employment issue and the Court ruled that discrimination existed. It said that Miss Marshall was discriminated against because she was dismissed solely on the grounds that she had reached the State's pension age when that was less for women than men. However, the Court also ruled that its decision could only be relied on in actions against Member States as employers, as they were under a direct obligation to observe the Treaty of Rome. This loophole for private sector employers was later closed by the British government in the 1986 Sex Discrimination Act.

In a further case, Mrs James, an employee of Barclays Bank, challenged the rules of her employer on retirement. The bank had amended its provisions on pension ages on two occasions, both to Mrs James' detriment. Firstly, the bank changed its retirement age to 60 for all staff from 1973 but did not backdate the provision. Secondly, after the 1986 Act, it allowed men and women above a certain grade to carry on until they were 65 and again Mrs James was excluded. She successfully argued her case through the Industrial Tribunal system and Barclays eventually conceded that they would offer Mrs James her job back or pay compensation (*Financial Times*, 20 November 1990).

In the third case related to pensionable ages it was a man who claimed discrimination. Douglas Barber was employed by the Guardian Royal Exchange Assurance Group whose pension scheme gave benefits to men and women at different ages. Some benefits also became available on redundancy but, again, at different ages. When Mr Barber was made redundant, he received various payments but his pension was deferred for five years because he had not reached the age of 62 set by the scheme. Women were entitled to payment from the age of 55. The European Court of Justice said: 'it is undisputed that a woman in the same position as Mr Barber would have received an immediate retirement pension as well as the statutory redundancy payment and that the total value of those benefits would have been greater than those paid to Mr Barber' (*European Industrial Relations Review*, July 1990, p. 20). This decision makes it much clearer that the European Court considers pensions to be part of pay and, therefore, covered by Community legislation in that respect.

In a subsequent case involving redundancy pay it was a woman who was the beneficiary and, although the claim was ultimately settled out of court, it was clearly influenced by European rulings. The case related to redundancy legislation which had restricted payments to men under 65 and women under 60. Klare Levy was made redundant at the age of 63 and the Department of Employment was forced to make a payment of £4,500 in order not to become involved in a legal tangle with the Community (*The Guardian*, December 1990). The 1989 Employment Act abolished the old discriminatory element in redundancy payment legislation.

The expansion of the retired population in the EC has meant an increased focus on the development of policy in this area. 1993 has been designated the year of the elderly and the Community has introduced an action programme to increase awareness and develop policies and programmes. It is also likely that there will be further legislation although there may be hesitancy among some Member States in accepting more radical proposals. The Social Affairs, Employment and the Working Environment Committee of the European Parliament has suggested a number of amendments to the Commission's more cautious approach to legislation. For example, the Committee argues for one Directive on flexible retirement systems and another to guarantee a minimum social provision for pensioners to be set as a percentage of the average income of individual Member States (Doc EN/RR/95372). This is an approach which has been taken by pressure groups such as Age Concern which notes that figures of 50 per cent for married couples and 33 per cent for single people might be considered target figures. The Committee has also asked the Commission to submit proposals on the harmonization of pensions among the Community States. Underlying this approach is one argument based on social justice but another which regards the elderly as a resource rather than a burden and looks for opportunities to reduce their isolation and encourage greater integration and links with young people.

Atypical Employment

As we saw in chapter 1, atypical employment contracts are becoming increasingly commonplace in Europe. It is important to place this development in its context and reiterate that the majority of European employees remain on full time work contracts of indefinite duration. Nevertheless, the expansion of other forms of work relationships is occurring and European States are responding by revising their employment law, both as a response and as a stimulus to further growth. In the main, these changes have been related to part time employment, fixed-term contracts and temporary employment arranged through agencies. It is these developments that we explore here but there are several other employment practices that are developing more slowly but often outside the scope of legal regulation. Examples include, home-work, tele-working, subcontracting, job sharing, and on-call contracts. Regulation is further inhibited by the amount of such work taking place in the informal economy. A further influence on policy making relates to the question of whether the development of atypical work is either voluntary or simply the result of employers taking advantage of unemployment and a weakened trade union movement to develop flexible employment practices. At one end of the spectrum might be short-term contracts with little job security and no holiday or sickness entitlements and at the other there might be the opportunity for phased retirement based on part time employment with a partial pension.

Part time work

Specific legal regulation in relation to part time work is much less common in Western Europe than that related to temporary employment. In many cases this is simply because the law does not define part time work and it makes no distinctions between such employees and those in full time jobs. The most straightforward approach to defining part-timers would be to indicate that they are those workers employed for less than the normal hours. This definition has only been adopted explicitly and directly in the Federal Republic of Germany where the 1990 Employment Promotion Act refers to weekly hours that are less than those of comparable full time employees in the same company. Italy has taken a similar approach although it excludes agricultural workers and defines hours by reference to collective agreements. Even this is not without its problems and the ILO has suggested using 'substantially' shorter hours in order to avoid any overlap with full-timers. This still leaves us with the problem of defining 'substantial' and a number of European countries have adopted cut-off points. In France, part-timers are those employed for 80 per cent or less of the statutory or collectively agreed working week or month. In Spain, part time work is less than two-thirds of the normal hours for a day, week or month.

A different approach to part time work has been to define exclusions from State benefits or employment protection. In this case the focus shifts to minimum rather than maximum hours. For example, in the Netherlands employees must be employed for one-third of normal hours in order to be covered by minimum wage protection. In the United Kingdom, employment security and redundancy rights only become operative if workers are employed for a minimum number of hours. In Denmark, the Federal Republic of Germany and Ireland there are hours cut-off points below which employees do not make contributions to social security systems and ultimately receive reduced or no benefits. There may also be savings to employers in relation to their reduced contribution to schemes.

The lack of a definition in many European countries effectively means that no distinctions are made between full and part time employees in relation to terms and conditions of employment. Pay and benefits are calculated on a proportional basis and part-timers are normally covered by employment protection legislation. There are a few exceptions to this situation. For example, in Ireland part-timers need to work for at least 120 hours a month to qualify for annual leave. In France, national sick pay only becomes payable if part-timers have worked for at least 200 hours in the three months preceding the illness. In the Federal Republic of Germany, the rights to extra leave for mothers and single fathers do not apply to part-timers. However, the overall picture is one of proportionally equal rights for part time employees and, where they do not exist, European Court rulings and proposed EC Directives are restricting the differences between part and full time work.

Alongside the statutory protection there have emerged government policies and collective agreements which have encouraged voluntary movements towards part time employment. We noted earlier how some countries were adopting more flexible policies for early and phased retirement and this has implications for part time employment. In Italy and France, for example, phased retirement has been used as a mechanism for bringing new workers into employment through part time work. In effect the retirer and the new worker are 'job sharing'. Collective agreements have generated the same sort of option elsewhere in Western Europe. In the German chemical industry in 1985 an agreement was reached allowing employees over 58 to reduce their working week to 20 hours and receive compensation equivalent to 70 per cent of gross average basic pay over the previous six months. The Chemical Workers' Union estimated that this would give an average of 85 per cent of previous earnings (*European Industrial Relations Review*, May 1985).

Part time employment used positively and based on voluntary arrangements can make an important contribution to changing patterns of employment. The danger is that it is used to cut costs and increase flexibility at the expense of job security, and in situations where no other work options are available.

Fixed-term contracts

Temporary employment can cover a variety of forms of work which may be full or part time, regular according to seasons or irregular according to work demands. In broad terms, it is less common in Europe than part time employment and more likely to be regulated by law. There is a broad division of approach between those countries which regard temporary contracts as much like any others and leave them unregulated and those whose general starting point is to view temporary contracts as anomalies. There are some countries were legal provisions are long standing – for example, Dutch law dates from 1907, Greek from the 1920s and Italian from 1962. However, because fixed-term contract work, apart from in industries such as agriculture and building, is a relatively new phenomenon, and 'rare and exceptional up to the 1970s' (European Foundation for the Improvement of Living and Working Conditions, 1988, p. 39), most of the law dates from that period. Given the hostility of the trade unions to temporary work and their influence in that period, much of the early legislation was restrictive. As fixed-term contract work expands there is pressure for these restrictions to be eased.

The normal pattern for full time employment remains indefinite-term contracts and the extent of temporary working is generally much less than for part time employment. However, the more recent pattern is one of growth: 'in France, about 70 per cent of new recruitment in 1988 consisted of fixed duration relationships; in the Federal Republic of Germany, about one third of new recruitment in the private sector is limited in time. In Spain, in the first half of 1989, about 80 to 90 per cent of all recruitment from the register of unemployed was for a fixed duration' (Commission of the European Communities, 1990a, p. 11). Spain has by far the largest fixed-term contract sector within the Community and the legal limitations have imposed very little restraint on their use. Indeed, government measures to combat unemployment have encouraged the spread of temporary jobs. In what follows, we focus our attention on fixed-term contracts and then look briefly at temporary employment agencies in the next section.

There are three broad approaches that could be adopted to fixed-term contracts. The first is to apply no statutory restrictions and to leave them to be negotiated between employers and workers. The opposite extreme is to ban temporary contracts completely or, more commonly, to allow them only in exceptional and carefully defined circumstances. The third approach is to allow the development of fixed-term contracts but to place restrictions on their operation. In reality the third approach has grown out of the second as temporary employment has expanded and a number of countries were reviewing their laws in the second half of the 1980s. Trade unions too, which had long been hostile to insecure employment, were being forced to accept new collective agreements or amended laws.

The countries least affected by change were those that had begun with the most minimal restrictions. The United Kingdom and Ireland have the least regulations and in Denmark there is little control once arrangements have been agreed with the trade unions. In the Netherlands there are few restrictions other than the rules on renewal and the obligation to observe normal terms and conditions of employment for all temporary workers with contracts of one-third or more of normal hours.

At the other end of this spectrum are countries such as Italy, Greece, the Federal Republic of Germany and Portugal which have lists of the circumstances in which fixed-term contracts can be agreed. These are, most commonly, for seasonal work, to cover for temporary absences, to provide for special skills and to cover short-term projects or increases in work. It follows from this approach that time limits are established for fixed-term contracts as well as regulations concerning their renewal. However, this is by no means universal.

In Spain the maximum duration of a renewed fixed-term contract is 36 months, in Luxembourg it is 24 months, in France and the Federal Republic of Germany (under the Employment Promotion Act) it is 18 months and in Italy there are maxima of 6 and 12 months in the private and public sectors respectively. However, in Italy's case alternative laws allow for greater freedom when fixed-term contracts are arranged through collective agreements. Initial contracts are normally made for less than the maximum period and in some countries there is a maximum number of renewals. In Greece, for example, two are allowed, in Sweden it is just one and the French have also reduced their provisions from two to one renewal.

Fixed-term contracts, by their nature, have known dates at which they will end but most countries allow for earlier termination where there is mutual consent or on the grounds of 'gross misconduct' by the employee. In France, Spain and Portugal there are extra payments at the end of a contract. In Spain this is equivalent to one day's pay per month worked, in Portugal it is two day's pay and in France a payment worth 6 per cent of the gross earnings during the contract is due (*European Industrial Relations Review*, 1990, p. 37).

Finally, it is normal practice for fixed-term contract workers to be on the same terms and conditions of employment as equivalent full time employees in the organization. This can create problems where workers with special skills outside the normal work done have been recruited and it also reduces the attractiveness of temporary employees to employers. In the United Kingdom, for example, fixed-term contracts of short duration may exclude employees from those holiday, pension and sick pay arrangements which are not statutorily enforceable.

Temporary employment agencies

In some Western European countries the concept of a third party hiring labour out to another has been vigorously opposed. The idea of someone selling another's labour and making a profit from that transaction has unacceptable links with slavery and forced labour and undermines the rights of the individual. A further factor undermining private agencies is the belief that regulating and allocating work is a function of the State. The first point is an anachronistic one in relation to modern employment agencies based on a voluntary transaction between each of the parties. Neither do they generally do the same job as State employment agencies. Nevertheless, in at least four Western European countries, Greece, Sweden, Italy and Spain, such agencies are formally banned. However, there is evidence to suggest that they operate informally in Sweden and Spain. One report on Spain 'estimated 200 agencies supplying the equivalent of 9,500 working years annually . . . while in Stockholm alone there are some 300 temporary office work agencies' (*European Industrial Relations Review*, 1990, p. 46).

Other European countries have sought to control the activities of temporary work agencies rather than outlaw them completely in a way that has been shown to be ineffective elsewhere. Legislative controls were introduced in France and the Federal Republic of Germany in 1972 and in Belgium in 1976. In the United Kingdom, the Employment Agencies Act of 1973 was supplemented by further regulations in 1976 and introduced a licensing system to protect individual employee rights. In essence, the controls outside the United Kingdom are related to the practices that each country adopts generally to fixed-term contracts. That is, there are limitations on their duration and renewal and, in some countries, the circumstances in which they can be used. In relation to pay and conditions of employment, in Belgium and Portugal for instance, temporary workers must receive the equivalent of permanent employees. In the Federal Republic of Germany a different approach is adopted and workers must receive a similar level to equivalent workers in the temporary employment business. In the United Kingdom and Ireland there are no legal regulations.

Finally, in most Western European countries which permit agencies, there are sanctions for those which act unlawfully. The removal of licences and hence the ability to continue in business is common as are fines. In the most extreme case, in France, there are prison sentences of up to six months and agencies may be banned from operating for ten years.

Atypical employment at the European level

The European Community has shown considerable concern about the increasing development of atypical employment and the wide range of legislation to control it in the different Member States. The Commission introduced a draft Directive on voluntary part time work in 1981 and an amended version in 1983 but it was not approved by the Council of Ministers. A similar fate awaited a draft Directive on temporary work which was introduced in 1982 and amended in 1984.

An alternative tactic has been to use the law, particularly in relation to the provisions on equal opportunities. Part-time work in particular is characterized by high levels of female employment. In one case relating to pensions and part time employment it was established that the non-payment of benefits or their reduction contravened Article 119 of the Treaty of Rome concerning equal treatment (Bilka Kaufhaus GmbH v. Karin Weber von Hartz). In that particular case it was established that the exclusion of part time workers with less than 15 out of 20 years' service from an occupational pension scheme was discriminatory. Other cases have followed this pattern and in July 1990 Maria Kowalska successfully argued that Hamburg's policy of paying 'golden handshakes' to permanent employees but not to part time workers was discriminatory. In the face of this piecemeal action and the failure to implement the draft Directives of the early 1980s, the European Commission has used the creation of the Single Market to introduce new measures. Introducing the draft Directives the Commission records that:

> ... given the number of workers concerned, it would be advisable, in order to identify and preclude the risks of distortion of competition resulting from the mobility of persons which will increase after 1992, to provide for harmonization of the rules governing the different types of employment relationships in the Community, in the following areas:

> • the very different practices noted as regards social protection and other social benefits, particularly in relation to part time employment;
> • the limits imposed on the duration and renewal of contracts and the establishment of an allowance in the event of an unjustified break in the temporary employment relationship;
> • the conditions under which licences are granted to temporary employment businesses, where they are lawful.

(Commission of the European Communities, 1990 (228 – final), p. 26)

The origins of this approach lie in the Social Dimension of the Single Market and, more specifically, the Social Charter. This refers to the improvement of living and working standards and refers directly to forms of employment other than open-ended contracts (Article 7). The underlying purpose of the Commission's approach is in line with the development of the Single Market and the elimination of potential 'distortions' in costs arising from differences in labour costs. Since the Treaty of Rome's inclusion of equality provisions, the social elements of the Community's actions has been based on market philosophies rather than workers' rights. This remains true of the draft Directives arising from the Social Charter although this has not prevented a number of employers' organizations and some governments being opposed to the changes.

The main thrust of the draft Directives is to equalize working conditions for part time and temporary workers in relation to full-timers on open-ended contracts. They are proposed under different articles of the EC Treaty which means that different voting provisions apply. The specific points of the draft Directives could have a considerable impact on those European States with little existing regulation of atypical work.

The first draft Directive requires a unanimous vote in the Council of Ministers and contains provisions for consultations with workers' representatives before the employment of atypical workers and for ensuring that companies make a statement indicating their needs for them. It also indicates that these workers are to be included when counting the workforce size for the establishment of works councils. Part-timers would have to be brought into the coverage of national and organizational social security schemes. This could conceivably be extended to schemes such as luncheon vouchers or even loans for travel season tickets. Workers on temporary contracts negotiated through employment agencies would be entitled to the same conditions of employment as if they were employed directly by the company.

The second draft Directive is proposed under an article that will lead to qualified majority voting in the Council of Ministers. This has a number of specific proposals that could have a very significant impact on Member States. Its effect is to ensure that part-timers who work for more than eight hours a week, and temporary employees, are entitled to pro rata equality in benefits. The Directive also addresses the issue of the duration and renewal of temporary contracts. The original formulation says that EC countries must pass laws so that temporary employment contracts do not exceed 36 months. An addition to this in the form of an amendment originating in the European Parliament would make restrictions much tighter by saying that 'a temporary employment relationship shall not be allowed to replace any existing permanent job'. The controversial nature of the Directives and the possibility of them being challenged make it unlikely that they will proceed as they stand.

The third draft Directive concerns health and safety. It is less controversial and is also subject to qualified majority voting.

Atypical employment and the British perspective

The United Kingdom has one of the least regulated labour markets in Europe and has few protective measures for atypical workers. Few organizations have concluded collective agreements to conform to European standards in spite of trade union pressure. This means that the proposed changes incorporated in the draft Directives are likely to have a major impact on British labour law. For this reason the CBI and the Conservative government have been vigorous in their opposition and have suggested that the changes will increase labour costs and reduce employment. The then Secretary of State for Employment, Michael Howard, said: 'the Commission's proposals seem deliberately designed to discourage part time work. It would be made more expensive, and employers who tried to take on new part time employees would be subject to a mass of new regulations' (*The Guardian*, 6 August 1990). The Engineering Employers Federation followed the government's general opposition though it felt that the provisions on part time work would be less onerous than those on temporary employment.

The draft Directives' proposals on consultation, information and representation are likely to have little impact on the United Kingdom given both the lack of works council systems and the absence of sanctions in the Directives. The right to be told why an employer is introducing temporary work does not carry with it any right to halt the process. However, the more specific proposals will change United Kingdom law although the cut-off point of eight hours a week for part-timers reduces the potential effects. Some workers will be brought into the provisions of State and company pension schemes for the first time and there would also be an extension of rights to areas such as family credit and invalidity benefit (*Employment Gazette*, September 1990). Employment protection legislation, redundancy and maternity rules might also have to be extended to give equal rights to part time and temporary workers. However, qualifying periods for protection from unfair dismissal do not need to be removed as long as they are equal.

The proposals on temporary work will also have an impact as these matters are currently left either to collective bargaining or for individual negotiation. Legal restrictions on the length and repeated renewal of temporary contracts are more or less unknown. However, the original proposal for three years of temporary work gives employers considerable leeway and so the impact is therefore likely to be lessened. If the amended draft, which restricts temporary contracts replacing permanent jobs, is accepted then there could be a very significant impact. Unless the circumstances are specifically defined trade unions could be given a powerful argument to prevent temporary work. It is more likely that there will be exceptions for cases such as temporary replacements to cover maternity leave and sickness absence.

In the initial period following Britain's membership of the Community the main impact of the EC on labour law was largely confined to equal opportunity issues. The legal decisions had an important impact on areas such as equal pay for work of equal value and pension rights. Outside that rubric the Community's influence remained restricted as the United Kingdom itself halted the implementation of draft Directives on employee participation and atypical employment. The Commission has now used the Single Market legislation to attempt to introduce measures that could potentially have a more significant impact on the United Kingdom than almost any other European country.

Termination of Employment

In most cases the ending of a contract of employment is through the mutual acceptance of notice. Difficulties arise when either the employee or the employer refuses to accept that the contract has been ended. In general, it is the employee who is the aggrieved party. However, there may be occasions when an employer does not wish a contract to end, as in the case of a particularly valued member of staff (a professional footballer or a computer programmer perhaps). An employer may also object to an employee's decision to end a fixed-term contract before its completion.

In this section we will focus on the individual termination of contract (collective redundancy is dealt with in chapter 6). We will look at variations in the periods of notice and differences in practice in what can be broadly defined as unfair dismissal. We will not discuss atypical contracts here and our discussion will largely be in relation to the protection of employee rights.

So, what are these employee rights? Historically, it has been the employer who has assumed the right to hire and fire labour. In that sense, individual employers have retained their 'rights' to employ who they see fit. However, the opposing concept of the individual's 'right to work' has imposed constraints on employers in two significant ways. Firstly, anti-discrimination legislation has restricted the employers' ability to refuse employment on a number of grounds including sex and, less commonly, race and religion. Secondly, once an individual is employed, there are restrictions in all EC countries governing periods of notice and 'unfair' dismissal.

In addition to these individual rights the concept of the right to work has taken on a broader dimension through the commitment of countries to full employment. Thus Article 23 (1) of the United Nations' Universal Declaration of Human Rights records that 'everyone has the right to work, to free choice of employment, to just and favourable conditions of work and to protection against unemployment'. It is beyond our scope here to develop a detailed analysis of government employment policies but we should note that the rapid rise in unemployment across Europe in the 1980s challenged the concept of the right to work. In particular, mass redundancies in the mining and manufacturing industries led to, often unsuccessful, trade union campaigns for jobs. These raised further questions about the rights of whole communities where they were dependent on one employer and the role of government in protecting and creating jobs.

In developing the individual job protection aspect of the right to work, the ILO has established a Convention on the termination of employment (158). This restricts dismissal by an employer to cases that are based on the operational requirements of the organization or where there are valid grounds based on individual capacity or conduct. It also enumerates reasons that are not valid ones for dismissal. These include 'union membership or participation in union activities at appropriate hours, seeking office or acting as a workers' representative, filing a complaint or participation in proceedings against an employer for violations of laws or regulations, race, colour, sex, marital status, family responsibilities, pregnancy, religion, political opinion, national extraction or social origin, absence from work during maternity leave and temporary absence from work because of illness or injury' (International Labour Organization, 1988a, p. 28).

This broad framework has been reflected in the development of labour law in Western European States although there remains considerable national diversity in the laws themselves and the way they are implemented. As a starting point we will consider the rights of individuals to notice at the termination of a contract.

Periods of notice

It is general practice in Western European countries for the period of notice served at the end of a contract of indefinite period to be covered by a legal framework. In a number of cases the matter is also managed through collective bargaining and it is possible for notice periods to be improved by such agreements. There are differences between countries in the way in which statutory regulations affect white collar and manual workers as well as variations in notice periods related to length of service.

In countries such as France, Spain, the United Kingdom, the Netherlands, Norway and Finland all full time employees are covered by the same legal standards. However, the Federal Republic of Germany, Belgium, Denmark and Austria have different legal arrangements for manual and white collar workers. In Belgium, this has led to considerable complexity in the calculation of notice periods for senior employees (earning above a certain wage level) and Blanpain (1985, p. 27) has recorded that 'there is no way of calculating the length of the term of notice with any real degree of certainty'. However, arithmetic formulas have been developed to cope with the problem. In Denmark, manual workers have no legal right to notice but their position is generally protected by the widespread effectiveness of collective agreements.

More generally, there is the issue of discriminatory practice in different lengths of notice for different occupational groups. There is a potential legal challenge if the practices infringe sex or race discrimination laws although this may be difficult to pursue and there have been no significant cases before the European Court. In Germany, however, there have been claims that the differences are unconstitutional and the courts have considered the matter, although

they have made no changes as yet. Leaving aside the legal implications, there is pressure for harmonization of conditions of employment such as these both from unions and some employers.
Single status agreements which do not distinguish between manual
and non-manual workers have become well known in the United
Kingdom through Japanese employment practices. There seems to
be little reason to retain these distinctions in the operation of notice
periods although some employers fear that harmonization upwards
would lead to much longer notice periods for manual workers. In
Greece, for example, if a statutory notice period were introduced
for manual workers on the same basis as for white collar staff it
could mean as much as five months' notice. In Germany the upper
limit for manual workers would be raised from three to six months.

Length of service related notice periods are a common feature
of the law in Europe. These range from relatively straightforward
schemes such as that in France, which offers one months' notice for
six months' to two years' service and two months' notice for two
years and above, to the more complex age and service related
schemes in West Germany and the Netherlands. In Germany, age
discrimination is related to occupational divisions, with longer notice
periods being available to non-manual workers over 25 years old
compared to manual workers who have to be over 35.

In a number of the EC States, notice periods are not effective
for new employees. In the United Kingdom, one months' service is
required, in Greece it is two months for white collar employees
and in Ireland the period is thirteen weeks. In other countries, the
concept of the trial period is more firmly established. In France,
while the legal notices are clear, trial periods may be allowed in
collective agreements and no notice at all need be required during
them. Belgium also has some provision for trial periods with notice
arrangements of seven days.

The only two EC countries whose provisions differ significantly
from the pattern established above are Italy and Portugal. In Italy,
the laws on termination of contracts in general have been described
as 'breathtaking in their byzantine complexity' (*European Industrial
Relations Review*, October 1988). Length of notice is largely established by collective bargaining and custom and practice which have
extended a decree dating back to 1922. Public sector workers have
their own arrangements and where no agreement can be reached,
individuals have recourse to conciliation through the courts.

In Portugal, the whole subject of dismissal has been the focus of major dispute. The original laws of 1975 placed severe restrictions on the ending of contracts which could only be through 13 legally defined 'just causes'. Attempts to introduce changes in the law were made in Parliamentary proposals in 1975, 1979, 1980, 1981, 1985 and 1988. The publication of new draft laws in 1988 led to a general strike but changes to give greater flexibility were finally introduced in 1989.

Unfair dismissal

If the different systems of notice periods have revealed a considerable complexity we would expect to find even further variations in unfair dismissal arrangements. This is partly due to the different historical circumstances and time periods when legislation was enacted. Constitutional 'right to work' standards have a long history in some countries and there are examples of protective legislation going back to 1859 in Austria, the 1920s in Germany and the immediate post-war years in Italy. However, the bulk of the legislation stems from the 1970s when trade union strength and social democratic governments in many countries combined to introduce new standards of worker protection. Weiss (1985, p. 3) indicates the turn-round in much European law when he notes of Germany that 'until 1951 the normal case was the legality of . . . dismissal, only in exceptional cases was it thought to be illegal. Now the normal case is the illegality and the legality has become the exceptional case'. While the German case may have come earlier than others it was reinforced by legislation in 1969 and 1972. In Portugal, on the other hand, legislation had to wait until political change removed the dictatorship, but what followed was highly protective for employees. This has now been challenged and the United Kingdom has led the way in 'deregulating' employment protection laws in the 1980s.

We begin our analysis of unfair dismissal by looking at the categories of workers who enjoy special protection. The employees most commonly covered by such arrangements are trade unionists and works council representatives; most countries also have restrictions on the dismissal of pregnant women and, in a smaller number of cases, there is special protection for the disabled and those involved in military service. In the Netherlands and Norway there are restrictions on the dismissal of workers on sick leave but perhaps the most comprehensive list can be found in Belgium where, alongside the more familiar categories, there is extra protection for works doctors, employees taking leave for political office, workers who handle toxic waste and candidates for health and safety committees (*European Industrial Relations Review*, 1989a, p. 4). Equal opportunities legislation will also impose restrictions on dismissal.

In a number of Western European countries there is legislation imposing compulsory consultation with trade unions and works councils. This is most common in the case of collective redundancies (see chapter 6) but it may also be used in individual cases. In Spain and Denmark, dismissals must be discussed with the trade unions and references to works councils are necessary in Austria, Luxembourg and the Federal Republic of Germany. However, consultation does not necessarily restrict freedom of action. In a survey of German works councils quoted by Weiss (1985), 66 per cent of referrals received agreement, in 20 per cent of cases no action was taken, in 6 per cent the council expressed reservations and in only 8 per cent were there objections. In 30 per cent of the objected cases the employer gave up the right to dismiss. While this 'success rate' for employees is low, it might be argued that the system of consultation itself reduces the number of arbitrary dismissals so that those arriving at the works councils are relatively clear cut.

In the Netherlands, Greece and Luxembourg, local offices of the appropriate government department have to be notified of dismissals. In the United Kingdom and Ireland there are no statutory procedures for consultation although this is effectively established through disciplinary procedures which will inevitably involve union representatives where they exist. In France, this mechanism is institutionalized and dismissed workers must be interviewed by management with a representative present.

The potentially fair reasons for dismissal follow similar lines in most Western European countries and are normally related to capability and conduct. However, there is some variation in how tightly these may be defined in legislation. Many countries have general protection from dismissal for employees without 'just' or 'serious' cause (for example, France, Austria and Italy). There have also been attempts to put legislative flesh on these bare bones. Dutch law, for example, contains a list of offences that are likely to justify summary dismissal which includes theft, refusal to work, persistent drunkenness, attacks on colleagues and gross negligence. In France there is a distinction between those types of action which justify summary dismissal and those for which an employee will retain the right to notice and severance pay. In Austria and the Federal Republic of Germany the concept of a socially unjustifiable dismissal has been developed. In the former country, this is defined as 'the legitimate and fundamental (social) interests of the employee' (*European Industrial Relations Review*, 1989a, p. 2). It is related to the concept of social comparison where 'a court rules on whether the proposed dismissal would affect this employee more unfavourably than other comparable employees' (ibid.).

Remedies for workers who feel they have been unfairly dismissed commonly go through two stages. The first involves the discussion with the works council or trade union that we have described. The second would be through appeal to whatever system of labour court or tribunal operates in the country concerned. These may offer reinstatement or compensation depending on the law and the circumstances of the individual case. This makes generalizations particularly difficult but it is clear that in a number of countries such as Spain, Belgium and the United Kingdom reinstatement is uncommon.

Much more significant as a remedy is some form of compensation and again there is a wide range of options. In the Federal Republic of Germany and the Netherlands employees may effectively retain employment and, therefore, their pay while their case is being heard. In successful cases in Greece, the law allows for a back payment from the time of dismissal until the court decision and an interest payment of 1.5 per cent a month. Greece, like France, also links payments to a separate system of severance pay. More common are systems that are related to length of service and, less frequently, age. For instance, in Germany, the system offers one month's salary for each year of service up to a maximum of 12 months' pay for those under 50 years old, 15 months' for those over 50 and 18 months' for those over 55. In Spain the compensation is considerably higher at 45 days' pay per year of service up to a maximum of 42 months' pay.

Such variation must be viewed in the context of the practical implementation of the policies and EC States differ significantly in their use of the law. For example, in Denmark dismissals are dealt with largely through the collective bargaining framework and only 30 to 50 cases are brought to tribunals annually, and there is a low employee success rate (*European Industrial Relations Review*, 1989a, p. 10). This compares with a quoted success rate in Italian courts of 72 per cent (Treu, 1985, p. 74).

As significant as the use of the law are the exemptions that exist. In France, there is a two years' service requirement, as there is in the United Kingdom. In Ireland this is one year and employees must work for over 18 hours a week. In the Federal Republic of Germany the qualifications are six months' service and ten hours a week employment in companies with over five employees. In France the figure is ten employees but it was in Italy that the most complex arrangements existed on the size of company. Conflicting laws from 1966 and the Workers' Statute of 1970 appeared to refer differently to companies. In the former case workers in companies with 36 or more employees were protected and in the latter case those in companies with more than 15. This was no minor legal quibble in a country with an economy where small and medium-size enterprises play such a significant part. The discrepancy appears to have been removed by a court decision in 1989 which has been followed by proposed parliamentary legislation.

As we have seen, the variety of European rules and laws on the termination of contract renders it impossible to make anything more than broad generalizations. It is clear that the EC States have all adopted some mechanisms for restricting the ability of employers to dismiss arbitrarily. The laws may have their roots in long-standing constitutional commitments to the 'right to work', in war-time legislation that involved governments in the allocation of labour or, most commonly, in the widespread employment protection legislation of the 1970s.

Consultation with unions or works councils on dismissals is commonplace and this may either be formally included in legislation or implied in good procedural practice. In the event of the failure of workplace negotiations to resolve disputes, EC countries each have their own arrangements of labour courts or tribunals to deal with cases. Reinstatement is a potential remedy in most European countries but compensation based on length of service is the most common practice.

Most Western European States have categories of workers who are clearly included or excluded from unfair dismissal legislation. The most common exclusions are related to qualifying service periods although hours of work and size of company may also be significant. On the other hand, we have seen that it is normal practice for there to be special protection from dismissal for trade union and works council activists – although this is observed with varying degrees of appreciation in some countries. Pregnant women are also commonly protected and there may be other sex-related provisions through equal opportunity legislation.

Termination of employment and the British perspective

As we have indicated, the law in Europe on unfair dismissal is diverse in its origins, provisions and practice. It is hardly surprising then that there has been little attempt to harmonize matters at a Community level and we again treat the United Kingdom and the EC together.

The first significant development of the concept of unfair dismissal in the United Kingdom did, however, receive an international impetus. The ILO had introduced a recommendation on the termination of contracts in 1963 (No. 119) and the then Ministry of Labour was asked to examine the question. It is notable that the overwhelming majority of unions at the time felt that the matter was best left to collective bargaining (Dickens et al., 1985, p. 9). However, the Donovan Commission suggested that legislation on unfair dismissal might provide a stimulus to the improvement of personnel practice as well as providing part of a floor of rights (Anderman, 1986, p. 417).

It is ironic that the United Kingdom's first legal enactment in relation to unfair dismissal was to be in Conservative Prime Minister, Edward Heath's, Industrial Relations Act. As an attempt to sugar the bitter pill of trade union reform, the provisions were a failure but they succeeded as a precursor of the succeeding Labour government's employment protection legislation. Thus, as was the case in a number of other Western European countries, the 1970s was the period that provided the basis for current employee rights. The Employment Protection Act 1975 introduced the essential components of unfair dismissal law in the United Kingdom. As in the other Western European States the provisions establish particular protection for trade unionists (and now non-unionists), they provide indications of the areas of potentially fair and, hence, unfair dismissal, they indicate the procedures necessary to resolve a dispute and they give details of the remedies.

Inevitably, the details of the Employment Protection Act have not remained unchanged given the room for interpretation through the appeal court system and the actions of the Conservative government under Mrs Thatcher. Most significant have been the various alterations of the qualifying rules. Changes were made in relation to both size of company and period of service. The current situation has removed the references to size but qualifying service has been increased from the Act's original six months to two years.

It is likely that future changes in dismissal legislation will remain firmly within the jurisdiction of the British government. The Commission has refrained from intervening in the tangled mass of individual national law. The Social Charter makes broad references to employment in its introduction and notes that 'employment development and creation must be given first priority in the completion of the internal market'. It adds in Article 4 that 'every individual shall be free to choose and engage in an occupation according to the regulations governing each occupation'. The Social Chapter issued after the Maastricht conference in 1991 makes specific reference to the 'protection of workers where their employment contract is terminated' but it adds that any decisions taken in that area will be subject to unanimous approval by the Member States.

Conclusion

The rights of individuals in employment have been the subject of wide ranging legislation and collective agreement in the post-war years. The initial framework of protection which was created in Western European States has since been challenged by changing government policies and the expansion of atypical work contracts. The result has been the creation of jobs that have fallen outside protective legislation and have often denied workers the opportunity to contribute towards their own security through State benefit and pension schemes. As Kravaritiou-Manitakis (1986) argues:

> The new forms of work . . . raise new and serious problems for labour law and social security in all the member states . . . the difficulties which they give rise to concern the elimination of worker protection, the erosion of acquired rights, the discrimination they cause and the principle of equality which they ignore. (p. 208)

In some respects, European Community Directives have attempted to make up these deficiencies through establishing equal opportunities legislation and introducing measures in line with the principle of equal treatment for all workers regardless of the form of contract.

However, the EC itself performs a balancing act between the demands of employers and workers, and it is important to remember that it introduces Directives in the name of the free market and equal competition rather than social justice.

Nevertheless, there has been a significant development in individual labour law across Western Europe, since the 1970s in particular. It is clear that a wide variety of practice remains in many of the areas that we have discussed in this chapter but it is equally important to note that most Western European States have accepted the principle of a safety net of individual employment rights in a number of similar areas.

6

Collective Rights at Work

For employees, some of the greatest advances in pay and conditions have been achieved by collective action, and the results thereof have been implemented by a series of rules governing relations between employees as a collective group and the employer or employers. While there have been moves to encourage greater flexibility in the labour market and to individualize employee relations, many significant rights are still protected in Western Europe on a collective basis, either as a result of legislation or collective agreements, or a combination of both.

The EC has generally had limited competence in the area of collective rights at work. Moreover, as was seen in chapter 2, some of the more significant proposals put forward by the Commission in this area have not found favour within the Council of Ministers. It was not until the signing of the Single European Act in 1986, with its accompanying Social Dimension, that there was a renewed interest in collective employee rights at work. Accordingly, in December 1989, eleven governments out of twelve (with the notable opposition of the British government) signed the Community Charter of Fundamental Social Rights for Workers which advocated a significant number of collective (and also individual) rights at work.

In this chapter we shall investigate four distinct issues relating to collective employee rights – working time, wages, redundancies and health and safety – all of which have been affected recently by developments in labour law and employee relations practices at the European level. We shall examine each issue from a comparative perspective, investigate salient proposals emanating from the European Communities and consider them in the light of prevailing industrial relations practices in the United Kingdom.

Working Time

Working time has been an important bargaining issue within an ever changing pattern of employee relations in Europe. In the 1970s and the early 1980s the emphasis lay with a reduction in working time, and European trade unions campaigned for a shorter working week. They claimed that this would provide broad social benefits and would make a contribution to solving the problem of unemployment. Subsequently, however, the emphasis has switched to the reorganization of working time, and employers have stressed the need for flexibility so as to be competitive in national and international markets.

Working time, in all its different aspects, varies considerably from one country to another. The maximum length of the working week is fixed by law in all countries in Western Europe (except Denmark and the United Kingdom, although in the latter there are restrictions for certain categories of employees – lorry drivers, young people and shopworkers – as a result of specific legislation). As can be seen from table 6.1, the legal maximum ranges from 39 hours in France, which was introduced in the aftermath of Socialist victory in 1981, to 48 hours in the Federal Republic of Germany, Greece, Ireland, the Netherlands, Portugal and Italy. However, in some countries (Germany, for example) the laws are relatively old and legislation has played a limited role in the more recent moves to reduce working time. Collective agreements provide the fundamental means for deciding the length of the working week (for instance, in Denmark and the United Kingdom). Collective agreements also ensure improvements in the basic legal provision in other countries. Of course, not all sectors of the economy have been able to negotiate these reductions, and the average working week established by collective agreement is 37.5 hours in Norway, 38 hours in the Netherlands and 39 hours in Denmark. Where figures are available, the working week tends to be shorter in the public sector (Greece) and for non-manual workers (France and the United Kingdom).

These figures do not necessarily represent the actual number of hours worked. In the manufacturing sector there was a considerable reduction in the number of hours worked in all Western European countries from 1970 to 1975, but not in the following decade up to 1985. In the Federal Republic of Germany, Norway and the United Kingdom, there was in fact a slight increase. The formal

Table 6.1   Normal weekly hours of work

	Legal provisions	Collective agreements[1],[2]	
		Range	Average
Austria	40	37–40	
Belgium	40	36–39	
Denmark	–	35–40	39
Finland	40		
France	39	35–39	39.05 manual
			38.85 non-manual
Germany	48	38–40	39.25
Greece	48[3]	35–40	37.05 public
			40 private
Ireland	48	35–40	
Italy	48	36–40	
Luxembourg	40	37–40	
Netherlands	48	36–40	38
Norway	40	33.6–37.5	37.5
Portugal	48	35–44	42
Spain	40	38–40	
Sweden	40	35–40	
Switzerland	45/50	40–45	42.6
UK	–	35–40	39.12 manual
			37.05 non-manual

[1] Figures relate to 1986 except for Germany (1987), Norway (1987) and the United Kingdom (1987)
[2] The ranges and averages are estimates based on available information; in many cases there are no official surveys or statistics
[3] 25 per cent premiums payable for hours worked beyond 40 a week

Source: adapted from International Labour Organization, 1988b

reductions in the length of the working week have been counter-balanced by the increase in the number of overtime hours worked. As a proportion of total hours worked in 1985, overtime represented as much as 8.8 per cent in the United Kingdom while only 3.7 per cent in Italy and 3.9 per cent in the Federal Republic of Germany. So as to ensure that the reduction in the length of the working week did not merely lead to an increase in overtime by those already in employment, some countries have introduced limits on the number of hours overtime that legally can be worked – two hours per day

Table 6.2 Minimum annual leave in legislative provisions

	Minimum annual leave in weeks[1]			Public holidays[3]
	1964	*1984*	*1988*	*1987*
Austria	2	4	5	13
Belgium	2	4	5	10
Denmark	3	5	5	10
Finland	3	4	5	8
France	3	5	5	10
Germany	2.5	3	3	11 or 13
Greece	1	4	4	4 + 3[4]
Ireland	2	3	3	8
Italy	2	_[2]	_[2]	11
Luxembourg	1.33	5	5	10
Netherlands	2.5	3	3	7
Norway	3	4.2	4.2	10
Portugal	0.67	3	3	12
Spain	1	5	5	12 + 2[5]
Sweden	4	5	5	11
Switzerland	1	2	4	8[6]
UK	2	–	–	8

[1] Where legislation provides for annual leave in days, a conversion has been made to weeks. Legislation varies on use of a five- or six-day working week for purposes of calculation of leave

[2] The right to paid annual leave is established in legislation, but the length is generally determined through collective bargaining

[3] As the number of public holidays varies in practice, only public holidays at the national level as stated in legislation have been indicated

[4] Optional

[5] Local

[6] Average – public holidays determined at cantonal level

Source: adapted from International Labour Organization, 1988b

in Austria, Belgium, the Federal Republic of Germany, Ireland, Italy and Luxembourg; ten hours per week in Austria, Belgium and Norway; twelve hours per week in Ireland, Italy and the Netherlands. (International Labour Organization, 1988b, p. 12, 16, 17)

The second major working time issue is the provision of paid leave and public holidays. As can be seen from table 6.2 a minimum period of annual leave is fixed by legislation in all countries except in the United Kingdom. Provision has increased markedly in most countries during the period between 1964 and 1988 with the result that employees are entitled to five weeks in Austria, Belgium, Denmark, Finland, France, Luxembourg and Spain. Moreover, in most of these countries further paid leave has been negotiated by collective bargaining. For the number of public holidays, Austria and parts of the Federal Republic of Germany lead the way with 13 days, but provision is less generous in Greece and the Netherlands. In addition, collective agreements in some countries have made it possible to augment the number of days off by taking a bridging day if the public holiday falls on a Tuesday or a Thursday.

As previously noted, the reorganization of working time has been emphasized recently. For employees, flexibility implies a move from a system which is uniform to one which favours individual needs, particularly those associated with child-care responsibilities, transport demands and leisure pursuits. For employers, flexibility implies adapting production to demand, using productive capacity to the full and therefore increasing labour productivity. For trade unions, the individualization of working time implies a threat to their capacity to control working conditions, thus reducing their overall bargaining position.

Flexibility in working time may come in many forms, flexitime, shift work, overtime and annualized hours. Flexitime is a system whereby employees are given the opportunity to determine the distribution of their working hours, normally around an obligatory core of attendance. It is in operation in many workplaces, although rarely in industrial jobs where production requirements require constant staffing levels. In the EC, shifts are worked by 20 per cent of employees on average, the highest figures being in Spain and the United Kingdom and the lowest in Ireland and Denmark. In manufacturing industry, the corresponding average figure is 37 per cent for the EC, but 67 per cent in the United Kingdom, the highest figure by far (Commission of the European Communities, 1990, p. 10). Recently, numerous agreements have been concluded, providing reductions in working time in exchange for 'flexible' forms of shift work. Examples include the BMCO plant in Regensburg, where employees work an average of 35.5 hours per week in exchange for a rolling two-shift system consisting of a nine-hour day and a six-day working week (i.e. including Saturday), and the Peugeot plant in Poissy, in which employees work 38.5 hours per week, but spread over four days, leaving three rest days off per week. Also, in the Rover plant in Longbridge the working week was reduced from 39 to 37 hours, in exchange for which employees agreed to seven-day working and a 24-hour continuous shift system (*European Industrial Relations Review*, June 1990, October 1990, January 1991).

Annualizing hours also makes it possible to side-step agreements on the length of the working week so as to respond to the seasonal or short-term requirements of the production process. In a survey of 17 countries in Western Europe it was noted that there were no known agreements on annualized hours in Austria, Denmark, Finland, Greece, Ireland, Italy and Portugal. However, annualization was formally introduced in Belgium in 1985, and the normal working time arrangements (8 hours per day, 40 hours per week) may be exceeded if a legally binding contractual agreement can be concluded. Another variant is the flexible system in practice in the metal-working industry in the Federal Republic of Germany where it has been agreed that the working week would be reduced to 38.5 hours in three different ways – by averaging out working time over a two-month period, by calling on some parts of the workforce to work more than the agreed maximum while others worked correspondingly less, and by providing extra days off to compensate for working a 40-hour week (*European Industrial Relations Review*, March 1987).

The controversy surrounding the issue of the reduction and reorganization of working time has been exacerbated by the issue of payment for hours no longer worked. In Belgium, the government intervened in the debate and put forward the so-called 3-5-3 formula. It agreed to reduce the working week by 5 per cent and to increase employment by 3 per cent, but at the expense of a 3 per cent reduction in wages. In the Federal Republic of Germany, the unsuccessful candidate of the Social Democratic Party for the 1990 election, Oskar Lafontaine, was in favour of a reduction in the length of the working week, but on condition that hours not worked were not paid for, a policy formally opposed by the largest national trade union IG-Metall, the metal-workers union (Bastien, 1989, pp. 284, 291). The controversy over the payment of hours not worked was resolved differently in France. The proposal made by the CGT and FO that employees working a 39-hour week should be paid the same wage as when they worked a 40-hour week was finally agreed by the French government, apparently as a result of prompting by President Mitterrand.

In spite of these major differences concerning the ways in which working time is organized, it is clear that 'the current trend towards increasing fragmentation of net hours worked is almost certain to continue' (*European Industrial Relations Review*, March 1987, p. 26). A tension will nevertheless remain between the need for flexibility of working time from an economic perspective and the need for minimum protection for all employees from a social perspective. It has been suggested that the collective agreements on the reduction of weekly working time (for example, those agreed within the German metal-working industry in 1984) may indicate the way forward – 'a combination of regulations by collective agreement with decentralised regulations on the enterprise or plant level' (International Labour Organization, 1987, p. 83).

Working time at the European level

Attempts to regulate working time at the international level are not new. The first labour standard agreed by the International Labour Organization (in 1919) was the Hours of Work (Industry) Convention which advocated the 48-hour week and the eight-hour day. Other conventions have subsequently extended the 48-hour week to a larger number of employees, introduced the notion of 24 hours' uninterrupted rest every seven days, a minimum of three weeks holiday for one year of service, maternity leave of a minimum of 12 weeks, paid educational leave and also prohibited the employment of women at night. Questions of ratification and, more importantly, implementation, are paramount. The Hours of Work (Industry) Convention has been ratified by 47 countries (of which 14 are industrialized countries). However, only the Convention on weekly rest in industry has been ratified by more than half of all industrialized countries (all the members of the EC except the Federal Republic of Germany and the United Kingdom). In addition, the ILO has been able to agree on a recommendation (No. 116) that each State should pursue a policy designed to provide the adoption of the principle of the progressive reduction of normal working hours with a view to obtaining a 40-hour week.

The Community has also attempted to intervene in the debate on working time. In 1975 the Commission of the EC proposed a Recommendation on maximum weekly hours (40) and minimum annual holidays (four) which was adopted by the Council of Ministers (*Official Journal* L 199/75), but which of course is not legally binding. A proposed Directive restricting night work was abandoned in the face of considerable opposition from employers in 1979. A Recommendation on the reorganization of working time was proposed in 1983, but was abandoned the following year in the face of stiff opposition from the British government.

The issue of working time was resurrected in the late 1980s in the wake of the publication of the Community Charter of Fundamental Social Rights for Workers which states that 'every worker within the EC should have the right to a weekly rest period and to annual paid leave, the duration of which must be progressively harmonised in accordance with national practices' (Article 8). In 1990 the Commission produced a draft Directive based on Article 118a of the Single European Act, thus linking working time with the issue of health and safety. It noted a considerable discrepancy between working hours and operating hours in industry and the retail sector in all countries within the EC, the average working hours and operating hours in industry being 39 and 66 per week and 39 and 53 in the retail sector respectively. Individuals' hours were becoming shorter while operating hours were becoming longer. This discrepancy led the Commission to 'consider the extent to which workers can rely on minimum rates concerning certain rest periods to protect themselves against excessively long working hours, which may be detrimental to the health and safety of the workers at their workplace' (*Official Journal* L 254/4/90). The Directive proposed the following:

- a minimum rest period of 11 consecutive hours per period of 24 hours (Article 3);
- one day off following the minimum rest period in every seven days (Article 4);
- a minimum period of annual paid leave, in accordance with national practice (Article 5);
- overtime should not interfere with the minimum daily and weekly rest periods (Article 6);
- night shifts should not exceed an average of eight hours in any 24-hour period (Article 7.1);
- a ban on two consecutive shifts where one of these involves night work (Article 7.2);
- in occupations involving special hazards or heavy physical or mental strain no overtime should be performed before or after a daily period of work that includes night work (Article 7.3).

These proposals provide for a significant number of exemptions, namely, in the case of *force majeure*, seasonal work and for certain activities which, by their very nature, may inevitably be in conflict with the above provisions.

The reaction from the two sides of industry was relatively critical. On the employers' side, UNICE rejected the legal basis of the Directive, Claiming that Article 118a does not specifically mention the issue of working time and so the harmonization of working hours is outside the competence of the Treaty. It also claimed that shift work and night work are not in themselves detrimental to health and safety. Working time is a matter for local regulation and practice, or for collective bargaining at the appropriate level. It argued that, because of the variation in different types of work, speed of work, habits, climate and sectors, it is not possible or sensible to try to devise legislation in Brussels to suit all situations in Europe – the minimum daily and weekly rest periods need not be the same in each Member State. Finally, the imposition of rest periods would be expensive, particularly for small and medium-size enterprises. On the trade union side, the European Trade Union Confederation (ETUC) welcomed the fact that Article 118a provided the legal basis for this type of measure, thus making it possible to use qualified majority voting within the Council of Ministers and therefore side-step the objections of some governments. However, according to the ETUC, the Commission did not respect the spirit of upward harmonization, since it is still possible to work 13 hours a day, which is more than the maximum of 12 hours or less in use in eleven of the twelve Member States (i.e. not the United Kingdom). In addition, there would be no upward harmonization if, in terms of paid annual leave, the proposal replicated existing national practice. The ETUC would prefer to see a statutory maximum figure, namely, eight hours per day and 40 hours per week, with collective bargaining providing possible adjustments and exemptions to cover overtime. The ETUC opposed the lack of restriction put on the notion of night work. Finally, within this draft Directive there were no protective measures for pregnant employees, for women returning to work after giving birth, and for young people under the age of 18. These initial draft proposals have been the subject of substantial review and, although some of the criticisms have been accommodated, they remain controversial.

Working time and the British perspective

In general terms, it could be expected that any harmonization of working time in Western Europe would benefit British workers, since on average, 'employees in Britain work longer hours, have shorter holidays and enjoy less legal protection than most of their European colleagues' (*The Guardian*, 6 May 1991). It has been calculated that more than 2.7 million British employees regularly work more than 48 hours per week (11.7 per cent of the workforce). Moreover, British employees are more likely to be engaged in night and shift work.

If passed by the Council of Ministers, it is likely that primary legislation would be needed to introduce the necessary changes, since statutory limitations on working hours or paid holidays pertain to very few sectors. The British government stressed the fact that the draft Directive would add to employers' costs, thus making it more difficult to compete in world markets, which would have a negative impact on employment. Indeed, the British government questioned the need for legislation on an issue which has traditionally been agreed upon in the United Kingdom through the process of collective bargaining (*European Industrial Relations Review*, October 1990, p. 17). It has also been claimed by the British government, that a plan to restrict the working week to 48 hours would add £5 billion to the wages bill, as a result of changes in shift patterns and reductions in flexibility. However, these claims need further substantiation. If it were decided that the weekly rest period should fall on a Sunday, this would have serious consequences for the increasing tendency to disregard the Sunday trading regulations. It is expected that the proposal would have negligible consequences for annual paid leave, since Article 5 of the original draft Directive makes it possible to continue with existing national practice.

Wages

Any attempt to examine wages from an international perspective involves the problem of the availability and comparability of existing data. Eurostat, the official statistics agency of the EC, has still not been able to persuade all Member States to use the same base for their data collection. Moreover, wages are viewed differently by both sides of industry and so differing sets of statistics are collected. For employers, wages are an essential element of labour costs, which are themselves an essential element of national and international competitiveness. For employees, wages cannot be divorced from prices, an essential element of social and economic prosperity. What is clear, however, is that there is enormous variation as regards labour costs and real wages.

Total labour costs cover direct pay, employers' statutory social insurance contributions and other indirect elements of labour cost, for example, the expense of providing benefits. According to a study by the Swedish Employer's Confederation, Great Britain had the lowest hourly total labour costs in Western Europe in 1988, with the exception of Ireland, Greece and Portugal. The Federal Republic of Germany, the highest on the list, had labour costs which were approaching double the British figure and five times the Portuguese figure (*IDS European Report 340*, April 1990, p. 10). As can be seen from table 6.3, unit labour costs in manufacturing for the period 1979–1990 have only risen marginally in Japan, but this is generally not the case in Europe. The average year to year percentage change in unit labour costs in manufacturing in the United Kingdom was 5.0, which is marginally lower than the EC average (5.1) and such countries as Denmark, France, Italy, Spain and Sweden.

As for earnings, average gross hourly earnings for manual workers in industry stood at 7.3 ECU in the United Kingdom, which was marginally higher then the EC average (April 1989). They stood at 11.1 in Denmark and 9.1 in the Federal Republic of Germany, but 5.2 in Spain, 3.1 in Greece and 1.6 in Portugal. For non-manual workers in industry, monthly earnings stood at 1,923 ECU in April 1989 in the United Kingdom, a figure which is above the EC average; they stood at 2.429 in Luxembourg, 2,295 in the Federal Republic of Germany and 2,151 in Denmark, the only countries with higher figures in the EC, while at the lower levels, the Greek figure stood at 776 and the Portuguese figure was 437 (*Eurostat Rapid Reports*, 8/1990). To attain these levels, hourly earnings in manufacturing increased more during the period between 1979 and 1989 in the United Kingdom (10.1 per cent per year) than, for example, in Belgium, Denmark, the Federal Republic of Germany, France, the Netherlands and, indeed, more than the EC average (8.0 per cent) (Organization for Economic Co-operation and Development, 1991a).

There has been considerable discussion in the British press of the large increases obtained by the managing directors of some companies, particularly newly privatized ones. One survey noted that, during the period from July 1989 to July 1990, directors' nominal base pay rose more in the United Kingdom than in the other Western European countries, but that real increases in the United Kingdom

Table 6.3 Unit labour cost in manufacturing – year-to-year percentage changes

	1979	1980	1981	1982	1983	1984	1985	1986	1987	1988	1989	1990	Average 68–73	Average 73–79	Average 79–90
Austria	-1.2	4.8	8.3	3.3	-0.4	-0.9	1.7	3.7	1.3	-4.7	-0.5	1.0	5.5	5.3	1.5
Belgium	3.1	4.2	3.7	-1.5	-3.2	3.5	4.0	2.9	-1.7	-3.0	–	0.2	4.0	7.5	1.0
Denmark	6.5	4.6	8.3	8.5	1.9	6.2	6.1	8.4	8.4	0.4	2.1	2.9	7.2	9.4	5.4
Finland	3.8	8.6	10.5	7.1	3.3	4.2	3.6	2.7	0.7	2.1	4.8	7.8	8.5	12.4	5.0
France	8.3	14.8	12.4	10.7	7.6	6.7	4.2	2.5	2.3	-0.8	-0.1	2.9	5.4	11.2	5.2
Germany	2.7	7.8	4.8	3.3	-0.6	1.1	2.2	5.0	6.1	-0.4	–	2.3	6.9	4.9	3.3
Ireland	13.0	19.5	9.3	16.4	-3.3	-3.9	-1.0	2.5	-4.9	-6.3	-3.8	3.2	10.9	13.5	2.2
Italy	10.7	11.9	17.8	15.1	11.2	4.3	6.6	3.2	3.4	2.4	7.7	7.5	9.0	15.9	7.9
Netherlands	2.3	4.2	1.8	4.3	-1.9	-5.5	1.2	1.9	2.3	-1.9	-2.8	1.1	5.8	5.8	0.6
Norway	0.1	10.7	11.2	6.5	4.2	2.7	5.6	10.9	9.1	4.2	-1.5	1.3	5.8	11.1	6.2
Portugal	15.5	22.6	20.7	19.9	19.9	18.1	19.3	16.8	13.6	9.9	10.2	16.3	7.0	21.6	17.1
Spain	18.7	11.9	9.6	7.9	7.0	3.5	5.1	9.4	5.6	3.0	5.8	6.1	5.6	23.4	6.9
Sweden	-0.1	9.5	10.4	4.1	1.3	4.9	7.8	6.7	5.6	5.9	9.2	12.9	5.5	11.2	7.0
Switzerland	0.3	1.6	6.5	7.1	7.4	2.2	1.7	3.2	2.7	2.8	3.3	4.7	0.7	3.4	3.7
UK	17.9	22.1	9.1	3.3	-1.3	1.3	3.5	3.8	0.2	0.7	4.8	8.9	9.1	18.0	5.0
Total EEC	8.5	12.3	9.0	6.8	3.2	3.1	4.2	4.7	3.9	0.8	3.0	5.4	6.9	10.4	5.1

Note: Percentage changes from previous year

Source: Organization for Economic Co-operation and Development, 1991a, p. 97

trailed behind those in Italy, France and Belgium. Even with these increases, however, and with the generally more generous range of extra benefits (share options and company cars) gross earnings of executives in the United Kingdom are considerably lower than those prevailing in all Western European countries (with the exception of Ireland and Portugal) (*IDS Employment Report 349*, January 1991).

It is, of course, real wages that are of most interest to employees since they take into account increases in the retail price index. According to a Eurostat survey, real average hourly earnings of manual workers have not moved uniformly during the 1980s in the countries of the EC. Between 1980 and 1985 real earnings increased in the United Kingdom, but decreased in Belgium, Denmark, Luxembourg, the Netherlands and Portugal. In the period 1985–9, the British figure was positive, and it was only in Greece where there was a fall in real hourly earnings. Figures show that real wages of non-manual workers in industry increased more in the United Kingdom during the period 1985–9 than in any other EC country. Moreover this figure was lower than for the same category of employee in the service sector – wholesale, retail and credit institutions (*Eurostat Rapid Reports*, 8/1990).

Within the perspective of the Single European Market, and hence increased trans-border labour mobility, it is not merely the real wage which is critical but what that wage buys. Eurostat has produced figures in terms of the purchasing power standard (PPS) – units of purchasing power – which allows the elimination of difference in price levels between countries. According to figure 6.1 the average hourly earnings of manual workers in industry as expressed in PPS for April 1990 was highest in Denmark, followed by the Federal Republic of Germany, Luxembourg, the Netherlands, and then the United Kingdom. Average gross monthly earnings of non-manual employees in industry (measured in PPS) for 1989 was highest by far in Luxembourg, followed by the United Kingdom which even outstripped the Federal Republic of Germany.

These average figures may disguise a more complex reality. In a study carried out by the European Federation for Economic Research on trends and distribution of incomes in the Federal Republic of Germany, France, Italy, Spain and the United Kingdom, it was shown that 'the UK is the only country where a significant increase in inequalities occurred between 1973 and 1984' (European Federation for Economic Research, October 1987, p. 13). A further study on the structure of earnings in eight Member States

Figure 6.1 Average hourly earnings of manual workers in purchasing power standards (April 1990)

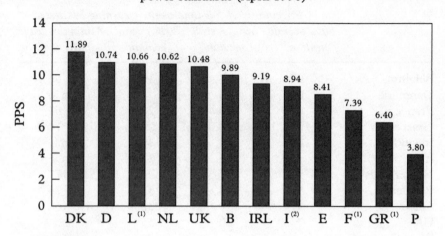

(1) October 1989
(2) Eurostat estimation

Source: *Eurostat Rapid Reports*, 5/1991

of the EC (Federal Republic of Germany, France, Italy, the Netherlands, Belgium, Luxembourg, Ireland and Denmark, but not the United Kingdom) underlined a clear difference between manual workers and non-manual workers, in France and the Benelux countries on the one hand and the Federal Republic of Germany, Italy and Denmark on the other. In the first group, the average earnings of non-manual workers were 40 per cent or more higher than those of manual workers (+61 per cent in France and Belgium, +44 per cent in Luxembourg, +40 per cent in the Netherlands), whereas they were only 20 per cent higher in the Federal Republic of Germany and 22 per cent higher in Italy or Denmark. In the first group of countries the average earnings of manual workers were lower than the lowest earnings of non-manual workers (i.e. of clerical staff), whereas the opposite applies in the Federal Republic of Germany and Italy.

The average earnings of women in Europe are 31 per cent less than those of men. The variation is most obvious in Belgium (−51 per cent) and least so in Italy (−20 per cent). Between these two extremes there are Ireland (−38 per cent), the Netherlands (−35 per cent), Luxembourg (−35 per cent), the Federal Republic of Germany (−32 per cent), France (−27 per cent) and Denmark (−24 per

Table 6.4   Low Pay in the European Community

| | Percentages of full-time workers earning less than: | | | |
	50% overall median[1]	66% overall median	80% overall median	Minimum wage/ median (%)
Belgium	0	5	19	66
Denmark	0	0	1	n.a.
France	0	14	28	61
Greece	10	16	26	70[3]
Ireland	10	18	30	n.a.
Italy	9	15	25	n.a.
Netherlands	5	11	24	77
Portugal	5	12	31	74
Spain	9[2]	19	32	60
UK	7	20	35	n.a.
West Germany	6	13	25	n.a.

[1] The overall (males and females together) median wage in each case is taken from the earnings survey used to obtain the low-pay figures. The date and coverage of the surveys varies across countries
[2] 42% of the median wage
[3] 70% of the average wage

Source: Bazen and Benhayoun, 1992, p. 625

cent). These figures take into account both the fact that women workers are generally at a disadvantage over men because of poorer qualifications and shorter periods of service and the fact that there may be wage discrimination against women. Most significantly, however, is an occupational structure across Europe which tends to locate women among the low paid (CERC, 1990).

While in absolute terms the low paid are more likely to be found in the poorer States of southern Europe, low pay is an issue in all EC countries, since it clearly refers to those in the lower level of income distribution in each country. While the relative incidence of low pay is difficult to compare because of the way in which certain groups (part time workers etc.) are included in the figures, it is clear that low pay is more of an issue in some countries than in others. Table 6.4 indicates the proportion of workers earning less than half, two-thirds and 80 per cent of median earnings in EC countries. While the figures need to be interpreted with some care, it is clear that low pay is an issue in the United Kingdom, the only country which has more than a third of full time workers earning less than 80 per cent of median earnings. In France and Belgium, on the other hand, a negligible proportion of the workforce earns less than 50 per cent of the median, since the national minimum wage is set at a level higher than 60 per cent of median earnings (Bazen and Benhayoun, 1992, p. 625).

The minimum wage

In order to minimize pay inequalities, and to protect vulnerable workers in sectors where collective bargaining provisions are weak or non-existent, the vast majority of countries in Western Europe have introduced some form of minimum wage regulation. In some countries, for example, France, Luxembourg, the Netherlands, Portugal and Spain, there is a statutory minimum wage which is fixed by government. In others a minimum wage level is set by collective agreement at the national level (Belgium and Greece) or at the industry level (Denmark, the Federal Republic of Germany and Italy). In the Greek case, for example, the Federation of Greek Industries and the General Confederation of Greek Labour meet annually to decide upon a figure and, if negotiations fail, then the minimum wage is set as a result of a process of arbitration. In the German case there is evidence to show that the minimum wage acts as a reference point for companies not covered by collective agreements. In a further group of countries within the EC, minimum wages for certain categories of employees or for certain sectors of employment (generally where union organization is limited) have been set by wages councils, as in the United Kingdom, or the joint labour committees, as in Ireland. In the United Kingdom, however, there have been recent changes. The Wages Act (1986) considerably reduced the powers of wages councils, and they can no longer set wages for employees under the age of 21 and more than one set of minimum hourly rates and overtime rates for adults. In 1993 legislation was introduced to abolish wages councils, and this means that the United Kingdom is the only country in Western Europe with no minimum wage protection.

The level of the minimum wage varies considerably from one country to another, as can be seen from table 6.5. In the prosperous countries of northern Europe the minimum wage stood in 1990 at £550–600, whereas in the countries of southern Europe the figure stood at £123 in Portugal, £185 in Greece and £253 in Spain.

Table 6.5   Summary of minimum pay rates in Western Europe
(1990)

	Minimum (adult monthly) wage	Qualifying age
Belgium	35,700 Belgian francs (approx. £599)	21.5 years
France	5,286.32 French francs (approx. £545)	18 years
Greece	55,595 Drachmas[1] (approx. £185)	18 years
Luxembourg	32,599 Luxembourg francs[2]	
	(approx. £556)	18 years
Netherlands	1,987.70 Gulden (approx. £611)	23 years
Portugal	31,500 Escudos[3] (approx. £123)	20 years
Spain	46,680 Pesetas (approx. £253)	18 years

[1] For unmarried clerical workers
[2] For unskilled workers without dependants
[3] For industry and commerce

Source: IRS Bulletin, 25 January 1991, p. 5

The minimum wage has been a subject of intense debate in all Western European countries. In France, for instance, increases are linked to the rise in the price index, itself a controversial figure and contested for years by trade union confederations. The Confédération Générale du Travail (CGT), for example, set up its own price index which incorporated a wider set of variables and thus provided a considerably higher figure than the government index. The automatic nature of minimum wage increases has also been a source of great controversy. In Italy, wages rose automatically in line with the price index, the so called *scala mobile*, until 1983. Then in the tripartite 'January Agreement', it was decided that for a three-year period (1983–5) wage increases should be made in terms of inflation forecasts and not historic inflation rates, which clearly had a significant impact on the real value of the minimum wage. Governments have also chosen to manipulate the level of the minimum wage in other ways. As part of its anti-inflation policy, the Dutch government froze the minimum wage from 1984 to 1987, as did the French government in 1982. However, on some rare occasions governments have chosen to increase the minimum wage more than the rise in the retail price index – for example, in France in 1981 and again in 1990. Moreover, the French government decided to uprate minimum wages in line with pay increases in the wider economy, even through it is only legally obliged to increase them by half the annual increase in the purchasing power of the average hourly wage. A further point – the timing of increases is significant. If minimum wages are updated annually, minimum wage earners in countries with high inflation suffer a loss of purchasing power, and in some countries special provisions exist to avoid this. In France minimum wages are upgraded each time price rises exceed 2 per cent, and in Greece updating takes place every quarter.

The minimum wage at the European level

The attempt by the Commission of the European Community to participate in the debate on minimum wage levels is not the first instance of an international response to low pay. The constitution of the ILO lists 'the provision of an adequate living wage' as a means of combatting social unrest, and it has produced a number of Recommendations and Conventions (Nos 26, 94, 95, 99) seeking to establish legally binding minimum wages over the years. Clearly, given the immense diversity of economic conditions throughout the world, it is extremely difficult to come to a consensus on the definition of 'an adequate living wage'. The ILO prevaricates somewhat by stating that countries should have as their objective the payment to the employed a wage adequate to maintain a reasonable standard of life as this is understood in their time and their country.

With the creation of the Single European Market, it is clear that the disparity in wage levels between different countries of the Community could be considered as a factor undermining competition, encouraging 'social dumping' and threatening economic and social cohesion. The Community Charter of Fundamental Social Rights for Workers states that 'all employment shall be fairly remunerated' (Article 5), and goes on to say that 'workers shall be assured of an equitable wage, i.e. a wage sufficient to enable them to have a decent standard of living'. 'Fair', 'equitable' and 'decent' require further qualification, and the Commission is engaged in an exercise to establish such definitions. This said, there is no likelihood of the introduction of a European minimum wage. Within the Social Charter itself, the element of subsidiarity is very strong – 'all employment should be fairly remunerated', but 'in accordance with arrangements applying in each country' – and the Action Programme accompanying the Social Charter only contains a proposal for an EC opinion on 'equitable remuneration', a non-binding instrument which can be ignored by Member States. Moreover, the Social Chapter appended to the Treaty on European Union which was negotiated at the Inter-governmental Conference in Maastricht in December 1991 specifically excluded the issue of pay from EC decision making. However, as Bazen and Benhayoun (1992) have pointed out, 'If the Commission is committed to the notion of ensuring that workers receive an equitable wage across the Community, further measures will be required' (p. 633).

Minimum wage and the British perspective

Given the mildness of the EC proposal on an equitable wage and the limited likelihood of it being implemented, it is surprising that the issue of minimum wage provision engendered such animated debate in the United Kingdom. In evidence to the House of Lords Select Committee and the European Community, the CBI described all minimum wage legislation as 'dangerous for employees' and the Engineering Employees' Federation was of the opinion that 'if every employee could turn to some machinery to establish a "decent" wage, it would cause a wages spiral'. The TUC and the Low Pay Unit, on the other hand, supported the introduction of a national minimum wage, the later calling for a figure of two-thirds median full time earnings. The issue of the minimum wage became one of the major political footballs in the run-up to the 1992 election. The Labour Party proposed a floor for wages at 50 per cent of the mid-point of men's earnings (£3.40 per hour in 1991) rising to two-thirds over time. Michael Howard, the then Secretary of State for Employment, counter-attacked by highlighting employment effects of the introduction of minimum wage provision. He claimed that the inflationary effects of the Labour Party proposals would increase labour costs dramatically, which in turn would lead to a two million increase in the number of unemployed. These figures too need further substantiation. They would seem to be based on the strict retention of wage differentials throughout the economy. However, as was indicated by Tony Blair, the then Labour Party front bench spokesperson on employment, the Governor of the Bank of England would not get a 25 per cent increase on his £155,000 salary just because the cleaning lady did (*The Independent*, 12 June 1991).

Both, Howard and Blair, quote OECD reports on the French

situation to back up their arguments, but they carefully use different OECD reports. Blair quoted Bazen and Martin who, in the conclusion to their article on the impact of the minimum wage on earnings and employment in France, noted: 'increases in the real value of the SMIC [the minimum wage] have exerted significant upward pressure on real youth earnings. We have not been able to establish satisfactorily, however, that increases in real youth labour costs have had a negative impact on youth employment' (Bazen and Martin, 1991, p. 215). Howard, on the other hand, quoted an OECD survey on the French economy which stated 'that the increase in the relative value of the SMIC in the 1980s is likely to have reduced employment levels, especially for youths and the unskilled'. According to Evans, however, 'research has failed to find satisfactory evidence to link minimum wages with poor employment performance in France' (*Financial Times*, 14 June 1991). Moreover, one element neglected by the two political protagonists is that it is not clear whether the French case would automatically replicate itself in the United Kingdom.

Collective Redundancies

Jobs have disappeared in Western Europe as a result of a series of waves of collective redundancies which have in turn occurred as a result of cyclical decline in economic activity linked to the aftermath of the oil crises, the structural decline of various industries, changes in working practice due to the introduction of new technologies and industrial reorganization, and the consequences of government policy.

Redundancies, of course, do not have to result automatically from these changes in the labour market. They may be avoided by enabling employees to work on a different basis, as the result of retraining or changes in working practices, or by switching to new or different products or services, a process which often takes place. Evidence would show nevertheless that employers tend to take refuge in collective redundancy schemes, particularly when the ensuing economic costs can be passed on to external bodies. We examined unemployment in chapter 1, but it is important to note here that many of the job losses in manufacturing industry took place as plant closures and wholesale redundancies rather than through slow decline and so-called 'natural wastage'. Whole industries have been decimated, for example, coal and steel; others are on the brink of extinction, the merchant shipbuilding industry being a case in point. From 1975 to 1982 employment in shipbuilding declined by 60 per cent in Sweden, 41 per cent in the Federal Republic of Germany, 33 per cent in Belgium and Denmark, 31 per cent in the Netherlands, 27 per cent in France and 26 per cent in the United Kingdom. A large number of yards closed, Nakskov Vaerft and Helgingör Vaerft in Denmark, NDMS in the Netherlands, Erksberg, Oresundsvarvet, Uddevallavarvet and Kockums in Sweden, and AG Weser in the Federal Republic of Germany (Stråth, 1987). As can be seen from table 6.6, employment in new shipbuilding has continued to decline, so that by 1987 only 75,404 people were employed in the industry. Since then, other yard closures have taken place – for example, Dunkirk, la Seyne and Nantes in France, and Sunderland Shipbuilders in the United Kingdom.

All countries in Western Europe have responded to the need to help protect employees in the event of collective redundancies and all countries in the European Community have introduced some form of statutory regulation to implement the 1975 EC Directive on collective redundancies. The most salient three features are definitions of collective redundancies, information and consultation procedures and arrangements for compensation. In the United Kingdom, a collective redundancy refers to the termination of contract of more than one employee, but in Belgium, collective redundancies exist if within a period of 60 days a decision has been taken to dismiss for operational reasons at least 10 employees in firms with between 21 and 99 employees, at least 10 per cent of the workforce in companies with between 100 and 299 employees and at least 30 employees in companies with 300 employees or more.

Procedures for making collective redundancies vary somewhat from one country to another. In Belgium, for example, workers' representatives must be informed in writing. The works council is entitled to make its own counter-proposals, but has no formal right to veto the original proposal. The firm must inform the regional office of the National Employment Office before it makes its final decision, and it may not give employees notice of redundancy until 30 days have elapsed subsequent to the notification of the original intention. In the United Kingdom the employer must tell union representatives in writing the reasons for the proposed dismissals, the number of redundancies, the selection rationale and the ways in which the dismissals are to be carried out. During consultations,

Table 6.6 Employment in new shipbuilding

	1980	1981	1982	1983	1984	1985	1986	1987
Belgium	6,523	6,347	4,680	4,104	4,060	3,923	2,995	2,548
Denmark	11,400	11,350	11,800	11,200	10,300	10,200	7,000	7,000
Germany	24,784	26,521	27,600	25,966	22,189	22,260	18,184	12,875
Greece	2,627	3,393	2,900	2,812	2,000	2,000	1,709	1,621
France[1]	22,200	22,200	21,600	21,000	16,940	15,058	13,700	8,940
Ireland	750	762	882	550	n.a.	n.a.	n.a.	n.a.
Italy[2]	18,000	16,500	13,750	12,800	12,800	12,000	11,570	9,500
Netherlands[3]	13,100	13,100	12,800	11,250	10,330	6,236	5,400	3,600
UK[4]	24,800	25,345	25,000	20,486	14,655	10,200	8,500	8,000
EC 10	124,229	125,518	121,012	110,168	93,274	81,877	69,058	54,084
Spain[5]	n.a.	n.a.	n.a.	n.a.	n.a.	18,000	18,000	17,300
Portugal	n.a.	n.a.	n.a.	n.a.	n.a.	5,370	5,087	5,020
EC 12	n.a.	n.a.	n.a.	n.a.	n.a.	105,247	92,145	76,404

[1] 1986–7 Employment in civil new shipbuilding, as well as para-naval activities (transformation, military and offshore shipbuilding). According to this method, previous years were: 1975, 32,500; 1980, 23,700; 1985, 17,700

[2] 1985–7 estimated. 1987: 2,780 unemployed should be added to the figure; of these, 2,000 represent a structural over-capacity for whom no new jobs can be found

[3] 1986–7 estimated

[4] 1985–7 excluding Harland & Wolf (Northern Ireland), estimated as 1985–6, 4,000, 1987, 3,500

[5] 1987 estimated

Source: Eurostat (1990) *Panorama of EC Industry*

employers are required to consider union proposals and, if they are rejected, reasons must be given for this. In other countries there are priorities for deciding which employees should be made redundant. Spain, for example, has a national policy whereby employees aged over 40, the longest serving within each occupational category, employees with large families, the disabled and workers' representatives have priority in retaining their jobs.

Redundancy payments differ considerably. In Belgium, for example, in addition to normal pay for the period of notice, employees subjected to collective redundancy qualify under a national collective agreement for special monthly payments from their employer. In larger companies, where collective redundancies involve significant numbers of employees, it is normal for employers and trade unions to negotiate a 'social plan' offering a package of measures to offset the effects of redundancies, and this will often provide for additional payments. In France, employees with two years' service and who are employed on an unlimited contract are entitled to one-tenth of a month's salary for each year of service, and a further one-fifteenth of a month's salary is paid for each year's service over ten. In both countries, these provisions may be improved upon by collective agreement. The situation in the Federal Republic of Germany is quite different because there are no rights to payment by law. However, payments may be laid down by collective agreement or by 'social plans' which are negotiated locally by management and works councils (*European Industrial Relations Review*, 1989a).

Legislative and collective bargaining arrangements have made it slightly more difficult for employers to 'hire and fire' at will, since the information and consultation procedures may be protracted and the compensation arrangements may be relatively costly. This was considered to be the case in France in the mid-1980s. France was the only Western European country to have a system which required prior authorization of redundancies by its Labour Inspectorate. The negotiations and discussions with labour inspectors were thought by employers to be too convoluted and time-consuming and in 1986 a law, introduced by the newly elected right-of-centre government, aimed to return to companies a greater responsibility in the management of their workforce. As a result, the need for prior authorization was abolished, as was the need to check the validity of the employers' grounds for announcing redundancies. When a left-of-centre government was re-elected in 1988, it produced a bill which, while not returning to the situation before

1986, aimed, in theory, to make the need for redundancies less pressing by encouraging forward planning and retraining, and redeployment by means of enhanced information and consultation with workers representatives. The law required that employers meet with works councils to give details of planned future employment levels and accompanying actions. Secondly, the law provided for State-financed incentives for companies that undertake long-term training initiatives for workers needing to adapt to changes in work and in employment levels. Thirdly, it has been made more difficult to dismiss workers over 55, a group particularly at risk. Fourthly, employers are now required to produce a 'social plan' – a set of measures for avoiding redundancies, limiting their number and enabling redeployment. Fifthly, labour inspectors have a new role and are able to make formal suggestions on 'social plans'. Sixthly, employers are required to offer a retraining agreement to all employees made redundant. Moreover, when employees contest the grounds for their redundancies, the burden of proof lies with the employer who will now have to provide evidence to justify their decisions. Finally, all employees made redundant are theoretically given priority for re-employment (*European Industrial Relations Review*, July 1989, pp. 23–4). This latest law tips the balance back in favour of employees, and it remains to be seen if it will have the desired effect and if it will be retained by the right-of-centre government elected in 1993.

Collective redundancies at the European level

Within the framework of the approximation of existing employment conditions, the EC took an interest in the issue of collective redundancies for the first time in the mid-1970s. A European multinational company, *Akzo*, was involved in a restructuring exercise requiring 5,000 collective redundancies, and it was engaged in identifying the most cost-effective countries in which to make them. This spurred on the Council of Ministers to adopt a Directive establishing a body of rules to be applied to all Member States, but leaving it up to Member States to apply or introduce more favourable provisions for employees (Blanpain, 1991, pp. 153–4). The Directive defined collective redundancies as 'dismissals effected by an employer for one or more reasons not related to the individual workers concerned'. Redundancies are defined as collective, if the number of redundancies is:

- either, over a period of 30 days
  1　at least 10 in establishments normally employing more than 20 and less than 100 workers,
  2　at least 10 per cent of the number of workers in establishments normally employing at least 100 but less than 300 workers,
  3　at least 30 in establishments normally employing 300 workers or more;
- or, over a period of 90 days, at least 20, whatever the number of workers normally employed in the establishments in question.

The Directive does not stop the employer making redundancies, it merely aims to protect workers' rights by obliging companies to give them and their representatives notice before redundancies could proceed (30 days), which would in theory give time to negotiate an alternative to redundancies or, otherwise, the terms and conditions of a redundancy package. The employer is obliged to consult the worker's representatives with a view to reaching an agreement (Article 2.1). To enable worker's representatives to make constructive proposals, the employer must supply them with all relevant information and must in any event give in writing the reason for the redundancies, the number of workers normally employed and the period over which the redundancies are to be effected. The employer is obliged to forward to the competent authority a copy of the information given to the workers (Article 2.3). Consultation should cover ways and means of avoiding collective redundancies or reducing the number of workers affected, and mitigating the consequences (75/129/EEC).

At the end of the 1980s the Commission published a draft Directive on collective redundancies which aimed to take the process a little further. It sought to respond to the transnational nature of decision making in companies and to extend regulations to non-EC based parent companies. The draft Directive requires that consultation procedures should begin 'in good time' and that these consultations should cover ways of minimizing the number of employees affected, and that in Member States which do not have established procedures for information and consultation, appropriate mechanisms for consultation should be set up. In addition, the draft Directive required that Member States should take necessary measures so that redundant workers have the right to redundancy payments reflecting their length of service and wage levels or unemployment benefit. Finally, a significant innovation, the draft

Directive allowed for sanctions ('appropriate remedies') to be taken against companies failing to comply.

These proposals were not received with great enthusiasm by the representatives of either side of industry at the European level although a new Directive was eventually agreed. UNICE was opposed in principle to this draft Directive, claiming that there was no need for transnational measures. It also criticized the reference to the payment of compensation since this would interfere with national social security systems (which are beyond the competence of the EC) and it opposed any reference to sanctions which could be taken against recalcitrant firms. The ETUC was more positive but expressed disappointment that the draft Directive was based on Article 100 which requires unanimity in the Council of Ministers. According to the ETUC, the draft Directive was found wanting in a number of major areas: firstly, it failed to anticipate the possibility of redundancies by ensuring that workers' representatives were involved at an earlier stage in employment planning; secondly, it failed to prevent redundancies by plans for redeploying and retraining existing employees; the draft Directive should give public authorities proper powers to intervene in the decision-making process leading up to a situation where redundancies were proposed; finally, quantitative thresholds should be lowered, to ensure that larger numbers of firms were covered.

Collective redundancies and the British perspective

After the introduction of the original Directive, the United Kingdom government had two years to ensure that it introduced appropriate legislation at the national level. The Commission delivered a 'reasoned opinion' of the implementation of the Directive, which stated that the Employment Protection Act (1975) failed to provide for the designation of employee representatives for bargaining and other purposes where this did not occur voluntarily in practice. The Commission also indicated that the definition of 'redundancy' was broader in the 1975 Directive than in the Employment Protection Act (1975), with the result that it was theoretically possible to dismiss the entire workforce and then re-employ them. This first point of criticism was addressed by Article 4 (4) of the new draft Directive, which advocated the creation of further mechanisms where national laws and practices for information and consultation procedures do not exist. This may make it possible for employers to encourage the creation of non-independent staff associations to the detriment of existing trade unions. In 1993, the UK government's Trade Union Reform and Employment Rights Act introduced a number of changes to bring British law into line with the original Collective Redundancies Directive and the more recent provisions.

Health and Safety

Health and safety at work is a key employee relations issue which affects the lives of all employees and also their immediate family. Public authorities at all levels have recognized their responsibility in ensuring that employees enjoy safe working conditions and as a result have introduced a wide range of appropriate measures. At the European level health and safety at work has become particularly important since being identified in the Single European Act as one of the issues requiring decisions within the Council of Ministers based on qualified majority voting.

There is considerable variation in the incidence of accidents at work. Comparability is problematical as there are definitional variations and evidence of under-reporting of accidents, but the most widely used yardstick, the rate per 1,000 workers, makes it possible to compare countries with different size working populations. Unfortunately it has the disadvantage of excluding working time (whether expressed in terms of contractual working time, part time work, overtime or holidays). However, some countries in Western Europe – Belgium and Sweden for example – have tried to obviate this discrepancy by presenting their accident at work statistics in terms of the rate per one million working hours.

Figures collected by the OECD show that there has been a considerable decline in the number of fatalities per 1,000 workers since the late 1960s, as can be seen from figure 6.2. Since 1965 fatality rates have declined by about two-thirds or more in France, the Federal Republic of Germany, Sweden and the United Kingdom, by about half in Austria, and by one-third in Norway. These significant reductions in fatalities at work can be explained by a variety of reasons: improvements in medical care and in the efficiency of the emergency services, changes in the pattern of employment with a move from the industrial to the less hazardous tertiary sector, the introduction of automation in the more dangerous work processes,

Figure 6.2 Occupational fatality rates (per 100,000 employed)

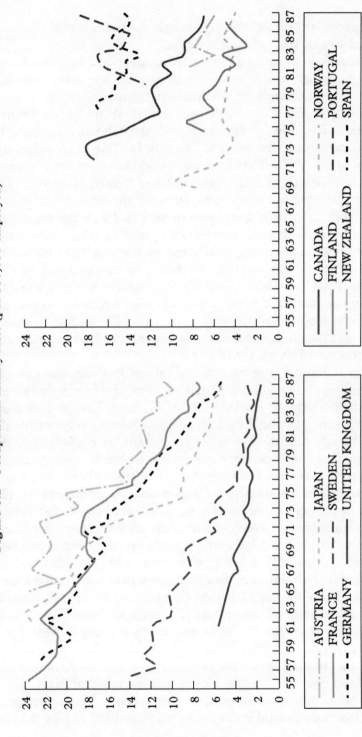

Source: Organization for Economic Co-operation and Development, 1989, p. 138

the improvement in machinery design and the introduction of improved health and safety legislation.

The situation is slightly different for occupational injuries. As can be seen from figure 6.3, there has been a decline since the mid-1960s in the incidence of occupational injuries, but to a lesser extent than for fatalities. Rates declined by about half in France, the Federal Republic of Germany and the United Kingdom, by about 30 per cent in Austria and Sweden. Decline has levelled out, however, in the 1980s in some countries and has even been reversed somewhat in Portugal and Spain and the United Kingdom. The factors influencing the relationship between the worker, technology and the working environment seem to have had a greater impact on reducing fatalities than on occupational injuries. The incidence of fatalities may have been more affected by the quality of life-saving medical advances whereas the incidence of occupational injuries may have been more influenced by the increase in more accurate reporting (as compared with fatality statistics which have generally always been reported accurately), thus artificially leading to slower declines statistically (Organization for Economic Co-operation and Development, 1989, p. 146).

Figures 6.2 and 6.3 show that the rate of fatalities and occupational injuries in the United Kingdom compares relatively favourably with the rates in the majority of Western Europe countries. This is explained by the British Health and Safety Executive by 'the relative strengths of the British safety system, as a whole, and the part played by the regulatory authorities within it, though clearly important, may not fully explain this. They are in themselves a part of a complex set of wider social and economic influences . . . The increase in the serious injury rate in some sectors in Great Britain in line with increased employment . . . is an indication that Great Britain's relatively good industrial accident record cannot be taken for granted' (Health and Safety Executive, 1991, p. 22).

Approaches to monitoring health and safety at work reveal a considerable level of diversity between countries in Western Europe. In some of the Member States of the EC, such as Greece, Italy, Luxembourg and Portugal, the basic provisions relating to health and safety are laid down within written constitutions. In others, such as France, the Federal Republic of Germany, the Netherlands and Spain these basic provisions are set out in national legal codes. Finally, protection of all individuals is provided by civil or common law in Denmark, Ireland and the United Kingdom, and by the civil

Figure 6.3 Occupational injury rates (per 1,000 employed)

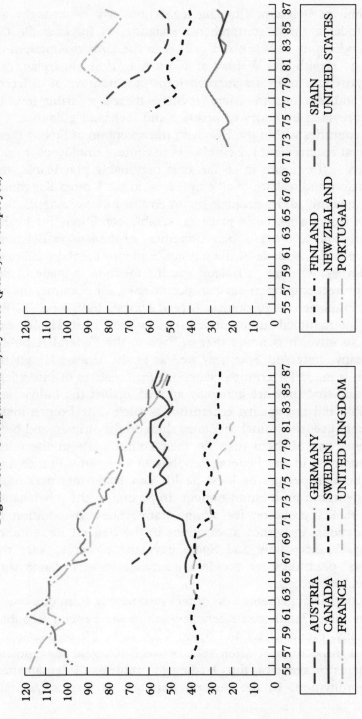

Source: Organization for Economic Co-operation and Development, 1989, p. 145

code alone in Belgium. Ensuing legislation may be brought together under a single comprehensive statute, as for example the Health and Safety at Work Act (1974) in the United Kingdom or the Safety, Health and Welfare at Work Act (1989) in Ireland, or it may exist in a more fragmented form in a number of different laws. In addition, in some Member States there is a further level of control provided by codes of practice and technical guidance.

In all countries within the EC (with the exception of Spain) there is a general requirement for employers to protect employees' health and safety – 'to ensure in so far as is reasonably practicable, the health, safety and welfare of all employees' in the United Kingdom, or more quaintly and patronizingly 'to ensure *with the diligence of a good father* that work takes place in suitable conditions for health and safety, and to observe the requirement of the law' in Belgium. In Italy mention is made of the physical and also mental welfare of all employees, whereas in Ireland specific mention is made of the need to protect employees against specific risks, for example, the inhalation of dangerous substances (*Social Europe*, 2/1990 pp. 37–8).

In an international survey undertaken by the British Health and Safety Executive, it is noted that in France, the Federal Republic of Germany, Italy and Spain, as well as in the United Kingdom, provision is made for criminal sanctions for breaches of safety legislation and that they are generally applied against the individuals responsible and not against enterprises as such. The French make much more use of criminal sanctions than do the British, and both make more use of them than do their counterparts in the other three countries. In the Federal Republic of Germany, France and Italy, labour inspectors or local health unit inspectors may issue enforcement and prohibition notices. In Spain, on the other hand, the law makes provision for administrative fines. In addition to these sanctions, insurance associations in the Federal Republic of Germany, France, Italy and Spain have the power to vary the employers' premiums for accident insurance in accordance with their accident records.

Inspection arrangements also differ considerably from one country to another. Health and safety at work in the Federal Republic of Germany, France, Italy and Spain tends to be the responsibility of several inspectorates, often split between different government departments or agencies, thus leading to problems of demarcation and co-ordination. In the Federal Republic of Germany, State labour inspectors are employed by the different *Länder*, and technical inspectors are employed by insurance associations. The former concentrate around one-tenth of their time on health and safety issues, the rest being spent on environmental matters and working conditions. The latter are primarily responsible for health and safety at work within different industrial sectors. In France labour inspectors come from the Ministries of Transport, Agriculture and Employment and spend approximately one-third of their time on health and safety issues. 'Advisory engineers' from the insurance associations investigate accidents and advise employers, and thus play an important ancillary part in inspection. In addition, there are other agencies which play an inspection role. In Italy labour inspection is primarily carried out by local health units which come under the auspices of the Ministry of Health. Inspectors from the Ministry of Employment are responsible for investigating accidents and for general health and safety inspection in those parts of the country where the local health units function imperfectly. In Spain labour inspectors spend about one-seventh of their time on health and safety issues; they are provided with technical and specialized assistance by a National Institute of Health and Safety at Work, which is also a part of the Ministry of Employment (Health and Safety Executive, 1991, pp. 2–4).

Employers and trade unions are of course closely associated with numerous aspects of health and safety issues. At the national level, they jointly manage the accident assurance associations in the Federal Republic of Germany, and they are represented on the governing bodies of research institutes in France, Italy and Spain. In the United Kingdom, on the other hand, they participate, with government representatives, in policy formulation and the preparation of regulations. At the workplace level, trade unions have an opportunity to influence policy and practice on health and safety issues in all Member States of the EC. In all countries there are legal or contractual requirements which ensure some form of workplace representation in the field of health and safety. In countries such as the Federal Republic of Germany, Italy and Luxembourg, health and safety issues are dealt with by the works councils. In Belgium, France and Spain, there are separate health and safety committees. In the United Kingdom, safety representatives are appointed by recognized trade unions and, if they so wish, a health and safety committee may be set up (European Trade Union Institute, 1990b).

This means that the extent to which employee representatives may influence decision making varies considerably from one country to another.

Health and safety at the European level

The basis for EC action in the field of health and safety is to be found in Articles 100 and 118 of the Treaty of Rome; the former was concerned specifically with the approximation of laws to ensure the operation of the Common Market, and provides for the adoption of Directives, while the latter was concerned with employment, working conditions, the prevention of occupational accidents and diseases and occupational hygiene, and only requires the Commission to promote close co-operation between Member States. In the early years, the Commission concentrated its attention on gathering information. In terms of action the first key date was 1974 when the Council of Ministers resolved to initiate a Social Action Programme which aimed to improve employees' living and working conditions, with specific reference to improvements in health and safety at work. This Programme prompted the adoption of two Directives: provision of safety signs at work (77/576/EEC); protection of health of workers exposed to vinyl chloride monomer (78/610/EEC); and a Resolution on an Action Programme for Health and Safety at work (78/C/165/1). Further Directives were to follow: protection of workers from the risks related to exposure to chemical, physical and biological agents at work (80/1107/EEC, 'the harmful agents Directive'); major accident hazards of certain industrial activities (82/501/EEC, 'the Seveso Directive'); protection of workers from the risks related to lead (82/605/EEC), asbestos (83/477/EEC), noise (86/118/EEC); and protection of workers by the banning of certain specified agents and/or certain work activities (88/364/EEC).

A turning point came with the signing of the Single European Act. The new Article 118a introduced qualified majority voting within the Council of Ministers for health and safety issues, thus making it possible to side-step the objections of reluctant governments. Member States were to pay particular attention to encouraging improvements, especially in the working environment, as regards the health and safety of workers, and set as their objective the harmonization of conditions in this area while maintaining the improvements already made. In addition, it was stated that the Community would adopt minimum requirements for gradual implementation, having regard to the conditions in each of the Member States. This commitment to high standards was, however, reduced by a clause which stated that these improvements should not impose unfair burdens on small and medium-size businesses. There is clear potential for some confusion as to the interpretation of this article. In its broadest sense, the term 'working environment' goes beyond the place where work is done and could refer to the wider social environment. The term 'health and safety' could refer not only to the physical well-being of employees, but also to their mental state, thus potentially opening up Community responsibility to a wide range of issues. At this time other Directives were approved relating to construction products (89/106/EEC), machinery (89/392/EEC) personal protective equipment (89/686/EEC), and dangerous substances and preparations (89/677/EEC).

A further significant development was the adoption of the Framework Directive on the introduction of measures to encourage improvements in the safety, hygiene and health of workers at work. This established a number of minimum standards and general principles for employers in the public and private sector to follow in protecting health and safety, including the prevention of occupational risk, and the provision of information and training. Employers are required to implement health and safety measures on the basis of the following general principles of prevention:

1 avoiding risks
2 evaluating the risks which cannot be avoided
3 combating the risks at source
4 adapting the work to the individual, especially as regards the design of workplaces, the choice of work equipment and choice of working and production methods, with a view, in particular, to alleviating monotonous work and work at a pre-determined work-rate and to reducing their effect on health
5 adapting to technical progress
6 replacing the dangerous by the non-dangerous or the less dangerous
7 developing a coherent overall prevention policy which covers technology, organization of work, working conditions, social relationships and the influence of factors related to the working environment
8 giving collective protective measures priority over individual protective measures and
9 giving appropriate instructions to the workers.

In addition, the employer is required to take into account the nature of the activities of the enterprise and/or establishment and:

1   evaluate the risks to the safety and health of workers, *inter alia* in the choice of work equipment, the chemical substances or preparations used, and the fitting-out of workplaces
2   where he entrusts tasks to a worker, take into consideration the worker's capabilities as regards health and safety
3   ensure that the planning and introduction of new technologies are the subject of consultation with the workers and/or their representatives, as regards the consequences of the choice of equipment, the working conditions and the working environment for the safety and health of workers and
4   take appropriate steps to ensure that only workers who have received adequate instructions may have access to areas where there is serious and specific danger. (89/391/EEC)

The Framework Directive did not however provide employees with a right to 'stop the job', nor to refuse to work in dangerous circumstances, a right which does exist in certain countries. Moreover, given that many of the minimum standards have been achieved in some countries, particularly in northern Europe, it is possible that they will no longer feel any need to improve their existing national standards.

This Framework Directive has opened the way for a number of so-called 'daughter' Directives relating to minimum health and safety requirements for the workplace (89/654/EEC), the use of work equipment (89/655/EEC), the use of personal protective equipment (89/656/EEC), the manual handling of loads where there is a risk of back injury (90/269/EEC) and work with visual display units (90/270/EEC).

All these Directives require that employees should receive appropriate health and safety information and appropriate training, and they and/or their representatives should have consultation and participation rights as regards the issues covered. Interestingly, these Directives may be adapted in the light of technological progress, new findings and/or as a result of future Directives, and this work is to be delegated to the Commission acting on the advice of a committee of representatives from Member States using qualified majority voting. Although Member States should inform the Commission of the ways in which they have implemented these Directives, there is still a clear doubt hanging over the effectiveness of the

Directives concerning the means available for ensuring employers' compliance, an issue which will be highlighted once the Directives have been translated into national law and then tested out in practice. It is only then that it will be possible to gauge the extent to which European legislation has improved, or worsened, national practice in terms of health and safety protection.

Health and safety and the British perspective

In general terms, it would seem that the United Kingdom will be drawn into a more legalistic approach to the resolution of health and safety problems. The Health and Safety Commission has been highly critical of this development. It has drawn attention to the 'highly prescriptive' nature of law which is made acceptable in other Member States 'by the continental normative pattern where literal interpretation is not expected'. There may be pressure, as in some northern European States, to ban processes or substances, or to apply strict quantitative limits, where in the United Kingdom a more flexible approach has been considered 'both desirable and necessary'. The impact of the qualified majority process within the Council of Ministers has 'changed the nature of the negotiating process' and 'made the United Kingdom more vulnerable in certain respects'. The Health and Safety Commission has pointed out that there may be a more rapid collapse of bargaining positions within the Council of Ministers, and a shorter time period in which to bring to bear technical and other arguments. In these conditions, 'our large body of recently achieved law is at risk to the rapid counterplay of argument and compromise, with the risk that less carefully constructed and industrially-acceptable solutions will emerge' (Health and Safety Commission, 1990, p. 15). British 'vulnerability' lies in the fact that the United Kingdom will be required to implement more and more health and safety legislation coming from the EC with which it may not agree.

Directives take some time to be transformed into national law, and it takes some time again before it is possible to ascertain how they have been implemented and whether this will make an impact on health and safety compliance in the United Kingdom. However, one observer, on behalf of the CBI, has noted two major areas which 'will need careful analysis and thought before being translated into United Kingdom jurisprudence'. Firstly, the Framework Directive stipulates that employers should undertake precise and specific functions, whereas the Health and Safety at Work Act lays down general duties for employers – 'the directives do not give employers due discretion to do their job properly: they prescribe a number of precise and often technical duties relating to some risks, but too often they fail to prescribe some of the more general and more important obligations'. Secondly, in the United Kingdom employers have to discharge their duties in the field of health and safety 'so far as reasonably practical'. By contrast the Framework Directive includes a *force majeure* clause which may be interpreted in some countries as a qualification on employers' obligations. The British approach, however, would require the letter of the law to be applied, which would mean that employers in the United Kingdom could lose the right to use their own judgement (Eberlie, 1990).

On the other hand, according to Walters (1990) 'the framework Directive has a number of provisions with which British legislation could be significantly improved especially in ways that would enhance its operation in workplaces where the SRSC (Safety Representatives and Safety Committees) regulations are already implemented', particularly the employer obligation to consult safety representatives on the designation of safety specialists and the use of outside specialists. This could be even more significant if this provision on safety specialists was interpreted as a requirement to provide an integrated occupational health service, and if safety representatives were given the right to submit observations to visiting inspectors. Safety representatives should also have more specific protection against victimization by employers for their health and safety activities. The framework Directive could however undermine trade union rights to representation ·in the field of health and safety, since it refers to 'workers and/or their representatives' which in certain circumstances could make it possible to by-pass trade unions.

Conclusions

Collective rights in the workplace are underpinned in most Western European countries by legislation, the provisions of which are then complemented by collective agreement. This system provides a minimum standard of cover for all employees, even those in the most vulnerable sectors of society, and a relative level of flexibility in terms of local labour market needs and demands. The major exception to this rule is the United Kingdom which has traditionally tended to favour a voluntaristic approach based on collective bargaining alone. This variegated Western European model is best typified in this chapter by the sections on working time and wages, but cannot be sustained so easily for the issues of health and safety at work and collective redundancies which tend to demonstrate a basic legalistic approach with collective agreement improvements in all countries, even in the United Kingdom. It could be argued that health and safety at work is an exception, because it has traditionally been considered primarily as an element of health provision and not merely as an employee relations issue, hence the need for State intervention. The issue of collective redundancies is also an interesting case apart, but for a different reason, namely, the embryonic Europeanization of employee relations. The European Community has introduced a measure of EC-wide legislation on collective redundancies, and consequently all Member States have been obliged to introduce appropriate national legislation on this issue, which has then been topped up by collective agreement to reflect the needs and the demands of the different local labour markets.

Increasingly, the EC has shown an interest in a range of employee relations issues relating to collective rights in the workplace. The overall agreement on the Social Charter and the subsequent Action Programme has given the Commission of the EC an opportunity to push ahead with a variety of different legislative proposals, and, as was seen in this chapter, the Council of Ministers has already agreed Directives on collective redundancies and a variety of health and safety issues. However, it has not yet come to any agreement on the other two subjects, wages and working time. The Commission has put forward a draft Directive on working time, an issue which traditionally in the United Kingdom would have been left solely to employers and trade unions to decide upon within the process of collective bargaining. At the time of writing, the British government is challenging the legal basis of the Directive. A more sensitive issue, the minimum wage, has been treated with greater circumspection by the Commission and it has only attempted to put forward an Opinion.

It is not yet fully clear what the impact of EC initiatives will be on employee relations in the United Kingdom. It is possible that some draft Directives will not receive the approval of the Council of Ministers. It is also possible that they will only make their passage through the Council of Ministers if they have been emptied of content. When the Social Chapter accompanying the Treaty on

European Union comes into force, the United Kingdom will presumably not be required to implement any of the new social policy measures which can be decided by qualified majority voting within the Council of Ministers. Where new Directives have been approved, particularly in the field of health and safety at work, it is too early yet to identify the real impact in terms of changes in practice. What is clear however, is that it is no longer possible to consider a range of employee relations issues concerning collective rights at work in a geographical and socio-economic vacuum, with no reference to other Western European countries.

Conclusions

The pattern of employee relations in Western Europe has undergone considerable change during the 1980s and remains extremely varied. Elements of divergence have appeared within a broader framework of convergence. Given further pressures emanating from multinational economic forces and supranational political institutions, an embryonic Europeanization of employee relations has been identified.

A range of factors linked with increasing global competitiveness within and outside Europe has led employers to restructure production and to demand greater flexibility in the labour market. This has been associated with higher levels of overall unemployment, a progressive switch from the industrial to the service sector, an increase in so-called atypical employment (part time and temporary work), particularly in countries such as the United Kingdom and the Netherlands, with the result that within Western Europe core and peripheral labour markets have developed.

There are still considerable differences between the voluntarist tradition to be found in the United Kingdom and the legalist traditions prevalent in most countries of continental Europe, which have often been the source of major misunderstandings within the decision-making bodies of the European Community. There are, however, signs of change, particularly where the deregulation of the labour market has been encouraged. In many countries, governments have attempted to disentangle themselves from certain employee relations practices. For example, there is considerable speculation about the 'decline' of the Swedish model, a process which accelerated with the change of government in Sweden at the beginning of the 1990s. In other countries, the United Kingdom for example, successive Conservative governments have introduced a variety of laws designed specifically to undermine the position of

one of the social actors, the trade unions. Also, while some governments have still been prepared to integrate the social actors, trade
unions and employers' federations, into a neo-corporatist decision-
making process, others have been more interested in steadily dismantling these structures and in excluding the trade unions, in
particular, from this form of consultation and decision making.
This has led to the further resolution of numerous employee relations
issues by means of collective bargaining even in countries with a
legalist and neo-corporatist tradition. However, some governments
continued to operate sporadic wage policies in the 1980s, and others
have aimed to control wage inflation by means of 'cash limits' in
the public sector and calls for wage moderation throughout the
entire economy. Finally, there would seem to be evidence of a
change in the notion of the State as a 'model employer', as a result
of the restrictions placed on trade union activity, the withdrawal of
bargaining rights in certain sectors and the creation of a hostile
environment dominated by privatization.

Among social actors, change has been uneven. Trade unions
have tended to be on the defensive in most Western European
countries. While membership has remained relatively static and at
a high level in Scandinavia, it has fallen significantly in other countries, notably France, the Netherlands and the United Kingdom.
Decline has not been automatic but has tended to occur when
trade unions have been faced with a number of variables – declining manufacturing industry, growth in the service sector and in the
number of small and medium-size enterprises, increases in so-called
atypical work, changes in management practice and occasional
open hostility from governments. Divergence in membership patterns has been countered to a certain extent by convergence over
structures and aims. Some individual trade unions have merged
and, with the general decline in the importance of ideological and
confessional differences, trade union confederations in a number
of countries – Belgium, Italy and Spain, for example – have been
more prepared to co-ordinate some of their activities. Only France
and, to a lesser extent, Portugal remain troubled by rivalry and
discord.

Employers and managers have been faced with the complex
problems of the management of change. Manufacturing industry
in Western Europe has been confronted with the challenge of
increased energy costs following the oil price rises, the growth of
competition from the newly industrialized countries and economic

recession. Given the declining influence of organized labour and the deregulatory policies of many European governments, management has taken the opportunity to restructure employee relations policies. There has been a clear trend towards the decentralization of decision making within a corporate framework, the growth in human resource management policies and internationalization of management careers. Public sector managers have also had to develop policies which cope with downward shifts in resource allocation and employment alongside programmes of privatization.

The relations between social actors, trade unions and employers show signs of continuity and change. The structure of collective bargaining is complex and somewhat resistant to change. Many features remain stable and, in most Western European countries, national sector-wide bargaining is predominant. However, some decentralization has taken place. Where national economy-wide bargaining has been the norm, there are examples, such as Sweden, where these structures are starting to break down; in other countries with national sector-wide bargaining, regional and company-wide bargaining have developed. There is an overall consensus in most countries of Western Europe about the need for some form of statutory employee representation, although it is clear that the information, consultation and participation rights enjoyed by employees vary greatly from one country to another. There has been relative stability in this form of representation, but change has been noticeable with the introduction of non-mandatory, management-led initiatives, such as quality circles, which stand outside and compete with more formalized participation structures and information bodies. The breakdown in relations between social actors has been less noticeable than in earlier decades. Levels of industrial conflict have declined overall in Western Europe during the 1980s, but the pattern of strike activity remains remarkably varied. Some countries – Austria, the Federal Republic of Germany, the Netherlands and Switzerland – are almost strike-free, whereas Greece, Ireland, Italy and Spain, have significantly higher levels of conflict. No single academic argument, whether institutional, political or economic, can account for these variations, but it would seem that, in the 1980s at least, there has been a significant link between levels of nominal wages and levels of strike activity.

In most Western European countries, employee rights have been underpinned by legislation and reinforced by voluntaristic means. As part of the neo-corporatism of the 1970s a range of new rights emerged in areas such as employment protection and equal opportunities. While trends have been similar, terms and conditions of employment differ widely across Western Europe. At one end of the spectrum, in the Federal Republic of Germany for example, wages are high, the working week is short, holidays are long, equal opportunities are comparatively well developed and health and safety at work is well protected. At the other end of the spectrum, in Ireland, Portugal and Greece for example, terms and conditions of employment are generally less attractive. The ways in which these terms and conditions of employment are decided vary somewhat, but patterns nevertheless emerge. Health and safety at work is an issue which is often regulated within a more legalistic framework, even within the United Kingdom. However, other issues are decided upon differently. In most Western European countries legislation underpins numerous employee rights within the workplace, thus ensuring a minimum level of cover for all employees, even those in the most vulnerable sectors of society. It is then usual to improve these basic terms and conditions by means of negotiation. In the United Kingdom, on the other hand, most terms and conditions of employment have been decided upon by means of collective bargaining alone. Increasingly, some aspects of terms and conditions of employment are influenced by policy-making at the European level. Decisions affecting collective redundancies and equal pay for men and women, for example, have generally been subject to EC Directives, which has meant that further legislative changes have been introduced at the national level.

The Europeanization of employee relations remains patchy. Forces advocating collective solidarity and harmonization stand alongside forces advocating *laissez-faire* flexibility. While similar developments are taking place within the industrial domain (the restructuring of labour markets, the partial decentralization of collective bargaining, the reduction of trade union influence, the decline of neo-corporatism), the results of these developments are also engendering more divergent practice – for instance, the restructuring of labour markets has led to a variety of types of employment and the decentralization of collective bargaining has led to differing patterns of negotiation. Moreover, within the political domain this incipient Europeanization has been checked at the level of the European Community by the re-emergence of national sovereignty as an issue under the guise of subsidiarity.

The Europeanization of labour markets is still relatively limited,

Western Europe remaining a configuration of porous regional and national labour markets. Freedom of movement of workers – one of the tenets of the Treaty of Rome and of a Common Market – has not led to migration from one country to another, with the exception of Luxembourg which has experienced high levels of inward migration from other EC countries. The vast majority of workers within the Member States remain resolutely at home, except for holidays, and so still act specifically in response to the constraints of regional and national labour markets.

The European Community has become a significant actor in the field of employee relations in Europe. The Single European Act gave a boost to this development. A Social Dimension was proposed to accompany the Single European Market, and the Community Charter of Fundamental Social Rights for Workers advocated minimum European standards for various employee relations issues. The Social Chapter of the Treaty on European Union specifically increased the competence of the European Community in the field of employee relations, at least for the eleven signatories other than the United Kingdom. In addition, by adopting majority voting in the Council of Ministers, the Member States agreed to facilitate decision making. This was established by the Single European Act in the field of health and safety and by the Social Chapter in the field of working conditions, information and consultation of workers, equality between men and women with regard to labour market opportunities and treatment at work, and the integration of persons excluded from the labour market. The acid test is the ability of the European Community institutions to agree on these measures and, in a more problematical and uncharted area, to ensure that they are properly implemented. The first tentative steps towards a diluted form of European neo-corporatism were taken with the agreement within the Treaty of European Union that the Commission should formally consult the representatives of management and labour on the future possible direction of Community action and proposals.

It would seem difficult for the major social actors at the European level to stand back from these developments. The ETUC has more and more trade union confederations within its ranks and now counts the sectoral Industry Committees as full members, with the result that it speaks on behalf of the vast majority of trade unions in Western Europe. Employer's organizations are also expanding and reviewing their European activities, and there is an increasingly significant role to be played by UNICE and CEEP. These three organizations are faced with the contrasting pressures of the need to be effective political lobbyists and the reluctance of affiliated organizations to relinquish their power to transnational corporate bodies. In addition, multinational companies themselves are effective lobbying bodies, particularly on issues such as European Works Councils. The ETUC, UNICE and CEEP have engaged in a series of discussions at the European level, and this has led to the signing of a number of common opinions. More significantly they signed a framework agreement in 1991 which allows for collective bargaining at the European level. The spirit of this agreement was incorporated into the Treaty on European Union, thus providing enhanced authority and further encouragement for a form of Europe-wide collective bargaining which has yet to be defined and developed. While most multinational companies aim to isolate employee relations issues within a resolutely national or indeed sub-national context, some have begun to contemplate the Europeanization of their employee relations activities. A dozen of so companies have agreed to set up transnational information bodies, a trend which may be reinforced either by individual company initiatives or in response to the EC draft Directive on European Works Councils.

It remains to be seen whether these recent developments will lead to the further Europeanization of employee relations. The new decision-making competences and procedures within the European Community should make it easier to agree upon a wider range of EC laws and policies. However, the propensity of some governments and employers' organizations to refuse to link a Social Dimension to the *laissez-faire* economics of the Single European Market should not be underestimated. The tentative step to introduce elements of European neo-corporatism and collective bargaining will strengthen the position of the social partners at the European level. However, for them to act effectively it will be necessary to reinforce and streamline decision-making structures. In the field of collective bargaining, it remains to be seen whether the social actors at the European level can obtain an appropriate mandate from their respective affiliated organizations to engage in meaningful negotiations, whether an appropriate level of demarcation between the national and European levels can be established and whether a consensus about the aims and contents of collective bargaining can be found.

These developments will, of course, be hampered or encouraged by other developments within and outside the European Community. The agreement with the EFTA countries to establish a European Economic Area may further encourage the Europeanization of employee relations, particularly if EFTA countries with a strong tradition of highly regulated employee relations attempt to transfer their national practice to the European level. The moves towards economic and monetary union within the European Community may necessitate a level of economic convergence which is not easily detached from some form of consensus on the Europeanization of employee relations. However, on the other hand, future presidents of the Commission may be less interested than Jacques Delors in stressing the importance of the Social Dimension. Future elections to the European Parliament may produce a majority less committed to the resolution of employee relations issues at the European level. The changes in Central and Eastern Europe may well exercise a destabilizing effect on the process of Europeanization, either because social and economic divergence within the entire continent will increase or because migratory flows in the direction of countries of the European Community will lead to disruption in their labour markets. The emphasis on subsidiarity expressed at the Lisbon European Council meeting in June 1992 may reinforce the desire of some national governments to decide employee relations issues at the national level. Finally, the faltering support for European solutions, as typified by the debates surrounding the ratification of the Maastricht Treaty, may lead to retrenchment behind national borders which will inhibit future moves towards the Europeanization of employee relations.

Bibliography

Adam, G. (1978) 'La négociation collective en France', *Droit Social*, November, pp. 385–91.

Anderman, S. (1986) 'Unfair Dismissals and Redundancy'. In Lewis, R. (ed.), *Labour Law in Britain*. Oxford: Basil Blackwell.

Armstrong, P., Glynn, A., and Harrison, J. (1984) *Capitalism Since World War Two*. London: Fontana.

Ash, N. (ed.) (1989) *The Single European Market*. W.E.A. Studies for Trade Unionists. London: Workers' Education Association.

Bachy, J. P. (ed.) (1986) *Report on Flexibility in the Labour Market*. Commission of the European Communities.

Baglioni, G. and Crouch, C. (eds) (1990) *European Industrial Relations*. London: Sage.

Bakker, I. (1988) 'Women's Employment in Comparative Perspective'. In Jensen J. et al. (eds), *Feminization of the Labour Force*. London: Polity Press.

Bamber, G. J. and Lansbury, R. D. (eds) (1987) *International and Comparative Industrial Relations*. London: Allen and Unwin.

Barnouin, B. (1986) *The European Labour Movement and European Integration*. London: Frances Pinter.

Bassett, P. (1986) *Strike Free*. London: Macmillan.

Bastien, J. (1989) 'Les Syndicats européens face au temps de travail', *Sociologie du Travail*, 3, pp. 283–300.

Bazen, S. and Benhayoun, G. (1992) 'Low pay and wage regulation in the European Community', *British Journal of Industrial Relations*, 30, 4, pp. 623–38.

Bazen, S. and Martin, J. P. (1991) 'The Impact of the Minimum Wage on Earnings and Employment in France', *OECD Economic Studies*, 16, Spring, pp. 199–221.

Bean, R. (1985) *Comparative Industrial Relations*. London: Croom Helm.

Bendiner, B. (1987) *International Labour Affairs*. Oxford: Clarendon Press.

Berghahn, V. R. and Karsten, D. (1987) *Industrial Relations in West Germany*. Oxford: Berg.

Bergougnoux, G. (1990) 'Projets européens, les politiques d'entreprise: BSN', *Droit Social*, 7–8, pp. 671–2.

Beyme, K. von (1980) *Challenge to Power*. London: Sage.

Blanpain, R. (ed.) *International Encyclopaedia for Labour Law and Industrial Relations*. Deventer: Kluwer.

Blanpain, R. (ed.) (1985) *Comparative Labour Law and Industrial Relations*. Deventer: Kluwer.

Blanpain, R. (1987) 'Recent Trends in Collective Bargaining in Belgium'. In International Labour Organization, *Collective Bargaining in Industrial Market Economics: A Reappraisal*. Geneva: ILO, pp. 177–89.

Blanpain, R. (1991) *Labour Law and Industrial Relations of the European Community*. Deventer: Kluwer.

Boca, D. del (1988) 'Women in a Changing Workplace: The case of Italy'. In Jensen J. et al. (eds), *Feminization of the Labour Force*. London: Polity Press.

Boyer, R. (1988) *The Search for Labour Market Flexibility*. Oxford: Clarendon Press.

Brewster, C. and Smith, C. (1990) 'Corporate Strategy: A No-Go Area For Personnel?', *Personnel Management*, July, pp. 37–40.

Brewster, C. and Teague, P. (1989) *European Community Social Policy: Its Impact on the UK*. London: Institute of Personnel Management.

Bridgford, J. (1990) 'French trade unions: crisis in the 1980s', *Industrial Relations Journal*, 21, 2, pp. 126–37.

Bridgford, J. (1991) *The Politics of French Trade Unionism*. Leicester: Leicester University Press.

Bridgford, J. and Morris, P. (1987) 'Labour Confederations and Socialist Governments in France, 1981–1986'. In Brierley, W. (ed.), *Trade Unions and the Economic Crisis of the 1980s*. Aldershot: Gower, pp. 46–63.

Bridgford, J. and Stirling, J. (1988) 'Ideology or pragmatism? trade union education in France and Britain', *Industrial Relations Journal*, 19, 3, pp. 234–47.

Bridgford, J. and Stirling, J. (1991) 'Britain in a social Europe: industrial relations and 1992', *Industrial Relations Journal*, 22, 4, pp. 263–72.

Brierley, W. (ed.) (1987) *Trade Unions and the Economic Crisis of the 1980s*. Aldershot: Gower.

Brown, R. (ed.) (1988) *The European Employer*. London: British Institute of Management.

Buckley, M. and Anderson, M. (eds) (1988) *Women, Equality and Europe*. London: Macmillan.

Byre, A. (1988a) 'Applying Community Standards on Equality'. In Buckley, M. and Anderson, M. (eds), *Women, Equality and Europe*. London: Macmillan.

Byre, A. (ed.) (1988b) *Human Rights at the Workplace*. London: Policy Studies Institute.

Cecchini, P. (1988) *The European Challenge: 1992*. Aldershot: Wildwood House.

CERC (Centre d'Etude des Revenus et des Coûts) (1990) *Structure of Earnings in Eight Member States of the European Community*. Paris: CERC.

Clegg, H. (1976) *Trade Unionism Under Collective Bargaining*. Oxford: Basil Blackwell.

Coates, K. and Topham, T. (1977) *The Shop Stewards' Guide to the Bullock Report*. Nottingham: Spokesman.

Coldrick, P. (1990) 'Collective Bargaining in the New Europe', *Personnel Management*, October, pp. 58–61.

Commission of the European Communities (1980) *Problems and Prospects of Collective Bargaining in the EEC Member States*.

Commission of the European Communities (1984) *The Prevention and Settlement of Industrial Conflict in the Community Member States*.

Commission of the European Communities (1989a) *Employment in Europe 1989*.

Commission of the European Communities (1989b) *Report on Social Developments, Year 1988*.

Commission of the European Communities (1989c) *Schemes with an Impact on the Labour Market and their Statistical Treatment in the Member States of the European Community*.

Commission of the European Communities (1990a) *Employment in Europe 1990*.

Commission of the European Communities (1990b) *Explanatory Memorandum on the Proposals for Directives Concerning Certain Employment Rights*.

Commission of the European Communities (1991) *Employment in Europe 1991*.

Commission of the European Communities (1992) *Employment in Europe 1992*.

Corcoran, J. (1988) 'Enforcement Procedures for Individual Complaints: Equal Pay and Equal Treatment'. In Buckley, M. and Anderson, M. (eds), *Women, Equality and Europe*. London: Macmillan, pp. 57–70.

Council of the European Communities (1990) *Resolution of the Council on the Fight Against Racism and Xenophobia*. Council of the European Communities.

Dahrendorf, R. et al. (1986) *New Forms of Work and Activity*. Dublin: European Foundation for the Improvement of Living and Working Conditions.

Dale, A. and Glover, J. (1989) 'Women at Work in Europe', *Employment Gazette*, June, pp. 299–308.

Daniel, W. W. and Millward, N. (1983) *Workplace Industrial Relations in Britain*. London: Heinemann.

Davies, R. J. (1979) 'Economic Activity. Incomes Policy and Strikes – a Quantitative Analysis', *British Journal of Industrial Relations*, 17, 2, pp. 205–23.

Dickens, L. et al. (1985) *Dismissed*. Oxford: Basil Blackwell.

Eberlie, R. F. (1990) 'The New Health and Safety Legislation of the European Community', *Industrial Law Journal*, 19, 2: 81–97.

Economic Commission for Europe (1988) *Economic Survey of Europe in 1987–1988*. Secretariat of the Economic Commission for Europe.

Edmonds, J. (1992) 'Bargaining for First-class Rights', *Fabian Review*, 104, 2, pp. 6–7.

Eurodoc, (1985) *Joint Declaration by the European Parliament, the Council and the Commission on Attitudes and Organisations Motivated by Racism and Xenophobia*. Commission of the European Communities.

European Federation for Economic Research (1987) *Programme for Research and Actions in the Development of the Labour Market*.

European Foundation for the Improvement of Living and Working Conditions (1988) *New Forms of Work*. Dublin: EFILWC.

European Industrial Relations Review (1989a) *Termination of Contract in Europe*. London: EIRR.

European Industrial Relations Review (1989b) *The Regulation of Industrial Conflict in Europe*. London: EIRR.

European Industrial Relations Review (1990) *Non-Standard Forms of Employment in Europe*. London: EIRR.

European Industrial Relations Review (1991) *The Social Charter and its Action Programme*. London: EIRR.

European Trade Union Institute (1984) *The Trade Union Movement in Greece*, Brussels: ETUI.

European Trade Union Institute (1987) *The Trade Union Movement in France*. Brussels: ETUI.

European Trade Union Institute (1988) *Pensioners in Western Europe*. Brussels: ETUI.

European Trade Union Institute (1989) *Positive Action for Women in Europe*. Brussels: ETUI.

European Trade Union Institute, (1990a) *The European Trade Union Confederation*. Brussels: ETUI.

European Trade Union Institute, (1990b) *Workers' Representation and Rights in the Workplace in Western Europe*. Brussels: ETUI.

European Trade Union Institute (1991) *Agreements on Workers' Information and Consultation Rights in European Multinationals and an Evaluation of Experience*. Brussels: ETUI.

Euzeby, W. (1989) 'Non-contributory Old Age Pensions: A Possible Solution in the OECD Countries', *International Labour Review*, 28, 1, p. 15.

Evans, P. and Lorange, P. (1989) 'The Two Logics behind Human

Resource Management'. In Evans, P., Doz, Y. and Laurent, A. (eds), *Human Resource Management in International Firms*. Basingstoke: Macmillan.

Evans, P., Doz, Y. and Laurent, A. (eds) (1989) *Human Resource Management in International Firms*. Basingstoke: Macmillan.

Evans, P., Lank, E. and Farquhar, A. (eds) (1989) 'Managing Human Resources in the International Firm'. In Evans, P., Doz, Y. and Laurent, A. (eds), *Human Resource Management in International Firms*. Basingstoke: Macmillan.

Fox, J. (1986) *Investing in People: Towards a New Style of Industrial Relations*. Nottingham: Trent Polytechnic.

Fredman, S. and Morris, G. (1989) *Personnel Management*, August, pp. 25–9.

Fürstenberg, F. (1987) 'Federal Republic of Germany'. In International Labour Organization, *Collective Bargaining in Industrial Market Economics: A Reappraisal*. Geneva: ILO, pp. 177–89.

Garson, J-P. (1992) 'International Migration: Facts, Figures, Policies', *OECD Observer*, 176, pp. 18–24.

Gerhardt, P. et al. (1985) *The People Trade*. London: International Broadcasting Trust.

Gladstone, A. (1984) 'Employers' Associations in Comparative Perspective: Functions and Activities'. In Windmuller, J. P. and Gladstone, A. (eds), *Employers' Associations and Industrial Relations*. Oxford: Clarendon, pp. 24–43.

Goetschy, J. (1991) '1992 and the Social Dimension: Normative Frames, Social Actors and Content', *Economic and Industrial Democracy*, 12, pp. 259–75.

Gold, M. and Hall, M. (1990) *Legal Regulation and the Practice of Employee Participation in the European Community*. Dublin: European Foundation for the Improvement of Living and Working Conditions.

Goodhart, D. (1992) 'Opting Out and Cashing In', *Financial Times*, 28 February 1992.

Guéry, G. (1991) *La Dynamique de L'Europe Sociale*. Paris: Dunod.

Guest, D. (1989) 'Human Resource Management: Its Implications for Industrial Relations and Trade Unions'. In Storey, J. (ed.) *New Perspectives on Human Resource Management*. London: Routledge.

Guigni, G. (1987) 'Italy'. In International Labour Organization, *Collective Bargaining in Industrialised Economies: A Reappraisal*: Geneva: ILO, pp. 115–241.

Hakim, C. (1990) 'Core and Periphery in Employers' Workforce Strategies; Evidence from the 1987 E.L.U.S. Survey', *Work Employment and Society*, 4, 2, pp. 157–88.

Hall, B. and Wilson, P. (eds) (1989) *The North of England: Prepared for 1992?* Socialist Group/European Parliament.

Hall, M. (1992) 'Behind the European Works Councils Directives: The European Commission's Legislative Strategy', *British Journal of Industrial Relations*, 30, 4, pp. 547–66.

Health and Safety Commission (1990) *Plan of Work for 1990–91 and Beyond.* London: HMSO.

Health and Safety Executive (1991) *Workplace Health and Safety in Europe.* London: HMSO.

Hegewisch, A. (1991) 'The Decentralisation of Pay Bargaining – European Comparison', *Personnel Review*, 20, 6, pp. 28–35.

Heller, F. A. (1986) 'Does Formal Policy or Law as used in Europe Contribute to Improved Employee Information and Participation?'. In Vandamme, J. (ed.), *Employee Consultation & Information in Multinational Corporations.* Beckenham: Croom Helm: pp. 69–92.

Hemming, R. and Mansoor, A. M. (1988) *Privatization and Public Enterprises.* Occasional Paper of the International Monetary Fund.

Herzog, M. (1980) *From Hand to Mouth.* London: Penguin.

Hibbs, D. A. (1978) 'Industrial Conflict in Advanced Industrial Societies', *American Political Science Review*, 70, 4, 1033–58.

Hobsbawm, E. (1975) *The Age of Capital.* London: Weidenfeld and Nicholson.

Hoskyns, C. (1988) 'Give Us Equal Pay and We'll Open Our Own Doors'. In Buckley, M. and Anderson, M. (eds), *Women, Equality and Europe.* London: Macmillan, pp. 33–5.

Hunter, L. (1988) 'Some Aspects of Flexibility Decisions'. In Nadel, M. H., *New Forms and New Areas of Employment Growth.* Brussels: Commission of the European Communities, pp. 219–27.

Hutsebaut, M. (1989) *The Future of Social Security in Western Europe.* Brussels: ETUI.

Hyman, R. (1989) *The Political Economy of Industrial Relations.* London: Macmillan.

Hyman, R. (1991) 'European Unions: Towards 2000', *Work, Employment & Society*, 5, 4, pp. 621–39.

Hyman, R. and Streeck, W. (eds) (1988) *New Technology and Industrial Relations.* Oxford: Basil Blackwell.

Incomes Data Services (1988) *1992 Personnel Management and the Single European Market.* London: IDS/IPM.

International Confederation of Free Trade Unions (1988) *The Challenge of Change.* Brussels: ICFTU.

International Labour Organization (1981) *Workers' Participation in Decisions within Undertakings.* Geneva: ILO.

International Labour Organization (1984) *World Labour Report: Volume 1.* Geneva: ILO.

International Labour Organization (1987) *Collective Bargaining in Industrialised Market Economies: A Reappraisal.* Geneva: ILO.

International Labour Organization (1988a) *Summaries of International Labour Standards*. Geneva: ILO.

International Labour Organization (1988b) *Working Times Issues in Industrialised Countries*. Geneva: ILO.

Jackson, M. P. (1987) *Strikes*. Brighton: Wheatsheaf Books.

Jacobi, O. et al. (1986) *Economic Crisis, Trade Unions and the State*. Beckenham: Croom Helm.

Jensen, J. et al. (eds) (1988) *Feminization of the Labour Force*. London: Polity Press.

Keller, B. K. (1991) 'The role of the state as corporate actor in industrial relations systems'. In: Adams, R. J. (ed.), *Comparative Industrial Relations*. London: Harper Collins, pp. 76–93.

Kendall, W. (1975) *The Labour Movement in Europe*. London: Allen Lane.

Kerr, C. et al. (1962) *Industrialism and Industrial Man*. London: Heinemann.

Kidger, P. J. (1991) 'The Emergence of International Human Resource Management', *International Journal of Human Resource Management*, 2, 2, pp. 149–63.

Kravaritiou-Manitakis, Y. (1986) 'Repercussions of the New Forms of Work on Labour Law and Social Security'. In Dahrendorf, R. et al., *New Forms of Work and Activity*. Dublin: European Foundation for the Improvement of Living and Working Conditions.

Labour Party (1990) *Looking to the Future*. London.

Lane, C. (1989) *Management and Labour in Europe*. Aldershot: Edward Elgar.

Lewis, R. (ed.) (1986) *Labour Law in Britain*. Oxford: Basil Blackwell.

Lindley, R. M. (1987) *New Forms and New Areas of Employment Growth*. Brussels: Commission of the European Communities.

McCarthy, T. (1988) *The Great Dock Strike 1889*. London: Weidenfeld and Nicholson.

McDonald, O. (1989) *Own Your Own*. London: Unwin.

McIlroy, J. (1991) *The Permanent Revolution?* Nottingham: Spokesman.

MacInnes, J. (1987) *Thatcherism at Work*. Milton Keynes: Open University Press.

Marchington, M. (1987) 'Employee Participation'. In Towers, B. (ed.), *A Handbook of Industrial Relations Practice*. London: Kogan Page.

Marginson, P. et al. (eds) (1988) *Beyond the Workplace*. Oxford: Basil Blackwell.

Marginson, P. (1992) 'European Integration and Transnational Management-Union Relations in the Enterprise', *British Journal of Industrial Relations*, 30, 4, pp. 529–46.

Mellor, M. et al. (1988) *Worker Cooperatives in Theory and Practice*. Milton Keynes: Open University Press.

Milne, S. (1991) 'Germany 37, Britain 39', *The Guardian*, 25 October 1991.

Munck, R. (1988) *New International Labour Studies*. London: Zed Books.

Nadel, M. H. (1988) *New Forms & New Areas of Employment Growth*. Brussels: Commission of the European Communities.

Negrelli, S. and Santi, E. (1990) 'Industrial Relations in Italy'. In Baglioni, G. and Crouch, C. (eds), *European Industrial Relations*. London: Sage, pp. 154–98.

Northrup, H. R. et al. (1988) 'Multinational Union–Management Consultation in Europe: Resurgence in the 1980s', *International Labour Review*, 127, 5, pp. 525–43.

Oechslin, J. J. (1985) 'Employers' Organisations'. In Blanpain, R. (ed.) *Comparative Labour Law and Industrial Relations*. Deventer: Kluwer.

Olea, M. A. and Rodriguez-Sandu, F. (1985) 'Spain'. In Blanpain, R. (ed.) *Comparative Labour Law and Industrial Relations*. Deventer: Kluwer.

Organization for Economic Co-operation and Development (1989) 'Occupational Accidents in OECD Countries', *OECD Employment Outlook*, July, pp. 133–59.

Organization for Economic Co-operation and Development (1991a) *Historical Statistics 1960–1989*. Paris: OECD.

Organization for Economic Co-operation and Development (1991b) *The OECD Guidelines for Multinational Enterprises*. Paris: OECD.

Ozaki, M. (1987) 'Labour Relations in the Public Service: Labour Disputes and Their Settlements', *International Labour Review*, 126, 4, pp. 405–421.

Paldam, M. and Pedersen P. J. (1982) 'The Macroeconomic Strike Model: a Study of Seventeen Countries 1948–1975', *Industrial Labour Relations Review*, 35, 4, pp. 504–21.

Panitch, L. (1980) 'Recent theorizations of corporatism: reflections on a growth industry', *British Journal of Sociology*, 31, 2, pp. 159–87.

Pellegrini, C. (1987) 'Italian Industrial Relations'. In Bamber, G. and Lansbury, R. (eds), *International and Comparative Industrial Relations*. London: Allen and Unwin.

Pelling, H. (1971) *A History of British Trade Unionism*. London: Penguin

Phillimore, A. J. (1989) 'Flexible Specialisation, Work Organisation and Skills: Approaching the "Second Industrial Divide"', *New Technology, Work and Employment*, 4, 2, pp. 79–91.

Pollert, A. (1988) 'The Flexible Firm: Fixation or Fact?', *Work, Employment and Society*, 2, 3, pp. 281–316.

Poole, Michael (1986) *Industrial Relations*. London: Routledge & Kegan Paul.

Price Waterhouse/Cranfield (1990) *International Strategic HRM Report*. Bedford.

Quintin, O. (1988) 'The policies of the European Communities with special reference to the labour market'. In Buckley, M. and Anderson, M., *Women, Equality and Europe*. London: Macmillan: pp. 71–7.

Rainnie, A. (1989) *Industrial Relations in Small Firms*. London: Routledge.

Ramsay, H. (1990) *1992 – The Year of the Multinational? Corporate Behaviour, Industrial Restructuring and Labour in the Single Market*. Warwick University.

Read, M. and Simpson, A. (eds) (1991) *Against A Rising Tide: Racism, Europe and 1992*. Nottingham: Spokesman.

Redmond, M. (1985) 'Ireland'. In Blanpain, R. (ed.), *Comparative Labour Law and Industrial Relations*. Deventer: Kluwer.

Redmond, M. (1986) 'Women and Minorities'. In Lewis, R. (ed.), *Labour Law in Britain*. Oxford: Basil Blackwell, pp. 477–502.

Reutersward, A. (1990) 'A Flexible Labour Market in the 1990s', *OECD Observer*, 16, pp. 29–32.

Roberts, I. (1992) 'Industrial relations and the European Community', *Industrial Relations Journal*, 23, 1, pp. 3–31.

Rose, R. (1985) *Public Employment in Western Nations*. Cambridge: Cambridge University Press.

Rosenberg, S. (1989) 'From Segmentation to Flexibility', *Labour and Society*, 14, 4, pp. 363–467.

Ross, A. M. and Hartman, P. T. (1960) *Changing Patterns of Industrial Conflicts*. New York: Wiley.

Schregle, J. (1987) 'Workers' Participation in the Federal Republic of Germany in an International Perspective', *International Labour Review*, 126, 3, pp. 317–27.

Schmitter, P. C. (1981) 'Interest intermediation and regime governability in contemporary Western Europe and North America'. In: Berger S., Hirschman, A. and Maier, C. (eds), *Organising Interests in Western Europe*. Cambridge: Cambridge University Press, pp. 287–327.

Segrestin, D. (1990) 'Recent Changes in France'. In Baglioni, G. and Crouch, C. (eds), *European Industrial Relations*. London: Sage, pp. 97–126.

Sexton, J. J. (1988) *Long Term Unemployment*. Brussels: Eurostat.

Sisson, K. (1987) *The Management of Collective Bargaining*. Oxford: Basil Blackwell.

Stirling, J. (1991) 'This Great Europe of Ours: Trade Unions and 1992', *Capital & Class*, 45, pp. 7–16.

Stirling, J. and Bridgford, J. (1985) 'British and French shipbuilding: the industrial relations of decline', *Industrial Relations Journal*, 16, 4, pp. 7–16.

Storey, J. (ed.) (1989) *New Perspectives on Human Resource Management*. London: Routledge.

Storey, J. and Johnson, S. G. (1987) *Job Creation in Small and Medium Sized Enterprises*. Brussels: Commission of the European Communities.

Stråth, B. (1987) *The Politics of De-Industrialisation*. Beckenham: Croom Helm.

Strauss, George (1979) 'Workers' Participation Symposium Introduction', *Industrial Relations*, 18, 3, pp. 247–61.

Taylor, Andrew J. (1989) *Trade Unions and Politics*. London: Macmillan.

Teague, P. (1989) *The European Community: The Social Dimensions*. London: Kogan Page.

Thurley, K. (1990) 'Towards a European Approach to Personnel Management'. *Personnel Management*. August.

Thurley, K. and Wirdenius, H. (1989) *Towards European Management*. London: Pitman.

Thurley, K. and Wirdenius, H. (1991) 'Will Management become European?', *European Management Journal*, 9, 2.

Tomaney, J. (1990) 'The Reality of Workplace Flexibility', *Capital & Class*, 40, pp. 29–60.

Tomlinson, J. (1982) *The Unequal Struggle: British Socialism and the Capitalist Enterprise*. London: Methuen.

Treu, T. (1985) 'Italy'. In Blanpain, R. (ed.), *Comparative Labour Law and Industrial Relations*. Deventer: Kluwer.

Treu, T. (ed.) (1987) *Public Service Labour Relations*. Geneva: International Labour Organization.

Tsoukalis, L. (1991) *The New European Economy*. Oxford: Oxford University Press.

Vandamme, J. (ed.) (1986) *Employee Consultation & Information in Multinational Corporations*. Beckenham: Croom Helm.

Van der Vegt, C. (1988) 'Old and New Areas of Employment'. In Nadel, M. H., *New Forms and New Areas of Employment Growth*. Brussels: Commission of the European Communities.

Van Houten, G. (1989) 'The Implications of Globalism: New Management Realities at Philips'. In Evans, P. et al., *Managing Human Resources in the International Firm*. Basingstoke: Macmillan.

Vaughan-Whitehead, D. (1990) 'Wage Bargaining in Europe', *Social Europe*, 2/90.

Venturini, P. (1989) *The Social Dimension of the European Communities*. Brussels: Commission of the European Communities.

Visser, J. (1988) 'Trade Unionism in Western Europe: Present Situation and Prospects', *Labour and Society*, 13, 2, pp. 125–82.

Visser, J. (1989) *European Trade Union in Figures*. Deventer: Kluwer.

Visser, J. (1990) *In Search of Inclusive Unionism*. Deventer: Kluwer.

Vranken, M. (1986) 'Deregulating the employment relationship: current trends in Europe'. *Comparative Labour Law Journal*, 17, pp. 143–65.

Walsh, K. (1982) 'Industrial disputes in France, West Germany, Italy and the United Kingdom: measurement and incidence', *Industrial Relations Journal*, 13, 4, pp. 65–72.

Walsh, K. (1985) *Trade Union Membership*. Brussels: Eurostat, Commission of the European Communities.

Walters, David R. (1990) *Workers' Participation in Health and Safety*. London: The Institute of Employment Rights.

Webber, F. (1991) 'From Ethnocentrism to Euro-Racism', *Race & Class*, 32, 3, pp. 11–17.

Weiss, M. (1985) 'Federal Republic of Germany'. In Blanpain, R. (ed.), *Comparative Labour Law and Industrial Relations*. Deventer: Kluwer.

Windmuller, J. (1984) 'Employers Associations in Comparative Perspective: Organization, Structure, Administration'. In Windmuller, J. P. and Gladstone, A. (eds), *Employers Associations and Industrial Relations*. Oxford: Clarendon, pp. 1–23.

Windmuller, J. (1987) 'Comparative Study of Methods and Practices'. In International Labour Organization, *Collective Bargaining in Industrialised Market Economies: A Reappraisal*. Geneva: ILO.

Index